# WITH THE BEST OF INTENTIONS

### The Child Sexual Abuse Prevention Movement

# WITH THE BEST OF INTENTIONS
## The Child Sexual Abuse Prevention Movement

Jill Duerr Berrick
Neil Gilbert
University of California, Berkeley

THE GUILFORD PRESS
New York          London

© 1991 The Guilford Press
A Division of Guilford Publications, Inc.
72 Spring Street, New York, NY 10012

Printed in the United States of America

This book is printed on acid-free paper.

Last digit is print number:  9  8  7  6  5  4  3  2  1

Library of Congress Cataloging-in-Publication Data

Berrick, Jill Duerr.
    With the best of intentions : the child sexual abuse prevention
movement / Jill Duerr Berrick and Neil Gilbert.
        p.    cm.
    Includes bibliographical references and index.
    ISBN 0-89862-564-5  ISBN 0-89862-530-0 (pbk.)
    1. Child molesting—United States—Prevention.   I. Gilbert, Neil,
1940–    .  II. Title.
    [DNLM: 1. Child Abuse, Sexual—prevention & control—United
States.   2. Child Welfare—United States.   3. Sex Education—United
States.    WA 320 B533w]
HQ72.U53B47   1991
362.7'6—dc20
DNLM/DLC
for Library of Congress                                         91-24680
                                                                    CIP

# About the Authors

JILL DUERR BERRICK, Ph.D., is Director of the Berkeley Child Welfare Research Center at the Family Welfare Research Group. She is also a lecturer at the School of Social Welfare, University of California, Berkeley. Currently she is involved in a number of studies that focus on the well-being of children and families. Dr. Berrick was Project Director for the Elementary School Based Child Abuse Prevention evaluation, and research associate for the Preschool Based Child Abuse Prevention evaluation conducted by the Family Welfare Research Group. She has presented the results of her work at numerous conferences and before various academic forums. She has also published articles in *The International Journal of Child Abuse and Neglect, Children and Youth Services Review, Social Work in Education,* and *Issues in Child Abuse Accusations,* and is co-author of *Protecting Young Children from Sexual Abuse* (Lexington Books, 1989).

NEIL GILBERT, Ph.D., is the Milton and Gertrude Chernin Professor of Social Welfare and the Social Services at the University of California, Berkeley, and Director of the Family Welfare Research Group. Professor Gilbert served as a Senior Research Fellow for the United Nations Research Institute for Social Development in Geneva in 1975. In 1981, he was awarded a Senior Fulbright Research Fellowship to study social services in the British welfare state. In 1987, he was awarded a second Fulbright Fellowship to study European social policy as a Visiting Scholar at the London School of Economics and at the University of Stockholm Social Research Institute. Dr. Gilbert's numerous publications include 13 books and more than 50 articles, which have appeared in *The Wall Street Journal, The Public Interest, Society,* and leading academic journals. Dr. Gilbert has served on the editorial boards of *The Journal of Social Policy* (U.K.), *Social Work,* and *The Journal of Social Service Research.* He is editor of the Prentice-Hall Series in Social Welfare and the Praeger Publications Series on the Social Services.

# Preface

Over the past decade a social movement to prevent child sexual abuse has sprung up across the United States. Among the various campaigns and activities generated by this movement, classroom training programs constitute the major thrust of its organized efforts. Based on a feminist theory of rape prevention, which draws heavily on the ideology of empowerment, these training programs are delivered each year to millions of children in thousands of schools throughout the country. With the support of public funds, the movement has spawned a virtual industry around the development of books, curricula, videos, and an array of educational paraphernalia devoted to prevention training.

In an era when family supervision of youngsters has declined due to divorce and the increasing labor force participation of mothers, parents are anxious to ensure that their children are safe from harm—an anxiety fueled, no doubt, by an alarming surge in reports of child molestation. Responding to these fears, the rapid spread of sexual abuse prevention training programs rests largely on their promise to promote the safety of young children. This objective is to be accomplished through a process of empowerment that strengthens the child's ability to recognize and deal with the dangers of sexual abuse.

In the wake of their rapid implementation, a number of important questions about prevention training programs remain unanswered. Although parental consent is often required for children to participate in these programs, few parents are well acquainted with the actual content of sexual abuse prevention training curricula. As children are increasingly exposed to these programs, the approach to empowerment and its results are coming under more intense scrutiny. Parents, child welfare professionals, school administrators, and policymakers have begun to ask: Precisely what is being done in classrooms to empower children as young as preschool and first and third graders that can help them to prevent sexual abuse? How well does this training work? Are there any negative side effects? These are difficult questions, which social science research cannot always answer with great clarity. More often, like a candle, it casts a fuzzy light—a welcome companion, nevertheless, to those stumbling in the darkness.

In addressing these questions, this book seeks to illuminate the design, purpose, and consequences of sexual abuse prevention training programs delivered to young children, specifically those in preschool through the third grade. Starting with a review of the social movement to empower children and the controversy surrounding its efforts at the preschool level, we examine a range of prevention programs from several perspectives. The curricula are analyzed to provide a highly detailed account of the ideas and lessons that form the essential core of prevention training in the early grades. To assess the design of these curricula, feminist theory about what children should learn to empower themselves is compared with developmental theory about what children in the early years are able to learn. This is followed by a review of empirical evidence on how much young children actually learn from prevention training and what they seem to learn best. Recognizing that some of the information and ideas about preventing sexual abuse absorbed by 3- to 9-year-olds may produce disagreeable results, we explore the extent to which parents observe unanticipated consequences in their children's behavior after exposure to training. A broader philosophical issue is also examined concerning the relation between cultural diversity and the normative message about appropriate expressions of intimacy in family life conveyed by prevention lessons.

Although the typical program for prevention training focuses its main effort on children, in daily life it is parents and teachers who form the child's first line of defense against the dangers of an adult world. How do teachers and parents perceive sexual abuse prevention programs? What kinds of efforts do these adults make to protect the children in their care? The answers to these questions raise important issues about the extent to which children participate in prevention training with their parents' informed consent and how well teachers fulfill their reporting obligations in suspected cases of abuse.

Taking into account the evidence from various perspectives, a broad-based assessment emerges of the apparent strengths and weaknesses in the prevailing model of sexual abuse prevention training. In light of this assessment, we conclude by posing an alternative approach that involves a fundamental restructuring of the current programs for young children. It is in the nature of social movements to engender passion for a cause. "If you are not for us, you are against us" is an attitude that often accompanies such devotion to a cause. In this case, however, the essential matter is not whether one is for or against efforts to prevent sexual abuse of young children—as some of the movement's adherents would frame the issue—but whether the empowerment of young children is really the best path to this objective. The evidence, although not without qualification, tends to point toward policy initiatives that flow in another direction, one that sharpens family and community responsibility for the protection of its most vulnerable members.

# Acknowledgments

This book is the result of a 3-year research project made possible by a grant from the Conrad Hilton Foundation. The Foundation's interest in understanding and promoting effective efforts to prevent child abuse is a mission that our study sought to advance. We gratefully acknowledge the generous support for this study, which was bestowed with the friendly encouragement of Marge Balopole, the Hilton Foundation's program officer for our project. We also want to thank the Walter S. Johnson Foundation and the University of California, Berkeley, for providing the initial assistance that allowed us to get a timely start on this project.

Our work over the last several years benefited from the advice and cooperation of many colleagues and organizations. The project could not have been conducted without the participation of numerous children, parents, teachers, and program providers. We appreciate the time and effort contributed by all of these people. Special thanks are due to the prevention program administrators, Brenda Blasingame, Connie Dolinshek, Shayla Lever, Pat Osborne, Sherri Patterson, Cindy Phipps, and Pnina Tobin, and their staffs for the full degree of cooperation they extended throughout the study. We also enjoyed the counsel and support of Beth Hardesty Fife, Bob Green, and their staff at the Office of Child Abuse Prevention, California State Department of Social Services.

Many friends and colleagues at the Family Welfare Research Group (FWRG), School of Social Welfare, University of California, Berkeley, donated their good services to the project. We are particularly indebted to Nina Nyman for developing and testing the children's instruments and to Nicole LeProhn for initial work on the study design. Eve Vanderschmidt, Karla Pearcy, Tracy Schreiber, and Helen Ahn assisted in the collection and coding of data. Richard Barth drew our attention to the character of prevention training as a social movement.

We appreciate the constructive efforts of Gary Melton and N. Dickon Reppucci, each of whom read the manuscript and provided us with thoughtful suggestions that helped to clarify a number of important points. The process of bringing this manuscript to fruition was facilitated by the patience and kind support of Seymour Weingarten at Guilford Press. Although our work profited considerably from all of these excellent sources, we must claim full responsibility for any deficiencies that remain in the final product.

As dean of the School of Social Welfare, Harry Specht created a wonderfully supportive environment for policy-oriented research activities. On numerous occasions Jim Steele's administrative dexterity saved us from getting bogged down in the maze of university regulations. Susan Katzenellenbogen cheerfully managed the office work at FWRG and, along with Rebecca Albiani, prepared several drafts of the manuscript with painstaking care.

# Contents

# Empowering Children to Prevent Sexual Abuse: A Social Movement

$F$rom young victims of pederasty in ancient Greece to child prostitutes in modern society, the sexual exploitation of children has a long and odious history. Periodically, over the centuries, individuals and groups have launched notable efforts to safeguard children from sexual abuse and other forms of maltreatment. Legal protection against sexual abuse, for example, was first extended to children in the mid-1500s, when England passed laws protecting young boys from forced sodomy and prohibiting the rape of girls under 10 years of age.[1] But in late 18th-century Venice, Jean-Jacques Rousseau was still able to purchase a girl of 11 or 12 to be raised as a shared mistress with his friend. Up through the late 18th century, neglect and abandonment of children were commonplace. Rousseau admits to depositing five of his offspring in foundling homes. Records available for cities such as Toulouse, Lyon, and Florence reveal that between 25% and 43% of the children born in these communities were abandoned.[2]

By the late 19th century, the groundwork was being formed for modern efforts to aid children of abusive and neglectful parents. In 1874, Henry Bergh, first president of the Society for the Prevention of Cruelty to Animals, intervened in the case of Mary Ellen Wilson, an 8-year-old being physically abused by her parents; Bergh's good friend Elbridge Gerry was called upon to prosecute the case, which led ultimately both to Mary Ellen's placement in a children's home and the founding of the Society for the Prevention of Cruelty to Children under Gerry's leadership.[3]

At the turn of the 20th century, the Progressive Era raised social consciousness about other forms of maltreatment, particularly the exploitation of child labor. The New York Child Labor Act of 1903 owed much to the efforts of Robert Hunter, an influential social reformer with deep sympathies for the hard life of 1.7 million children under 15 years of age who toiled in factories, mines, and workshops. Of their plight, Hunter wrote:

> This destruction of the little ones now so unnecessary and so obvious is a kind of cannibalism. . . . There is a good deal more of such cannibalism in our modern world than we realize. The bodies and souls of many men and women are destroyed by the selfishness of our present-day society; but if we are to use the word "cannibal" in this new sense, let us begin by applying it to those employers, in the parasitic industries, who go to our legislative halls in order to defeat child-labor laws, using the argument that only by the toil of infants are they enabled to make profits.[4]

Eventually, child labor laws prevailed, and by the 1950s professional social work services to deal with child abuse and neglect were firmly institutionalized. It was not until the early 1960s, however, that physical abuse and neglect of children gained the prominent degree of recognition that marks contemporary acknowledgment of these problems. Much of the credit for expanding and sharpening public recognition of child maltreatment rests with Dr. Henry C. Kempe and his colleagues, who identified the "battered-child syndrome"—"a clinical condition in young children who have received severe physical abuse, generally from a parent or foster parent. The condition has also been described as 'unrecognized trauma' by radiologists, orthopedists, pediatricians, and social service workers."[5] Kempe's work alerted physicians to the fact that injured children were not always the victims of an accident, encouraged them to examine clinical findings and historical data supplied by parents with a critical eye, and reaffirmed their professional responsibilities to children.

## EMERGENCE OF CHILD SEXUAL ABUSE
## AS A SOCIAL CONCERN

Over the past two decades, increasing public and professional awareness of physical abuse has heightened sensitivity to child sexual abuse as a social issue. Public concern about the sexual abuse of children intensified as adult victims began to articulate their experiences of early molestation. These disclosures were spurred by the political and social climate of the 1960s and 1970s, a time that was conducive to women's expression of their anger about male oppression and dominance. Battered women were

particularly vocal in airing their grievances[6]; and women who had been raped began to insist on their right to safety.[7] Early consciousness-raising groups provided a comfortable environment that encouraged women to explore these personal issues. The most startling aspect of women's disclosures was the degree to which their experiences were shared; the amount of violence they had sustained, and their early age of sexual victimization. Women who remained silent for years came out with poignant autobiographical accounts of their rape and exploitation at an early age, which helped to identify these crimes against childhood as a social issue demanding investigation.[8]

The public response, in the early 1970s, was to allocate funds for the systematic study of child sexual abuse. Because the problem was articulated by women and seen as equivalent to the violations of rape, initial funding came from the National Center for the Prevention and Control of Rape, which provided resources for two studies to examine the scope of this problem.[9] Results from these studies, however, were not made available until the early 1980s. This was due, in part, to the difficulty in gathering information on such a sensitive and controversial subject. Thus, in the early 1970s there were few empirical studies concerning the incidence of child sexual abuse. At that time, the major data available on this problem were from the Kinsey survey, conducted 20 years earlier. Kinsey and his associates had found an incidence rate of 9.2% for sexual activity involving physical contact between preadolescent females and older males.[10]

Yet public concern ran deep, despite the lack of current estimates on the magnitude of child sexual abuse. Once it gained recognition, the horrifying nature of this type of abuse was difficult to ignore. In 1974 Congress passed the Child Abuse Prevention and Treatment Act.[11] The term "child sexual abuse" appeared in the Act, providing a legislative mandate for further analysis and discussion of the problem. This act created the National Center on Child Abuse and Neglect (NCCAN), established guidelines for community action in both treatment and prevention, and provided funding for research on the prevalence and implications of the problem.[12] Addressing all forms of child maltreatment, NCCAN was to design uniform criteria for determining abuse and neglect, and to develop model standards for managing reports of abuse.

Although officially recorded cases of child physical abuse and neglect are more prevalent than those involving sexual abuse, and in many instances more damaging, the sexual molestation of young children attracts greater attention from the media and evokes higher public anxiety. Lending fuel to these anxieties, awareness of the problem increased as states broadened their child abuse reporting laws to satisfy eligibility requirements for federal aid administered by NCCAN. Prior to the

passage of the Child Abuse Prevention and Treatment Act of 1974, only three states were able to satisfy these requirements; over the next four years 40 additional states had made the programmatic changes, including expansion of reporting laws, necessary to qualify for federal aid.[13]

As reporting laws expanded, systematic efforts were devised to measure the number of cases seen annually. These studies revealed that reports of all forms of abuse and neglect increased substantially, by about 150% from the mid-1970s to the early 1980s. The Study of National Incidence and Prevalence of Child Abuse reported another 51% increase from 1980 to 1986.[14] Although child sexual abuse accounted for less than 15% of the cases in 1980, reports on this form of maltreatment multiplied at an alarming rate. National estimates based on surveys by the American Humane Association show an increase of almost tenfold (from 7,559 to 71,961) in the number of reported cases between 1976 and 1983[15]; and by 1986, according to the US Department of Health and Human Services, the number of reported cases had reached 155,000; in California, reports of sexual abuse climbed almost fourfold between 1982 and 1986.[16] The experts widely believe that many, if not most, incidents of child sexual abuse are never reported. Because incidence studies disclose only part of the problem, a number of surveys were initiated to detect the proportion of the population that experiences sexual abuse during childhood. The findings from these prevalence studies reveal more about the ambiguities of this problem than its scope.

## A DIFFICULT PROBLEM TO MEASURE

The difficulty in documenting the scope of this problem is highlighted in the results of 15 surveys conducted since 1976, which attempt to estimate the prevalence of child sexual abuse through self-reports from victims. According to these surveys, estimates of the proportion of females sexually abused in the course of their childhood range from 6% to 62% of the population, with a median figure of 15%; for males the estimates range from 3% to 31% with a median of 6%.[17]

Some of the differences in these estimates can be explained by the alternative research methodologies employed, particularly sample selection and interview techniques.[18] Several studies were conducted with undergraduate students (usually enrolled in psychology or sociology classes)[19]; other studies included large probability samples of women from urban areas.[20] College surveys often involved paper-and-pencil questionnaires, whereas other studies have collected data through extensive personal interviews. Response rates also vary by study, yet there has been little discussion regarding the implications of nonresponse patterns until

recently.[21] Further, on a subject as sensitive and controversial as child sexual abuse, the candor and accuracy of responses must be treated with reserve; reasons for exaggerated accounts of abuse are as numerous as the reasons for hiding the truth.[22]

The factor that appears to explain the greatest discrepancy among studies, however, is each investigator's working definition of child sexual abuse. Obviously, the more broadly the act is defined, the more people who will be classified as victims. Child sexual abuse is variously defined as involving a range of behaviors including physical contacts (e.g., kissing, fondling, and intercourse) and noncontact experiences (e.g., sexual propositions, exposure to exhibitionism, and posing for nude photographs). For example, using a definition that included any unwanted contact as well as noncontact experiences before their eighteenth birthday with someone less than five years older than the respondent, Wyatt found a 62% prevalence rate of abuse for females.[23] Other researchers have employed narrower definitions. Finkelhor's study distinguishes between contact and noncontact experiences. His definition of childhood includes two age categories: children under the age of 12 who have had an experience with someone at least five years older and children between the ages of 13 and 16 who have had an experience with someone at least 10 years older.[24]

Just as the depths of this problem are difficult to gauge, so are its consequences. What impact does sexual abuse have on a child's life? The answer depends on several factors. The specific nature of the act, for example, is clearly relevant to its consequences for the victim.[25] One would not expect the same results from unwanted kisses, fondling, rape, and exposure to an exhibitionist. The relationship of the perpetrator to the child also appears to have an effect; the more closely related the victim is to the offender, the more serious the harm.[26] And the duration of abuse must be taken into account. Although little research has been conducted to determine the consequences of a single abusive incident, the evidence suggests that the longer the exposure to abuse, the higher the percentage of victims who feel that it has caused serious and lasting harm.[27]

Not all children exhibit immediate symptoms of abuse, nor do all adults show obvious signs of dysfunction as a result of childhood molestation. Some studies have found few, if any, negative outcomes as a direct result of sexual molestation.[28] Most studies, however, indicate painful reactions among victims; these include responses of guilt,[29] anxiety,[30] anger, and depression,[31] as well as a profound sense of loss that is carried over into adulthood.[32] Other reactions involve behavioral responses such as aggression,[33] suicidal ideation,[34] and self-mutilation.[35] Child sexual abuse also appears to have an impact on sexual functioning later in life.

Some victims become promiscuous in their behavior during adolescence and through adulthood;[36] others exhibit confusion regarding their sexual identity.[37]

The lack of clarity about the definition of child sexual abuse has given rise to a wide range of estimates concerning the size of this problem; some of these estimates are very large, suggesting that more than half of all women are sexually abused as children. Even the median figure among recent surveys of a 15% prevalence for females is not trivial. Uncertainty about the full dimensions of this problem, coupled with the growing body of evidence on its harmful effects have lent a certain urgency to the call for public action.

## FROM TREATMENT TO PREVENTION

Beyond funding studies to gauge the full dimensions of child sexual abuse and other forms of maltreatment, NCCAN's legislative charge was to be both treatment- and prevention-oriented. The Center's early efforts in the area of sexual abuse focused on funding treatment programs to work with offenders and their families. However, the evaluation of treatment programs for sex offenders showed indefinite results. Examining the treatment outcomes for 141 cases of child sexual abuse, Daro reports that clinicians judged 64% of the offenders (fathers and stepfathers) as unlikely to engage in future abuse of their children; although these offenders were in treatment, reincidence of sexual abuse was detected in 19% of the cases.[38] In the absence of a control group, of course, it is difficult to assess the extent to which these outcomes are attributable to treatment per se. Reviewing three studies of convicted child molesters that compared the recidivism rates of treatment and nontreatment groups, Finkelhor notes that two of the studies found no differences between groups over follow-up periods of 5 and 10 years; although the third study revealed meaningful differences in recidivism rates between sex offenders receiving treatment and an untreated group, the follow-up period was relatively short (only 3 years), and the treatment group consisted of men who had volunteered for services. Finkelhor concludes that none of the recidivism studies provides strong evidence in favor of the positive effects of treatment. Studies that do indicate successful treatment effects tend to employ "soft" outcome measures, such as attitude change and short-term self-reports of sexually abusive behavior.[39]

Although the treatment outcomes for child molesters remain highly uncertain, as already noted, there was a growing body of research documenting not only immediate, but long-term harmful effects of sexual abuse on young victims. Assessing more than 20 studies on the impact of child sexual abuse, Brown and Finkelhor observe that the evidence "conveys a clear suggestion that sexual abuse is a serious mental health problem consistently associated with very disturbing subsequent problems in a significant portion of its victims."[40]

The shortcomings of a treatment-oriented approach to child sexual abuse are evident. On the one hand, counseling and other treatments for offenders are costly, with outcomes of questionable efficacy. On the other hand, even if treatment were highly effective, the physical and psychological damage suffered by young victims is not easily mended. As with many social problems, prevention is a more attractive alternative than treatment.

Three levels of prevention—primary, secondary, and tertiary—are typically identified in analyses of preventive practice, with some differences in definition between the psychological/psychiatric literature and the literature on child abuse prevention. In the former, "primary prevention is the steps taken to prevent the occurrence of a disease, secondary prevention is early treatment of the disease once it has occurred, and tertiary prevention is the attempt to minimize the long-term effects of the disease."[41] In the child abuse literature, primary prevention is also defined as efforts aimed at preventing the occurrence of this problem in the general population; secondary prevention involves measures to stop abuse from happening, which are directed more narrowly toward high-risk groups; and tertiary prevention aims to reduce the severity and effects of abuse after it has occurred.[42]

The child sexual abuse prevention efforts examined in this book deal mainly with programs operating on the primary level. Efforts to achieve primary prevention focus on three broad targets: the problem-causing agent, the community, and the victim. Measures may be devised to eradicate, block, or otherwise neutralize the problem-causing agent, as in the draining of swamps to eliminate the breeding grounds of malaria-carrying mosquitoes. The community may be strengthened to resist the problem through education and involvement of its members, as in the development of neighborhood crime watch organizations, or the community may be reformed to alter the social conditions that give rise to the problem. Finally, the victim population may be immunized against the problem, as in the use of vaccines. Taking this last approach, programs aimed at sexual abuse prevention are addressed principally to children. The conventional metaphor is that of providing a universal "inoculation" that injects skills into children's cognitive systems, which strengthen their abilities to ward off physical or psychological hazards.

The campaign for the prevention of sexual abuse was initiated with strong backing from victims.[43] In 1971, the New York Radical Feminists sponsored a conference to discuss the feasibility of prevention services. At this conference, victims of rape and childhood molestation voiced considerable support for preventive action. Soon after, a collective of Women Against Rape (WAR) members in Columbus, Ohio, began to develop prevention techniques for children. Their efforts focused on programs to teach young children practices distilled from self-defense strategies that were originally designed for women.

The first Child Assault Prevention (CAP) program was launched when a local Catholic elementary school requested a prevention program from the WAR collective. A child had been raped, and school officials were trying to find a way of responding to this tragic event. They called on the women's collective to conduct a prevention training program for children; this marked the start of the CAP workshop that, over time, gained a national audience.

CAP may have been the first sexual abuse prevention program geared specifically toward children. Yet elsewhere in the country, similar approaches to the problem were emerging. In Hennepin County, Minnesota, for example, Cordelia Anderson worked in the county attorney's office doing research on sex offenders. Investigating their childhoods, she noticed a pattern of experiences that included early victimization. In thinking about how to present material to children that might help safeguard them against sexual abuse, Anderson came upon the idea of the 'touch continuum' (commonly referred to as the good, bad, and confusing touch). This framework for distinguishing physical contacts became the cornerstone for another prevention curriculum. Combining her ideas with the skills of a community troupe led to the formation of the Illusion Theatre, which produced a dramatized version of prevention techniques.

Between 1980 and 1985, the movement was given a significant boost through funding from NCCAN to design prevention curricula. In 1980, six large-scale projects were funded to develop sexual abuse prevention programs for children. The Illusion Theatre was encouraged to develop its presentation for older children.[44] In Washington, the "Personal Safety" curriculum was produced.[45] Geraldine Crisci, a leader in the child abuse prevention movement, wrote her initial children's curriculum (also titled, "Personal Safety") under the NCCAN grant.[46] Similar programs also evolved in Indiana,[47] New York,[48] and North Carolina. These early programs were widely distributed throughout the United States. Today every state in the nation has at least one program that focuses on children and attempts to strengthen their ability to prevent sexual abuse. An estimated 60% of school districts mandate prevention instruction in their classrooms,[49] and millions of children are trained in prevention techniques each year. Although the methods of presentation vary, the goals of most curricula are the same. Underlying these efforts is a common ideology of empowerment that imbues them with the force and cohesion of a social movement.

## FEMINIST THEORY AND THE PREVENTION MOVEMENT

While child sexual abuse prevention programs are closely associated with the larger field of institutional efforts dealing with child abuse and neglect, there is an important distinction between these two areas of service. Child abuse and neglect programs (which include detection, in-home services, and out-of-home placement of sexually abused children) operate within an institutionalized network of child welfare services mandated by the Social Security Act; delivered by professionals, mainly social workers, along with lawyers and doctors; and administered largely by established state and county Departments of Social Welfare. These child-protective service agencies are for the most part treatment-oriented. Their work tends to focus on the abused child's family, which is viewed both as the source of the problem and as the unit ultimately responsible for the child's protection. In comparison to these efforts, child sexual abuse prevention programs constitute more of a social movement than an institutionalized network of professional services.

By definition, social movements entail "a group venture extending beyond a local community or a single event and involving a systematic effort to inaugurate changes in thought, behavior, and social relationships."[50] The child abuse prevention movement is composed of numerous local community-based groups, whose members are overwhelmingly female; they include many sexual abuse victims and are linked by a common ideology. The role of ideology is an important feature of social movements. As Cameron observes:

> Ideologies, in brief, are systems of thinking and talking about a situation which are set up on the basis of a partial view of that situation, and which tend to support action now being taken. They are not exactly true or untrue. They are reasoned out and they are reasonable if we make certain assumptions (usually hidden) and omit certain observations. Their function is to provide an apology, a rationale, or a justification for something which we intend to do. . . . People in social movements use ideologies to convince themselves and others who share their position that the movement taken is the "right" one, so that they can have their own way and feel righteous too.[51]

Feminist theory is at the ideological core of the child sexual abuse prevention movement. More than any other ideas, this system of thinking has shaped the essential features of the training curricula for prevention programs. Feminist theory was designed by and for women to explain their experiences. It found early expression in the anti-rape campaign and was later distilled into an alternative theory for children. To understand how feminist theory came to influence child abuse prevention, a brief description of the adult component of this theory is first necessary.

Feminist principles pivot on individual empowerment and the defense of basic human rights. Rights to self-determination of sexual preferences and boundaries are central to the theory. Within the women's movement, any act initiated against a woman's will, without consent, should be countered, resisted, and overcome.

According to feminist analysis, rape is not viewed as a singular act of sexuality but rather as an expression of power and violence, focused diffusely upon women. The sociopolitical system in which rape occurs is seen as supported by well-established patterns of patriarchal dominance and male socialization.[52] Routine social practices, such as pornography and the objectification of women in the media, are viewed as primary factors in the community acceptance of degrading and inhuman attitudes toward women.[53] As Herman states, "without an understanding of the power relations between the sexes (i.e., male dominance and the erotization of dominance) it is impossible to explain the epidemiology of sexual abuse."[54]

From the feminist perspective, rape occurs as a result of socially defined constructs of acceptable behavior. When rape came to be understood in this way, radical feminists set out to bring down the existing power structure and to establish a normative revolution.[55] Other feminists, who may have been equally committed to these ultimate goals of the radical contingency, were able to focus on more immediate objectives. They looked first for ways to prevent the physical act of rape before combating the deeper sociopolitical ills. Self-defense training for women thus emerged with an eye to protecting individual women from sexual assault.

The theory behind the anti-rape campaign and women's self-defense has both philosophical and practical implications. The rape prevention movement was designed to propagate the idea "that direct confrontation of rapists [is] a way to exert community control over men's behavior."[56] The message conveyed to a woman through her training in self-defense is not only that she can protect herself from personal assault but also that she is a powerful being in a society that encourages her powerlessness. A woman's psychological and emotional experiences are also viewed as part of her defense. Relying on a sixth sense that was developed prior to the incursion of oversocialization, women are encouraged to intuit potential danger in their surroundings.

The feminist campaign against rape has a natural affinity with child sexual abuse prevention efforts because, according to the WAR collective,[57]

Women and children share a similar victim status in that both groups are dependent upon another group of people from whom rapists, or abusers, are drawn. Just as women have traditionally been dependent upon men, children are dependent upon adults for economic support, for social identity, for protection. In addition to this dependence children are vulnerable in other ways. Like women, children are physically smaller and muscularly weaker than their attackers.

Drawing on a feminist perspective in the design of its CAP training curriculum, the WAR collective has issued the most explicit statement regarding the application of feminist theory to prevention programs. Advocating for this approach, the program manual explains[58]:

> The sexual abuse of children, particularly the abuse of female children by adult males, demands that we extend our critique of rape prevention one step further. . . . The CAP Project stems from the same feminist critique of rape prevention, applied to the condition of children. . . . While precautions are often necessary, we do not advocate the restriction of children's activities. Rather we encourage children to solve problems using their own resources. This approach is considerably different than most child abuse programs which focus on community education, adult intervention, and parental responsibility.

Sociological literature abounds with various classification schemes that distinguish among different types of social movements. As an analytic device these typologies focus on a few important variables, which simplifies reality and allows for comparative study of related phenomena. One classification particularly relevant to child sexual abuse prevention efforts involves the distinction between value-oriented and norm-oriented movements. In value-oriented movements, collective behavior is mobilized by beliefs that the basic values of society are deficient and only radical change can set things right. In contrast, operating within the basic values of society, norm-oriented movements seek to alter the social rules and expectations governing behavior.[59] As expressed in the CAP program statement of philosophy, the child sexual abuse prevention movement is explicitly norm-oriented. Mobilized by the ideology of empowerment, the social norms that this movement endeavors to change are rules and expectations about children's behavior and the acceptable boundaries of physical intimacy.

The CAP program is widely used throughout the United States, with more than half of the 84 programs in California directly based on this model; its basic approach has influenced the entire field of sexual abuse prevention training. Carol Plummer, one of the pioneers in this field, describes the movement's faith in its theory and objectives: "If we inform children about sexual abuse, and ways to prevent it . . . we adults believe children can be empowered to avoid or interrupt their own victimization."[60] Indeed, whether teaching youngsters to rely and act on their feelings (as in the CAP program), to distinguish "good" touches from "bad" touches (as in the Illusion Theatre's program), or to act on a combination of feelings and rule-oriented lessons (as in the Talking About Touching program[61]), the sexual abuse prevention movement rests on a system of thought that promotes self-defense and the psychological empowerment of children. Conveyed through various messages and forms of instruction, this orientation is expressed succinctly in a children's rhyme taught by the Touch Safety Program:[62]

> *My body is my own*
> *Though I'm not fully grown*
> *I'm old enough to tell you so*
> *And I am saying, "No!"*

## CHILDREN'S PROGRAMS: ISSUES OF AGE AND EFFECTIVENESS

As the sexual abuse prevention movement gained momentum over the past decade, a virtual industry developed around the production and delivery of prevention curricula for children. Financed mainly by state and local governments and delivered by community-based service providers, these prevention training programs are designed to protect young children from sexual abuse. Between the intent of these programs and their outcomes, however, looms a huge zone of uncertainty. The programs were not built on rigorous systematic testing of curricula. They sprang almost full-blown out of a pressing need to respond to the alarming reports of child sexual abuse. For example, the CAP curriculum adopted much of its basic approach to training children (e.g., assertiveness and self-defense) directly from the instructional techniques of rape prevention programs originally designed for adult women. The relative haste with which these programs were formed is illustrated by the fact that in 1985, when the NCCAN was still requesting proposals to develop and test prevention curricula for children, the state of California had already passed legislation providing more than $10 million a year to implement sexual abuse prevention training and was in the midst of delivering these programs to every school in the state. The California initiative emerged as the most comprehensive sexual abuse prevention effort in the country.

Teaching children about how to prevent sexual abuse is a delicate business. With the rapid spread of prevention programs and the absence of careful testing, the effectiveness of these efforts remains to be demonstrated. Questions about the effectiveness of sexual abuse prevention training may be framed in terms of both what knowledge is gained from these programs and what the practical consequences of this learning are for the protection of children. The behavioral outcomes of learning, of course, are the stronger measures of effectiveness. A child may learn the signs of a potentially dangerous situation (e.g., uncomfortable touches, bad secrets, requests from strangers) and what she is supposed to do in these cases (e.g., say no, yell for help, kick, run away, tell an adult); unless she can act appropriately on this knowledge when faced with the event, however, the ideas absorbed in the classroom ultimately will have little effect on the prevention of sexual abuse.

Although behavioral response is the more powerful criterion of effectiveness, it is also considerably more difficult to measure than the knowledge gained from classroom lessons. Indeed, to test children on their actual behavior in response to classroom instructions about uncomfortable touches, yelling for help, running away, and physical self-defense would require placing them in threatening or seductive situations that are generally beyond the pale of acceptable social experimentation. With the exception of responding to strangers, there is little scientific evidence on the behavioral consequences of prevention training.

In regard to lessons about "stranger danger," several studies using simulated techniques have attempted to assess the impact of sexual abuse prevention training on children's responses to adults they do not know. Fryer, Kraizer, and Miyoshi, for example, conducted an experiment with kindergarten and first- and second-grade children that involved having the subjects approached in the hall of their school by a researcher in the role of a stranger; he asked each subject to come outside to his car and help him to carry in treats for his son's birthday party or puppets for a puppet show. The findings revealed that after participating in the training program, among the 23 students in the experimental group, the number refusing to accompany the stranger increased from 10 to 18; of the 21 control group students, 11 refused to go with the stranger on both the pretest and the posttest simulation.[63] In a similar vein, Poche, Yoder, and Miltenberger found that using a videotape and behavioral techniques were effective in training kindergarten and first-grade children to avoid strangers who tried to lure them into their cars.[64]

In general, studies simulating direct approaches by strangers show that child abuse prevention training can increase to some extent stranger avoidance by young children in particular situations. The extent to which these experiments mirror reality, however, is unclear. Strangers who prey on children try to select those who are the most vulnerable, their approach is often time-consuming and subtle, and sometimes they use force or threats of harm. As Melton suggests, the question remains whether the effects of training can be generalized or applied to other social contexts in which the stranger's approach is more cunning or threatening than those that can be simulated for research purposes.[65] Even the mild approaches simulated in these experiments have sparked controversy among child welfare specialists.[66] Some question the propriety of exposing children to possibly anxiety-provoking situations. Others are concerned about unintended side effects. Conte, for example, suggests that these studies may actually teach children that strangers do no harm. "Indeed," he writes, "it may desensitize children to the very behavior most programs seek to sensitize children to."[67] This debate on the use of simulated techniques underlines the tremendous difficulty in assessing behavioral outcomes to determine the practical effectiveness of prevention training programs.

Measures of the knowledge gained by children in prevention programs are less rigorous criteria of effectiveness than are behavioral results, but they are more accessible to social research. If behavioral outcomes are predicated on learning the information and ideas delivered through prevention curricula (an implicit assumption of these programs), then measures of knowledge gained are useful as conditional indicators of effectiveness. They tell us the extent to which programs achieve the preliminary conditions for children to realize behaviors that would help to protect them from sexual abuse. Since the mid-1980s more than a dozen studies have been conducted measuring the knowledge gained by subjects after exposure to prevention programs. Most of these studies were internal evaluations conducted by the program providers, with samples of fewer than 100 subjects; ages ranged from preschool through high school. (See Chapter 5 for a summary of these studies.)

With sexual abuse prevention curricula being delivered at every grade level, the issue of program effectiveness is joined to the strategic question: At what ages are children best able to absorb different concepts and lessons about prevention? This question underscores the need to incorporate insights from theories of cognitive development into the design of prevention curricula. Although feminist theory, which animates these curricula, addresses the skills and knowledge that children should possess to protect themselves, theories of cognitive development reveal the extent to which children can master these lessons in light of their developmental abilities. In analyzing prevention curricula, age and effectiveness are interrelated: some concepts may be more useful and communicable than others when offered at different age levels.

Reviewing recent efforts of the sexual abuse prevention movement, this book focuses on issues of age and effectiveness in children's programs in the early school years. The following chapters report on a range of evidence evaluating the knowledge gained through prevention programs offered to children in preschool and first and third grades. Examining results from a number of recent studies, our major emphasis is on the detailed findings of two large-scale evaluations conducted over the past five years by the Family Welfare Research Group at the School of Social Welfare, University of California, Berkeley.[68] In addition to outcomes for children, we assess the impact of these programs on parents and teachers. Different curricula designs are compared and analyzed in light of both developmental and feminist theory. The purpose of this study is to take a close look at the theory, practice, and evaluations of these programs before they become too firmly institutionalized. Drawing on the evidence, we explore some policy implications to guide the future direction of public efforts to protect young children.

# Age and Effectiveness: California's Preschool Controversy

Questions about the effectiveness of sexual abuse prevention training and the appropriate age to begin instruction are nowhere more pressing or complex than when applied to the youngest age group served by these programs—3 to 5-year-old preschool children. As part of the most comprehensive prevention effort in the country, California's Child Abuse Prevention Training Act of 1984 makes publicly funded training available to children in every preschool program in the state. The story of how this landmark legislation developed and responses to the assessment of its preschool component illustrate not only the issues of early childhood training but also some strengths and weaknesses of the child sexual abuse prevention movement.

## THE MOST COMPREHENSIVE PREVENTION LAW IN THE UNITED STATES

In 1984, twenty nine bills dealing with child abuse were introduced in the California legislature. Somewhat more than an ordinary level of legislative interest in the problem, this wave of lawmaking activity reflected a mounting concern for the safety of children. It was a concern impelled by a precipitous rise in reports of child sexual abuse (induced, largely, by the broadening of the state's reporting laws in 1981) and by several chilling cases of kidnapping and abuse that were widely publicized by the media. Between 1982 and 1984, for example, Californians were haunted by the kidnapping of 3-year-old Tara Burke, the disappearance of 8-year-old Kevin Collins, and the alarming charges of mass sexual abuse of preschoolers at the McMartin School.[1] These events conveyed in gruesome detail the reality behind many reports of child sexual abuse, the rate of which had increased by more than 70% over the two years.[2] Among the 29 bills submitted in response to the growing awareness and public anxiety about this problem, Assembly Bill 2443 stood out as the most comprehensive measure designed to prevent child sexual abuse.

The Child Abuse Prevention Training Act (hereafter referred to as the Prevention Act) was introduced as Assembly Bill 2443 by Assembly-woman Maxine Waters, chair of the Democratic Caucus and among the most influential members of the California legislature.[3] The Prevention Act proposed to give all children ages 2½ to 18 an opportunity to partici-pate in prevention training five times throughout their school careers—in preschool, kindergarten, early elementary grades, junior high, and high school. Initially, this program was to be state-mandated, with the training curricula based explicitly on that of the Child Assault Prevention (CAP) project originated by the Women Against Rape in Columbus, Ohio. In the bill's final draft, the state mandate was eliminated and the curriculum guidelines broadened to include models conceptually similar to CAP, but different in detail.

The prevention curricula outlined in AB 2443 were modeled on the CAP project largely through the efforts of Kate Kain, Director of the Child Assault Prevention Training Center of Northern California. The California CAP Center, organized in 1981, was one of the early sponsors of AB 2443, and Kain was among the small group of child advocates gathered by Maxine Waters to help draft the legislation. By 1983, the CAP Center had introduced its prevention training program to children in 30 communities throughout northern California. This widespread de-livery of the program conveyed an implication that the CAP model had been successfully piloted, despite the fact that no serious evaluation of these efforts had been undertaken. There was, however, much anecdotal evidence—letters from children, praise from parents, and other testimo-nies—that signaled public enthusiasm for CAP training.

Although California had a Republican governor who looked upon costly social programs with some reservation, the Prevention Act sailed through the state senate with virtually no opposition and drew only two opposing votes in the assembly. This rapid passage was set in motion through an extensive lobbying effort by CAP providers:

> In addition to generating a steady stream of written materials and striking dramatic personal testimony, the sponsors doggedly pursued legislators with phone calls and visits. The network of CAP program organizers, always alert to the bill's progress, continued their vocifer-ous endorsements. . . . At the same time, the media began to give increasing coverage to the bill. Supporters had systematically contacted

editorial writers at every major newspaper in California. As a result, pro-AB 2443 editorials were regularly appearing in newspapers across the state.[4]

The network of program providers lobbying on behalf of the Prevention Act had much to gain from the bill's passage. These were mostly small community-based agencies continually struggling for support. Public funding on the scale proposed in the Prevention Act would not only ensure their existence but widen their service domains. The legislation prescribed a special training and coordination role for the Northern California CAP Center, for example, which was funded at about $400,000 annually. But more than just financial support was at stake. With the imprimatur of government approval, the Prevention Act would legitimate and lend a high degree of credibility to child sexual abuse prevention curricula and the movement promoting these efforts.

The roots of interest group support for the Prevention Act went deeper than the obvious benefits to provider agencies. Among program organizers and staff there was a high level of individual commitment to the ideology behind the bill. The CAP providers' motivation was born, in part, out of shared experiences and personal interest in the feminist cause. The bill struck an emotional chord with providers, many of whom had firsthand experiences with child abuse.[5] This collective thread of personal experience united the group.

In the campaign to persuade legislators of its value, child abuse prevention training was also touted as a crime prevention strategy whose benefits would be cost-effective. Citing the costs of investigation and prosecution in alleged sexual abuse cases, CAP supporters set out their analysis in a widely distributed flier that claimed:

> AB 2443 saves money while it saves lives. The cost of a primary prevention program: just $7.00 per child. A typical case of child sexual abuse can require . . . child protective services, medical treatment, police, district attorney, courts, foster care or residential placement, supervision by a social worker, therapy . . . and can easily add up to $40,000!

As with the other evidence in support of the Prevention Act, the cost–benefit analysis was speculative and anecdotal—the data of journalism, not scientific appraisal. Indeed, little empirical evidence of program effectiveness was offered or called for during the legislative hearings. Faced with an impassioned and well-organized interest group, an anxious public, and the natural desire to protect young children, it is not difficult to see why legislators were virtually unanimous in their support of the Prevention Act. It is hard to imagine, however, what they thought might be transmitted in the classroom to 3-, 4-, and 5-year-olds that could help these children prevent sexual abuse. If opposition to the bill was lacking, so was a critical assessment of the evidence of its merits, particularly in regard to preschool children. The Prevention Act emerged from a decision-making process that did not follow the conventional models of social planning.

## A CASE OF "OPPORTUNISTIC" PLANNING

Efforts to describe social planning processes usually refer to what policy analysts call "rational" and "incremental" models.[6] The essential features of these well-known models emphasize different approaches to decision-making in the legislative arena. The rational model conceives of decision-making as an orderly, logical progression from diagnosis to action based on the articulation of objectives, collection of facts, and systematic analyses of evidence.[7] The approved course of action emerges only after a broad range of alternatives is carefully weighed. Assuming that knowledge is the driving force behind policy choices, this model is more reflective of how decision-making ought to proceed than of how it actually occurs. Even if detailed information about a broad range of viable policy alternatives were accessible on every issue, legislators would be hard pressed to understand such a bewildering array of data.[8]

Unlike the rational model, the incremental approach forgoes large-scale movement based on in-depth analysis of all possible courses of action in favor of achieving small remedial gains by way of limited comparisons between "what is" and "what is acceptable" in the way of change. Built on existing policies and programs, the incremental approach seeks to ameliorate problems through an ongoing process of moderate adjustments at the margins.[9] From this perspective, policy, as Lindblom puts it, "is made and re-made endlessly," as past experiences create a reasonable gauge of future progress.[10] In contrasting these two approaches, one should not form an impression that the incremental model is irrational. Drawing on fewer data and a more limited range of policy options than does the rational approach, it is a decision-making process that relies more on political negotiation than technical solutions to problem solving.

Neither the incremental nor the rational model of policy-making render an accurate description of the process that gave rise to child abuse prevention legislation in California. The development of the Prevention Act is best understood by a model that might be called "opportunistic planning." Braybrooke and Lindblom acknowledge that some policies are opportunity-based.[11] Other analysts have suggested alternative approaches to policy-making, such as the "nonincremental,"[12] "surprise,"[13] and "calculated risk"[14] models. But there has been little elaboration of the basic elements that distinguish these alternative processes. Table 2.1 illustrates the central features of opportunistic planning and shows how this model differs from rational and incremental approaches.

There is, of course, an element of opportunity in all political decision-making; good timing may not be everything, but it certainly helps, whether a rational or incremental model is employed. In both cases, however, opportunity is not the essential feature of the problem-solving environment. Unlike the rational model, opportunistic planning does not rely on a careful weighing of the facts and a broad examination of alternatives. Nor does it involve the vigorous political negotiation among competing interests that animates the incremental approach.

Opportunistic planning is a model of decision-making characterized by a convergence of public opinion, political considerations, and interest group objectives around a social problem. The joining of these influences creates an immediate call for action and elicits support for a broad programmatic solution that is, by appearances, feasible enough to satisfy the urgent concern that "something be done." Such were the circumstances that led to the rapid, almost unanimous passage of the Prevention Act in 1984. As shown in Table 2.1, the process of opportunistic planning has implications that extend beyond the initial phase of policy design to implementation and program evaluation.

## IMPLEMENTATION OF THE CALIFORNIA PROGRAM

With the Prevention Act's passage into law, the task of implementing a statewide training program for children was assigned to the Office of Child Abuse Prevention (OCAP) of the California Department of Social Services.[15] It was a formidable undertaking, and the legislation offered only vague direction on many of its aspects. There is, of course, a degree of latitude in implementing most legislation, depending on how clearly the means and purpose are defined. The sharper its guidelines, the fewer the administrators' choices and the higher the possibility that legislation will be implemented as intended.[16] Legislative guidelines, however, rarely cover the full range of questions that arise during implementation; thus, the administrative unit, such as OCAP, often comes to shape policy in the course of carrying it out.

As suggested in Table 2.1, the margin of administrative discretion in the implementation process varies with the decision-making model through which policy was originally established. If the Prevention Act were formulated under the rational model, for example, it would have

TABLE 2.1. Alternative Planning Models

| Planning model characteristics | Rational planning | Incremental planning | Opportunistic planning |
|---|---|---|---|
| Definition of the problem | Problem viewed as unique from all others; quantifiable | Seen in light of other related problems; quantification is secondary | Problem seen as large and growing, although its dimensions may not be well measured; demands quick action |
| Process of decision making | All relevant factors taken into consideration; full cost–benefit analysis of all alternatives | Factors related to other relevant policies taken into consideration; feasible, related alternatives considered | Urgent search for broad-based solutions; limited analyses conducted. |
| Ideological orientation | Comprehensive knowledge more important than ideology | Competing ideologies tempered by compromise and agreement | Ideology a major determinant of proposed actions |
| Interest group influence | Limited—more attention to facts | Moderate—competing interests are mediated | Strong—interest group structure unified and supported by public opinion |
| Policy approval | Lengthy process of weighing all alternatives; ratification based on logical analysis of benefits | Long-drawn-out negotiations with other relevant actors; bargaining to achieve agreeable end | Little bargaining or debate, rapid acceptance by all; intense attention to the problem until it is solved or media attention subsides |
| Implementation | Moderate margin for administrative discretion; many options and regulations set forth | Moderate margin for administrative discretion; administrator adjusts by increments; changes usually defined by the policy | Large margin for administrative discretion; all relevant variables have not been defined nor addressed by the policy |
| Evaluation | High regard for systematic assessment of outcome; empiricism revered | Moderate regard for systematic assessment of outcomes; compromise revered | Limited regard for systematic assessment of outcome; interest group ideology supersedes empiricism |

undergone an exhaustive analysis of implementation strategies and choices. Following this approach, OCAP would have been authorized to carry out legislation with well-defined objectives and detailed instructions for their achievement. With the incremental approach, OCAP would also have encountered a fairly well-defined set of procedures for implementation. Through the process of extensive negotiations, characteristic of this approach, many details of implementation would have been hammered out, narrowing the scope of administrative choice.

Opportunistic planning, however, creates a wider margin of administrative discretion. In a climate of urgency, stimulated in this case by the growing reports of child sexual abuse, the details of policy implementation are often absent from legislative debate. Indeed, the Prevention Act was passed without regard for the many technical and administrative issues that are normally resolved in more deliberate proceedings. These questions arose in the process of implementation; the most problematic was that of how best to serve the preschool population. The bill was vague in its directive for serving this group; specifically, it was unclear whether the program should be offered to children in family day care programs, day care centers, or half-day preschools. Logistics of service delivery also needed clarification, as did regulations regarding the frequency of service provision. In response to these issues, OCAP drafted a technical clean-up bill following AB 2443's passage. Prominent in the language of this bill was OCAP's emphasis on "age-appropriate training" for all children and a move away from specified ages for training.[17]

But matters of technical detail were not the only issues raised as the Prevention Act guidelines were translated from policy to program. More fundamental questions arose regarding the appropriateness of prevention training. Again, preschoolers were at the heart of the issue. Would they be frightened by program content dealing with sexual abuse? Would the programs hinder normal familial expressions of affection? Would children misinterpret their parents' touches as "bad" or "abusive"? Unintended consequences in any of these areas would have a negative effect on children and expose the entire prevention effort to serious criticism. Although little data were available to answer these questions during the early implementation of the Act, the uncertainties they expressed gained force with the unfolding of the McMartin case and other incidents.

In 1984, just one month after the Prevention Act was introduced to the legislature, the McMartin preschool case came to public attention. Dozens of preschool children claimed to have been sexually molested by their day care providers. Public shock and outrage over this incident lent impetus to the passage of the Prevention Act and the inclusion of preschoolers among the service population. Yet as the McMartin case unfolded, complications arose. Children began recanting their stories. Some admitted that the incidents they described had never actually occurred. Others' accounts of the events wavered from plausible reality to clear fiction.[18] Children's accusations grew questionable.[19] Prosecutors were criticized for being over-zealous; therapists appeared to be manipulating children and putting words into their mouths. Whereas eight workers were initially charged for their roles in the McMartin case, only two were finally brought to trial. All other defendants were released for lack of evidence. Five years later, after the longest and costliest criminal trial in history, the two defendants, Peggy McMartin Buckey and her son Raymond Buckey, were acquitted on 52 counts of child molestation. The jury was deadlocked on 13 additional counts brought against Raymond Buckey. He was retried on 11 counts and finally acquitted on all charges.

McMartin was not the only highly publicized case of child abuse marked by controversy and confusion. In Jordan, Minnesota, for example, charges against a community "sex-ring" stirred public fears. Here, scores of children claimed to have been victimized by parents and neighbors. Four of them even described episodes of ritualistic torture and murder. During the investigative process, however, many children recanted their stories (all homicide stories were withdrawn), and all 21 defendants were dismissed from the proceedings.[20]

Although less visible, individual cases of false or unsubstantiated allegations also occurred. In California a 5-year-old disclosed her grandmother's "bad touches" after viewing a CAP presentation. The allegation ultimately proved false, but the incident was of considerable embarrassment to the family and sparked public concerns about the CAP programs (L. Wimberley, personal communication, September 1988).

Many children's reports are indeed based on true incidents of molestation. However, as the rate of child abuse reports increased in the early 1980s, so too did the number of unfounded cases. False allegations of child sexual abuse impose a heavy, sometimes devastating, emotional toll on the accused and their families. As the number of unsubstantiated allegations mounted, a backlash began to emerge against what some people felt were programmatic and legislative excesses of the child sexual abuse prevention movement. The loudest criticism came from a group known as the Victims of Child Abuse Legislation (VOCAL), formed in 1984.[21] This organization was composed mainly of parents and professionals who claimed to have suffered from false accusations of child abuse. In the delicate balance between children's rights and parents' rights, VOCAL charged that the scales were being tipped against parents.

Within the professional child welfare community, questions about investigation and treatment of child abuse also were being heard. Of particular concern was whether the child welfare system had the capacity to manage the burgeoning volume of child abuse reports. Reporting laws had been expanded to include greater numbers of mandated reporters such as teachers, researchers, day care workers, doctors, social workers, and even photographic processors. At the same time, prevention programs were raising children's awareness and encouraging them to report "bad touches" and other adult behavior that made them uncomfortable. Although child welfare workers were required to investigate a growing number of reports, funding for additional staff was not forthcoming. The margin for error expanded. If inappropriate intrusion into families continued at the going rate, Besharov warned, the child welfare system would lose credibility.[22]

These growing uncertainties about the consequences of new reporting laws and prevention efforts, fueled in part by criticism from groups whose members had experienced some harmful consequences of these measures, emerged shortly after the passage of the Prevention Act. Although public support for the Prevention Act was still quite strong, the Office of Child Abuse Prevention (OCAP) could feel mounting though diffuse pressures as it set about implementing this program. There was an awakening sense that the Prevention Act might become a volatile program, particularly at the preschool level. This heightened administrative responsibility to examine program effectiveness and provide empirical evidence of results.

## EVALUATION OF THE PRESCHOOL COMPONENT

In 1987, Beth Hardesty Fife was appointed the new Director at OCAP. From the beginning of her tenure, Hardesty Fife, whose child was of preschool age, had questions concerning the appropriateness of the Prevention Act's preschool component. She asked for suggestions about revising service delivery and was interested in exploring options that might alter the current programs without provoking resistance from the field.

At the same time that OCAP was starting to question the consequences of preschool training, empirical data on sexual abuse prevention programs were being collected and analyzed throughout the nation. Several of the studies focused on the preschool level. A federally funded project conducted by the Family Welfare Research Group, at the University of California, Berkeley, was among the most extensive of these efforts. This study focused mainly on the knowledge gained after participation in prevention training by 118 children in seven of the Prevention Act–sponsored preschool programs. The results were not encouraging. Before and after exposure to the programs, children were asked to explain what they understood about and how they would respond to material from prevention training curricula such as touching, secrets, and strangers. Although some learning took place, overall the gains were quite low.[23] On this point the study concluded: "If we assume that both the testing effect and the erosion of learning over time are limited, the best that can be said for the preschool segment of child abuse prevention training is that in a few areas it appears to yield rather modest gains in knowledge."[24]

Moreover, there was some evidence that the children might not have been interpreting all of the lessons exactly as they were intended. After exposure to the prevention curricula, children responded more negatively to pictures of neutral physical interactions than before the program. It could not be ruled out that these negative effects were related to prevention training. Although parents expressed a highly favorable view of the programs, only about one-third of them participated in the parent component, and over 20% noted that they had observed some indication of increased anxiety, such as changes in sleeping patterns and fear of strangers in their children after prevention training.

The findings from the California study were widely publicized in the media and roundly criticized by program providers. Indeed, there was room for criticism. The sample of 118 children was relatively small, though one of the largest studied at that time; the study instrument was new; and the absence of random assignment to experimental and control groups limited how firmly conclusions might be drawn from the data concerning program effects.

Despite these limitations, the general conclusions of the California study were reinforced by findings from several other studies, which had been completed by 1988, on knowledge of prevention training gained by preschoolers. For example, although Borkin and Frank asked just one question of 84 preschoolers, only 31% of their sample could respond appropriately after participation in prevention training. It was a simple question: "What should you do if someone tries to touch you in a way that doesn't feel good?" Yet few of the children could offer even one of the safety rules—say no, run away, tell someone—they had been taught.[25] Because this study employed a posttest-only design with no control group, it is also impossible to know how many of those who responded correctly actually gained this knowledge from the program. Similarly, a survey of 183 preschoolers who were trained using the Talking About Touching curriculum revealed an average score of 47% on the curriculum content for which they were tested. When the sample was divided according to the degree of training received by program presenters, the average test scores ranged from 35% for the children taught by those with no special training to 58% for the group taught by presenters with enhanced training. This study suggests that after 20 lessons, the longest of all prevention curricula, preschoolers were still unable to answer more than half of the items on a small test that ranged from 0 to 13 points.[26] Again, because the study employed a posttest-only design, it is unclear how many of the six to seven correct responses were already known by the subjects before taking the program. Several other studies with smaller samples also found that while children made apparent gains in knowledge, they were unable to grasp a large proportion of the material being taught.[27]

The California findings were congruent not only with other preschool studies, but with a large body of developmental research as well.[28] Bolstered by an amply documented literature on the cognitive limits of the preschool child, the study raised compelling questions about young children's ability to grasp many of the abstract and often complex concepts in the prevention curricula. In light of these findings, several directions for change were identified. Specifically, the California study recommended shifting Prevention Act resources away from the current focus on classroom presentation for preschoolers toward programs designed to sharpen the vigilance of parents, teachers, and other responsible adult caretakers. The idea was to place the duty for protecting children closer to their families and the community. Along with efforts to increase teacher training and to reach parents more effectively, it was also recommended that classroom training be phased out at the preschool level. If prevention training of preschoolers were to continue, however, the study suggested that it be revised significantly, eliminating many of the complex concepts and developmentally inappropriate demands in the prevention curricula.[29]

Program providers disapproved of the recommendations. But the emerging evidence from preschool studies resonated with concerns that state officials had been expressing about these programs. If young children really could not understand much of what was being presented, why waste taxpayers' money? Even worse, what if they misunderstood the lessons and made unwarranted accusations against parents and teachers? The organization of VOCAL created the distinct, if still faint, rumblings of a potential backlash. If false accusations rose or other unintended consequences of preschool training appeared, the entire Prevention Act program could be jeopardized. With all of the uncertainties surrounding preschool training, state officials and OCAP administrators believed that the interests of young children would be better served with a different approach.

With the support of public officials higher up in the administration, Hardesty Fife moved to reform the preschool component. A memo was sent to all providers in the state regarding "Program Improvements to the Child Abuse Prevention Training Act." These improvements included the suspension of all direct training for preschool children. The memo noted, "If children cannot grasp the message [of self-protection], the potential confusion may create anxiety in both the child and the family."[30] Agencies were assured that their overall funding would not be affected by this administrative decision. They were just being asked to change their programs' emphasis to create a safer environment for children by strengthening parent and teacher training.

The administrative decision to suspend classroom training for preschoolers was not well received in the field. Ideologically committed to their curricula and convinced of the importance of their efforts to empower young children, providers feared that this change would undermine the foundation of the sexual abuse prevention movement. Their opposition was rapidly mobilized. Supported by the program directors, Kate Kain, Director of the Northern California CAP Training Center, launched a campaign to have preschool training reinstated. Charging that Hardesty Fife's decision had altered the basic intent of the Prevention Act, Kain immediately enlisted the aid of Assemblywoman Maxine Waters, the Act's author. Joining the fray, Waters organized meetings with providers and conferred with fellow legislators. She also confronted the State Director of Social Services (Hardesty Fife's supervisor). Although the words exchanged at this meeting are not on public record, there is good reason to believe that Waters played political "hardball." One version of these events is that Waters threatened to decimate the Department of Social Services budget if the Act's preschool component was altered.

Although the exact form of political pressure brought to bear on the Department of Social Services may not be entirely clear, the results were swift and intended. Three months following the initial decision, Hardesty Fife was instructed to reinstate preschool training in California—effective immediately. But the case was far from closed. She was also directed to form a blue-ribbon task force that would further examine the issues surrounding preschool curricula and develop guidelines for age-appropriate programming.

In October 1988, OCAP convened the Preschool Curricula Task Force, whose 14 members were drawn from a variety of fields, including child development, law enforcement, education, research, and prevention programs. Divided into three subcommittees, dealing with child abuse prevention programming, research and evaluation, and child development, the Task Force spent a year studying research findings, listening to expert testimony, observing prevention programs, and conducting informal surveys. A report of its findings and recommendations was issued at the end of 1989.

Although they did not go so far as to propose terminating all preschool classroom training, the Task Force issued a call to seriously limit these programs, their recommendations substantially confirming those of the California study completed the year before. Following the main recommendation of this earlier study, the Task Force observed:[31]

> Parents and teachers are the most important influences in a preschool child's life, and primary prevention programs are in a unique position to reach both groups with vital information about how to prevent child abuse . . . Protecting young children is an adult responsibility; certainly we cannot expect preschoolers to shoulder the burden of protecting themselves. The *Task Force believes, therefore, that the central focus of primary prevention during the preschool years should be on the training and education of parents and teachers*. In many cases this means considerable expansion of a program's adult education component. Even when a program does very little training of preschoolers themselves, it can do a great deal to prevent abuse by helping the adults in these children's lives to become better teachers and parents. (emphasis added)

As for the limited classroom training that might be conducted (again in line with the earlier study), the Task Force advised eliminating many of the complex concepts and developmentally inappropriate demands in the current prevention curricula. Among a long list of concepts and lessons they believed inappropriate for preschool curricula, the Task Force recommended against the following:

- Teaching preschoolers the abstract concept of "body ownership" ("your body is your private property").
- Teaching that touch experiences can be classified into categories such as "safe" and "unsafe," or "good," "bad," and "confusing."
- Presentation of specific acts of private-parts touching by demonstration or use of media.
- Teaching preschoolers about adults or older children harming them physically or sexually.
- Teaching physical self-defense skills to preschoolers.
- Teaching preschoolers to "get away" or "run away" from an abuser or abusive situation, which creates unrealistic expectations about their abilities to outrun or ward off adults.
- Teaching preschoolers about the concept of secrets (for which they have an immature understanding) in the context of child abuse prevention.
- Teaching preschoolers to "trust their feelings" as a way to avoid abusive situations.
- Emphasizing rules for preschoolers in the context of child abuse prevention.

- Teaching children "don't talk to strangers," which creates distrust and cuts children off from potential sources of help.
- Teaching preschoolers about fault and blame.
- Teaching assertiveness skills in the context of warding off abuse.
- Teaching preschoolers the concept of "children's rights" (which they could understand only as the opposite of "left" or "wrong").

This list of prohibitions cut right to the ideological core of prevention curricula. The commitment to empowering children could not be realized without teaching concepts of children's rights, body ownership, assertiveness skills, and the other lessons the Task Force reported as inappropriate for preschool-age children. Although the Task Force did not recommend to discontinue classroom training entirely, their proposals to delete the concepts and lessons that composed the essential content of preschool prevention curricula were of little consolation to the program providers. Faced with the resistance to change from program providers and the Prevention Act's political support, whether the Task Force recommendations will have any effect on the reform of preschool prevention training in California remains uncertain.

Both strengths and weaknesses of the child sexual abuse prevention movement were revealed in its response to the controversy over preschool training in California. Through its ability to mobilize political support and public opinion, the movement stimulated awareness of the problem and created a climate highly favorable to prevention efforts. In this climate, investing a righteous cause with ideological fervor, prevention service providers could deflect criticism of their programs and resist change. The ideological commitment to empower children, which endowed the movement with resolution and unity, also deprived it of a certain resiliency that might have encouraged more serious consideration of research evidence and a more flexible approach to protecting children.

As the controversy over preschool training simmers, a number of questions continually bubble to the surface: What exactly do these programs communicate to children? Are the ideas presented developmentally appropriate? How do preschool prevention curricula differ from prevention curricula for the early primary grades? Chapter 3 examines the curricula design of major school-based prevention programs found in California and across the nation, and presents a comparative analysis of these programs for preschool and first- and third-grade children.

# C·H·A·P·T·E·R  3

# Ideology and Curricula:
# A Comparative Analysis
# of Program Design

In recent years the child sexual abuse pre-
vention movement has spawned a veritable industry that produces an
array of educational paraphernalia used in a variety of programs. Comic
books, puppets, theater, films, role plays, and other methods have been
designed to engage children and deliver the prevention message.

One of the earliest forms of prevention education utilizes the medi-
um of theater. Illusion Theatre,[1] Bridgework Theatre,[2] and Bubbylonian
Encounters,[3] for example, are creative and entertaining programs that
can reach relatively large groups of children in a single performance.
Presentation fees are high compared to classroom-based programs, but
costs per child are mitigated by the size of the audiences. This approach is
especially common in the Midwest, possibly reflecting the fact that the
use of theater for prevention training originated in Minnesota. The visual
arts provide a similar approach to prevention. Scores of films and videos
have been developed to communicate information about how to prevent
sexual abuse of children of all ages.[4] Although sometimes used in-
dependently as a training instrument, film is more often employed as a
follow-up to classroom lectures.

Another method designed to reach large audiences involves the use
of printed materials such as comic books and coloring books. The childhood comic figure "Spiderman," for example, has two special editions
dedicated to the cause of preventing child abuse.[5] Spiderman discloses
his own sexual victimization as a child in one edition. In a later episode he
also speaks out against emotional maltreatment and cautions children to
tell an adult if they are abused. Coloring books are also a popular means of
communicating the prevention message, allowing children to follow the

story line while filling in the pictures.[6] With printed material, prevention ideas can be reinforced outside the classroom as parents help their children to read and color the books at home.

Although plays, films, and books are among the mediums used in prevention training, the approach most widespread throughout the nation draws on classroom programs involving lectures and discussions. Some of these programs focus on problem-solving rules and the development of decision-making skills.[7] Others communicate ideas about touching, personal space, and physical boundaries.[8] The degree to which children interact with presenters varies from program to program. The Behavioral Skills Training Program (a Washington-based program), for example, is a highly interactive course, built on modeling theories of behavioral change.[9] Although other programs include some modeling and role playing, because of classroom size and time constraints only a few children are able to participate in these activities.[10] Typically, these interactive techniques serve as a catalyst for classroom discussion.[11]

Classroom training is popular partly because of intimacy and convenience: Children can be reached in relatively small groups, space and time are usually available for their questions, and daily schedules are minimally disrupted. Compared to presentations in an auditorium, the classroom setting is more easily managed to ensure that all children have an opportunity to hear the message presented.

With regard to the general orientation of classroom training, a content analysis of 41 sexual abuse prevention programs across the nation identified "empowerment" as the guiding conceptual framework in 61% of the cases. Two percent of the programs were guided by developmental theory and 2% by learning theory. The remainder were not explicitly identified with a particular framework, but among the programs designed for preadolescent children, 86% of the materials mentioned "body ownership," and they all taught assertiveness skills, which are basic elements of the empowerment model.[12] Thus, some aspects of empowerment were present in nearly every program for children.

## PROGRAM DESIGN: STRUCTURAL CHARACTERISTICS

It is estimated that 400 to 500 curricula have been designed for sexual abuse prevention training programs.[13] They address the needs of children of all ages. Some of these curricula are local products whose use is limited to the communities in which they were developed; others, such as the Talking About Touching and the Child Assault Prevention programs are marketed nationally and reach a vast number of children. Beyond the program providers, few people, parents of participating children included (see Chapter 6), are familiar with the precise form and content of prevention curricula. Claims for the uniqueness of programs and their delivery of material tailored to age differences are difficult for parents and policy-makers to judge. Although many programs claim to be unique, in one way or another most of them attempt to empower young children.

Within a framework of empowerment, the issues remain: To what extent do alternative programs for the same age groups vary in their essential characteristics? And how much do programs for different age groups vary? In addressing these questions, it is necessary to take a close look at the way classroom programs are structured and exactly what they teach. To provide such a view, 15 curricula were selected for analysis from among those being used by California's 84 sexual abuse prevention programs under the Child Abuse Prevention Training Act of 1984. Representative of the most prominent models in the state, these curricula include seven preschool, four first-grade, and four third-grade programs. They consist of both locally developed courses and training manuals adopted from well-known nationally marketed programs. These 15 curricula may not capture the entire spectrum of sexual abuse prevention programs, but they mirror a considerable segment of prevention efforts throughout the nation and incorporate several of the most popular courses commercially available. Tables 3.1 and 3.2 outline the curricula under examination in terms of their most significant structural features and substantive content.

In reference to their structural characteristics, all of the programs are organized around some form of lecture or discussion. About half include role playing. The Talking About Touching program also includes optional take-home activities for the children, but it is not clear how often that option is exercised in practice. Puppets are sometimes used to animate the lessons, mostly in the preschool programs.

The relationships between the adults presenting the curricula and the children on the receiving end is an important element in prevention training closely associated with program auspices. In most instances, community-based agencies, whose primary charge is to develop and disseminate prevention curricula, offer the program to schools in their surrounding area.[14] The community-based approach relies on presenters from outside the school. Program staff are therefore strangers to the children and are available for a relatively short period. They cannot follow up on children's questions that might come to mind over the course of time nor check on the progress of those who might disclose incidents of abuse. But the community-based programs are in the vanguard of the child sexual abuse prevention movement. Staff fervently believe in their work and usually bring a high degree of enthusiasm to the training sessions.

TABLE 3.1. Preschool Program Characteristics

| Program: | Preschool Child Assault Prevention | Preschool Children's Self-Help Project | Preschool Touch Safety Project | Preschool Talking About Touching | Preschool YSAP[a] | Preschool CAPIE[b] | Preschool Project SAFE |
|---|---|---|---|---|---|---|---|
| Mode of presentation | Lecture/discussion; adult role plays; some child role plays | Lecture/discussion; songs, visuals, puppets; some adult role plays; some child role plays | Lecture/discussion; use of puppets, visuals, songs, storytelling | Lecture/discussion; uses pictures and stories to initiate problem solving | Lecture/discussion; use of puppets | Lecture/discussion; songs | Lecture/discussion |
| Program period | 3 days | 2 days | 3 days | 27 lessons | 1 day | 1 day | 1 day |
| Presenter | Outside presenter, volunteer or paraprofessional | Outside presenter, volunteer or paraprofessional | Outside presenter, volunteer or paraprofessional | Trained classroom teacher | Outside presenter, volunteer or paraprofessional | Outside presenter, volunteer or paraprofessional | School district personnel |
| No. of Presenters | 2 | 3 | 2 | 1 | 1 | 1 | 2 |
| Auspices | Community-based | Community-based | Community-based | School-based | Community-based | Community-based | School-based |

[a]YSAP is an acronym for Youth Safety Awareness Project.
[b]CAPIE is an acronym for Child Abuse Prevention, Intervention, and Education.

33

TABLE 3.2. School-Age Program Characteristics

| Program: | First-Grade CLASS[a] | First-Grade CARE[b] | First-Grade Child Assault Prevention | First-Grade Talking About Touching | Third-Grade Talking About Touching | Third-Grade Child Assault Prevention | Third-Grade Children's Self-Help | Third-Grade Touch Program |
|---|---|---|---|---|---|---|---|---|
| Mode of presentation | Lecture/discussion; use of puppets | Lecture/discussion | Lecture/discussion; adult role plays; some child role plays | Lecture/discussion; uses pictures and stories to initiate problem solving | Lecture/discussion; uses pictures and stories to initiate problem solving | Lecture/discussion; adult role plays; some child role plays | Lecture/discussion; adult role plays; some child role plays | Lecture/discussion |
| Program period | 2 days | 1 day | 1 day | 17 lessons | 12 lessons | 1 day | 2 days | 2 days |
| Presenter | Outside presenter, volunteer or paraprofessional | Trained school personnel | Outside presenter, volunteer or paraprofessional | Trained classroom teacher | Trained classroom teacher | Outside presenter, volunteer or paraprofessional | Outside presenter, volunteer or paraprofessional | Outside presenter, volunteer or paraprofessional |
| No. of presenters | 1 | 1 | 2 | 1 | 1 | 2 | 2–3 | 2 |
| Auspices | Community-based | School-based | Community-based | School-based | School-based | Community-based | Community-based | Community-based |

[a]CLASS is an acronym for Children Learning Assertion, Safety and Social Skills.
[b]CARE is an acronym for Child Abuse—Recognize and Eliminate.

In contrast to community-based efforts, school-based programs are administered and sometimes developed within the school system. In the Talking About Touching program, for example, classroom teachers are trained to use the curriculum designed by the Committee for Children in Seattle. Under the assumption that children learn more readily from familiar adults, the curriculum's goals are to "provide information and self-protective skills that will reduce children's vulnerability to abuse."[15] Classroom teachers present the lessons and are available to work with troubled children throughout the year. The Child Abuse-Recognize and Eliminate (CARE) program is an example of a school-based model developed and employed by the Los Angeles Unified School District. Teachers, nurses, and principals who volunteer to participate in this program receive training in how to present the CARE curriculum. They are then organized into teams that deliver prevention training in each school.

Program length varies across the grades as well as by curricula. Preschool programs are typically presented in 15- to 30-minute segments over the course of 1 to 3 days. School-age programs are somewhat longer, with segments lasting approximately 1 hour, and are usually conducted over 1 to 3 days. The exception to this general pattern is the Talking About Touching program; its curriculum ranges from 12 to 27 lessons according to grades.

Overall, auspices and length are the most notable variations in program structure. In the vast majority of cases, the differences in program length are not large; but they are nevertheless curious. It is unclear why the range of from 1- to 3-day presentations emerged in California. This variance was more a matter of curricula choices that appealed to local service providers than of state policy concerning the most effective and efficient length of training; funding under the Prevention Act was based not on program duration but on the number of children served within each school district.

## WHAT IS TAUGHT? THE CONTENT OF PREVENTION TRAINING

Sexual abuse prevention programs attempt to convey a number of ideas that might help children protect themselves. Sometimes couched in slightly different terms (e.g., good touch/bad touch or safe touch/unsafe touch) and often delivered through different examples, stories, and play techniques, these ideas fall into several broad categories. Before examining in detail the specific concepts covered by each curriculum, an outline of the broader context may provide a useful orientation to prevention lessons delivered in preschool and first- and third-grade classes. What follows is a description of these general categories of program content.

## Touch Distinctions

The original terminology for helping children to distinguish among physical contacts comes from Cordelia Anderson, who talked about a "touch continuum" that ranged from good, to confusing, to bad touching.[16] These distinctions are used today in many programs.[17] The terms are usually described by prevention curricula in relation to their affective response: "Bad touches hurt and make you angry" or "Good touches feel good."[18] These definitions rely on the child's emotional and physical perception of the experience to identify the kind of touch received. The Talking About Touching program recently shifted from the "good" and "bad" labels to the language of "safe" (or "appropriate") and "unsafe" (or "inappropriate") touching.[19] Although the labels changed, the meaning remained fairly constant—children determine the safety of a touch by the actual or potential injury that may occur to them.

Some programs have taken a more symbolic approach to the touch continuum. The CLASS program refers to "Red Light" touches and "Green Light" touches.[20] Initially, the curriculum had included three colors (red, yellow, and green) to symbolize different touches in terms of traffic safety. Children were told that green lights meant "go," red lights meant "stop," and yellow lights meant "be cautious." But the yellow light concept seemed to cause some confusion. One student observed, "When my dad sees a yellow light, he steps on the gas and *goes fast!*" Because children's understanding of traffic safety was a little vague on this point, the yellow light was discarded in the elementary school curriculum. Along with this change, however, the traffic safety implications related to good and bad touching were also abandoned. Under the revised curriculum, green light touches are defined as "safe touches" and red light touches are defined as "not safe touches."

The Children's Self-Help Project also uses symbols to convey the touch continuum. A good touch is represented by a heart, a bad touch by the term "no," and a confusing touch by a question mark (?). The use of symbols has a certain appeal to parents and teachers, who may see this method as a delicate approach to the scary subject of abuse. Yet it requires an ability to deal with abstraction that is beyond the reach of many young children. (See Chapter 4 for a more detailed discussion of this issue.)

## Rules about Touching

There is a lack of consensus among program providers about how children should be taught to interpret physical contact. In some programs children are told to determine the nature of a touch by the feelings it engenders. If they experience a "funny feeling" inside, this should be taken as a cause for concern. The lesson here is that by using intuitive signals to diagnose physical contact, children can detect the danger of abuse. As the use of intuition is a difficult skill to communicate to children, it has been supplemented in some programs and abandoned in others in favor of a more rigid orientation to rules.

Among the 15 curricula selected for analysis, some continue to rely on the use of intuition, while others have adopted the more recent rule-oriented approach. The CAP program teaches children, "When a touch makes you feel uncomfortable inside, you should always tell someone you trust."[21] The Children's Self-Help Project also trusts children's intuition to gauge the safety of a touch:

> "Funny feelings are kind of hard to describe, because everyone's funny feelings are different. A funny feeling is something inside you. It's maybe like a little voice that tells you something's not okay. The little voice is like a warning saying, 'Uh-Oh,' better say no."[22]

In trying to communicate the concept of intuition, the Touch Program compares it to:

> "A feeling like an alarm going off inside your body and tells you when something is wrong . . . The Uh-Oh feeling, or intuition. Your Uh-Oh feeling, goosebumps, thoughts in your head.[23]

Other programs have combined the two approaches. They teach children to rely on intuition in addition to providing straightforward rules about touching:

> "Anytime someone touches you on your private parts . . . or you feel uncomfortable or mixed up about a touch, say 'no' and tell someone. It's against the law.[24]

The idea that touching is related to the authority of the law is an interesting feature of the Talking About Touching program (discussed at greater length in Chapter 4). In that curriculum, children are directed to report physical contact under three different circumstances: 1) if they are touched on the private parts; 2) if they are uncomfortable; or 3) if they feel mixed up about the touch. Rather than choosing one approach, this curriculum gives children three separate and unrelated reasons for reporting a touch. Under the rule-oriented approach, children are told:

> "It is never okay for another, more powerful person to touch your private body parts except for health reasons. It's against the law."[25]

Following the example above, in many cases, children are given a strict rule ("it is *never* okay") and then an immediate exception to the rule ("except for health reasons"). The exceptions to the rules vary by program. The CARE program simply tells children that adults must have a "very good reason" if they touch children's private parts.[26] The Talking About Touching curriculum excuses touches "in love relationships between two adults."[27] The message is a complex one, and prevention providers are not yet in agreement about it.

## Children's Rights and Body Boundaries

The concept of children's rights is central to many programs. Children are taught that they can control access to their bodies and should reject any touch that is unwanted. All CAP workshops, for example, focus on the concept of empowering children by encouraging them to assert their rights. The CAP curriculum is most ardent in communicating assertiveness skills.

In referring to children's body rights, one CAP program succinctly explains: "Your body is yours alone."[28] The Children's Self-Help Project offers the following description of children's rights:

> You have the right to feel safe from forced or tricked touch [*sic*]; the right to ask questions about forced or tricked touch to private parts of your body or the other person's body; and the right to say 'no' to forced or tricked touch [*sic*].[29]

In some programs, body rights are introduced through examples such as children's rights to eat and to sleep. Although not part of the written curriculum, on one occasion CAP presenters were observed embellishing the lessons with a suggestion that children even have a right to watch TV.[30] How well youngsters understand the concepts of individual rights and body boundaries is unclear, but these ideas are prominent among prevention lessons for both children and parents. In educating parents about their need to recognize children's rights, a CAP parent manual states:

> Children begin to want their own room, closed doors, private time alone. It's important to foster that [*sic*] so the child learns that they [*sic*] have the right to control their own body and personal space. An analogy can be drawn between a bedroom door (closed) and sexual assault. If a door is closed, like your bedroom door, then another person should not enter without your permission. Later, a child will generalize this to mean, "No one can do anything to me without my permission."[31]

## Private Parts

Most sexual abuse prevention curricula attempt to describe the body's "private parts" so that children will understand exactly where it is they should not be touched. The approach to this topic varies as do the areas of the body identified as "private parts" by different programs. Despite the strong interest in conveying this knowledge, few program providers apparently are comfortable in offering children detailed and explicit information about their bodies. Instead, many curricula become prudishly euphemistic when addressing this topic, perhaps to make program content more palatable to parents and teachers.

Private parts are often described as "those areas covered by a bathing suit."[32] Privacy is conveyed to children by stating, "they (the parts covered by your bathing suit) stay covered unless you take a bath or change into pajamas, or go to the doctor."[33]

Taking a somewhat more tangible, if not completely explicit view, the Children's Self-Help Project defines children's private parts as "the mouth, the chest, between the legs, and the bottom."[34] And in the Talking About Touching curriculum, teachers are allowed some discretion in presenting this subject; they may use either the veiled bathing suit definition or more direct identification of anatomical parts. The training manual for teachers of this curriculum states:

> In the discussion of touch, it is rare that a child will mention sexual touch. It is important to introduce this concept to the children. An easy way to do this is to talk about private body parts as the parts of the body that are covered by a bathing suit. If you are in a position to do so, it is preferable to use medical names of body parts, but in many schools it will be easier to use the swimsuit idea.[35]

Although the "swimsuit idea" is usually welcome in schools, it does not always convey the appropriate information to children. For example, girls often wear one-piece bathing suits; are they to assume that the entire torso is off limits? When boys wear bathing shorts, do their private parts include everything from their waist to just above the knees? There is much room here for confusion, especially when dealing with young children who are inclined toward a literal interpretation of this message.

## Prevention Skills

Children are taught a variety of skills to prevent abuse. All of the curricula advise them to say no firmly if someone tries to harm them and to tell an adult they trust about the episode. This lesson is expressed in phrases such as: "No is a safe, strong and free word;[36]" "you can say 'no' or 'stop' "[37]; "he should say, 'stop that, I don't like that.' He should use a big strong voice."[38] Children are encouraged not only to assert themselves if harassed but to report the incident. They are instructed to "tell someone you trust"[39]; a variety of individuals are recommended, including "your family, teacher, school counselor, brownie leader, minister or police"[40] or "Mom, Dad, siblings, cousin, teachers, baby-sitter, grandparents, or call 549-KIDS."[41]

Other prevention skills involve teaching children how to alert neighbors and community members that something is wrong. They are coached to "yell and say what is wrong. No one can understand us when we cry. Make a lot of noise."[42] Or "yell if you need to get attention."[43] Two programs offer children lessons in a special type of yell:

> "This is a safety yell so you should only use it when you're in trouble. The yell doesn't come from the top of the throat, it comes from the small place between your ribs."[44]

The "safety yell" is deep, rather than the more common children's screech and is expressed in a way that "people will know it is serious and will come to help when they hear it."[45]

These various skills try to communicate a sense of empowerment to children, suggesting ways to handle threatening situations. One program takes the idea of empowerment further than any other. As an outgrowth of women's self-defense programs, CAP teaches children to fight back if they are grabbed by an assailant. The children are advised:

> Kicking is a good idea . . . You can kick him in the shin . . . Scraping down the shin and stomping on the stranger's foot are also good ideas. Use the heel of your shoe to scrape down the stranger's shin. The part of your foot called the instep, or the arch, is very sensitive. There's [sic] a lot of little bones there so that when you stomp on the stranger's instep, it really hurts him. Your elbow is a good weapon because it's sharp. Push your elbow really hard into the stranger's stomach. If you're tall enough you can aim for the throat . . . If the stranger puts a hand over your mouth, you can bite or grab a hold of his little finger. Brace your other fingers against the back of the stranger's hand, and pull his finger back as far as you can.[46]

Children are advised to follow these "safety precautions" because program providers believe that they will work. Yet there is no mention of the actual danger children may face if they fight back against an offender.

## Secrecy

Touching shrouded in secrecy is one of the most obvious signals of child sexual abuse. A secret is something told to another person, which they are not to tell to anyone else. As an interaction that involves both giving and keeping, "secrets" are difficult to describe to children; the definition is complex and therefore hard to convey. Also, secrets are usually a rich and pleasurable part of children's early school years, not an act generally to be guarded against.

Most programs try to address this issue by dividing secrets into two categories. "A good secret," as one curriculum explains, "might be a surprise for someone"[47]; "a good secret is a secret that makes you feel good when you tell it—like a surprise."[48] However, "some secrets are not good, like touching or looking at your private parts. Bad secrets have no time limit. They are usually scary."[49] Children are taught that bad secrets, usually described in relation to bad or unsafe touching, should never be kept.

## Blame

Children who are sexually abused sometimes feel guilty and blame themselves for letting it happen. Those who feel guilty are often reluctant to report their abuse and unable to halt its recurrence. In response to these feelings of guilt associated with abuse, many curricula try to assure children that no matter what the circumstances, sexual abuse is never the victim's fault. For example, "If [this has] ever happened to you, remember: it was not your fault, it is never your fault when a bigger person/adult does something wrong. It is never too late to tell someone."[50]

## HOW MUCH DO PROGRAMS DIFFER? A COMPARATIVE ANALYSIS

As indicated in the overview of program content, the majority of prevention curricula in California and across the county are built around the idea that children have personal rights and should be empowered to exercise those rights. With a full understanding of their rights, children are taught to assert themselves in order to prevent being molested. Programs also try to teach children how to distinguish between different kinds of touching. Here, touching is usually defined along a continuum from good to bad, the latter identified in terms of physical contact with a child's private parts. Children are shown how to protect themselves if an adult tries to seduce them sexually; these protective measures include saying no, running away, standing an arm's distance away, yelling, or using self-defense skills. They are also instructed to report any inappropriate touch to a parent, teacher, or adult friend. Finally, they are told that "bad touching" is often shrouded in secrecy and that these "bad secrets" must be revealed. Programs impress upon children that if they have suffered sexual abuse it is not their fault; the adult abuser is to blame and should be reported.

Although the exact terminology may differ, the general messages that prevention programs deliver appear highly comparable. To assess the degree of comparability, these prevention messages were decomposed into 29 specific concepts. The 15 sexual abuse prevention curricula covering preschool and first- and third-grade programs were analyzed to determine which of the 29 concepts were covered in each program. As shown in Tables 3.3 and 3.4, there are some differences in the concepts presented by these curricula. One program teaches about strangers, but another does not. Some programs discuss bribes; others do not. More striking than their differences, however, is the extent to which the substantive content covered in these programs overlaps. (For a more detailed analysis of the terms in which these concepts are expressed see Tables A.1, A.2, and A.3, in Appendix A.)

Overall, the number of concepts presented to children at every age level is quite high, particularly in light of the length of most programs. On the average, lessons for third-grade children contain 23 concepts; those for first graders, 24; and those for preschoolers, 18. Excluding the unusually long Talking About Touching programs, which consist of 12 to 27 lessons of 15 minutes each, the average length of classroom instruction is about 28 minutes for preschoolers, 67 minutes for first graders, and 83 minutes for third graders. This allows about 1.6 minutes per concept for preschoolers, 2.9 minutes per concept for first graders, and 3.6 minutes per concept for those in the third grade. Because older children are generally better prepared to absorb ideas about sexual abuse prevention than younger children are, the time spent per concept at the different grade levels is a curious reversal of what one would expect.

There are often differences between the range of material contained in a written curriculum and what program presenters actually teach in the classroom.[51] To gauge the extent to which the written curricula fully reflect program content, directors of the first- and third-grade programs were asked to fill out the list in Table 3.4 indicating which concepts were covered in their classroom presentations. According to the directors' responses as shown in Table 3.4, the range of materials presented in first- and third-grade programs increased by an average of almost two concepts per program, or approximately 8%. Assigned to a residual category, most of these additional ideas were not among the main concepts identified in the content analyses of curricula.

On the whole, prevention curricula appear to be shaped more by the ideology of empowerment than by any other considerations. Program providers claim that developmental factors weighed heavily in the design of prevention curricula; yet in a detailed content analysis of the major

TABLE 3.3. Preschool Program Concepts

| Concept | Preschool Child Assault Prevention | Preschool Children's Self-Help | Preschool Touch Safety Program | Preschool Talking About Touching | Preschool YSAP | Preschool CAPIE | Preschool Project SAFE |
|---|---|---|---|---|---|---|---|
| Good touches | | X | X | X | X | X | X |
| Bad touches | | X | X | X | X | X | X |
| Mixed-up/confusing touches | | X | X | X | X | X | |
| Good secrets | X | X | X | X | X | X | |
| Bad secrets | X | X | X | X | X | X | |
| What to do if told a secret | X | X | X | X | X | X | |
| Body rights | X | X | X | X | X | | X |
| People you know can abuse you | X | X | X | X | X | X | |
| Strangers | X | X | X | X | X | | |
| Say no | X | X | X | X | X | X | X |
| Run away | X | X | X | | X | X | X |
| Tell someone | X | X | X | X | X | X | X |
| Whom to tell | X | X | X | X | X | X | X |
| Keep telling if they don't believe you | | X | X | | | | |
| Stand at arm's distance | X | X | X | | X | | |
| Yell | X | X | X | | | | |
| Self-defense | X | | | | | | |
| Private parts | X | X | X | X | X | X | X |
| Rules about touching | X | | X | X | X | | X |
| When *can* people touch private parts | | | X | X | | X | X |
| When *can't* people touch private parts | | | | X | | | |
| Bribes | | X | | X | | | |
| Abduction | | | X | | | | |
| Intuition | X | X | X | X | | | |
| Guilt/blame | | X | X | X | X | | X |
| Bullies | X | X | X | X | X | X | |
| Physical abuse | | | X | | | | X |
| Emotional abuse | | | X | | | | |
| Neglect | | | X | | | | |
| Other | | | | X | | | |
| Total number of concepts | 17 | 21 | 26 | 21 | 18 | 14 | 12 |
| Minutes per program (approx.) | 45 | 30 | 45 | 405 | 15 | 15 | 15 |

# TABLE 3.4. School-age Program Concepts

| Concept | First-Grade CLASS | First-Grade CARE | First-Grade Child Assault Prevention | First-Grade Talking About Touching | Third-Grade Talking About Touching | Third-Grade Child Assault Prevention | Third-Grade Children's Self-Help | Third-Grade |
|---|---|---|---|---|---|---|---|---|
| Good touches | X | + | X | X | X | | X | |
| Bad touches | X | + | X | X | X | X− | X | |
| Mixed-up/confusing touches | | X | | X | X | | X | |
| Good secrets | X | X | X | + | X | X | X | |
| Bad secrets | X | X | X | X | X | | X | |
| What to do if told a secret | X | X | X | X− | | | X | |
| Body rights | | X | X | | | X | X | |
| People you know can abuse you | X | X | X | X | X | X | X | |
| Strangers | | X | X | X | X | X | X | |
| Say no | X | X | X | X | X | X | X | |
| Run away | | X | X | + | X | | X | |
| Tell someone | X | X | X | X | X | X | X | |
| Whom to tell | X | X | X | X | X | X | X | |
| Keep telling if they don't believe you | X | X | X | X | X | X | X | |
| Stand at arm's distance | | + | X | + | | X | X | |
| Yell | | | X | | | X | X | |
| Self-defense | | | X | | | X | X− | |
| Private parts | X | X | | X | X | | X | |
| Rules about touching | X | | X | X | X | | | |
| When *can* people touch private parts | X | X | X | X | X | | | |
| When *can't* people touch private parts | X | X | X | X | X | | | |
| Bribes | | X | X | X | X | | X | |
| Abduction | | | X | | | | X− | |
| Intuition | | X | X | + | | X | X | |
| Guilt/blame | X | X | + | X | X | | X | |
| Bullies | | | X | X | X | X | X | |
| Physical abuse | X | + | X | X | X | | X | |
| Emotional abuse | | | X | | | | X | |
| Neglect | X | | X | X | + | | X | |
| Other | X | | X | X | + | | X | |
| Total number of concepts | 18 | 24 | 27 | 25 | 23 | 13 | 25 | |
| Minutes per program (approx.) | 100 | 50 | 50 | 255 | 180 | 50 | 100 | 1 |

+Indicates that directors report this concept is taught in the program, although it was not found in written curriculum.

−Indicates that directors do not report this concept is taught in the program, although it was found in written curriculum.

44

curricula available to preschoolers, first graders, and third graders, program similarities stand out more clearly than do their differences. The primary differences in programs for younger children can be found in the methods of curriculum presentation. In this respect, providers are well attuned to the attention span of young children and their needs for varied activities. Appropriate methods and length of presentation, however, are no substitute for content tailored to children's abilities. Without careful regard for the cognitive limitations and the moral behavior of young children, the effectiveness of prevention curricula is ultimately compromised. In an effort to put these limitations into perspective, some of the prevalent features of children's development from preschool through middle childhood and how they bear on sexual abuse prevention training are examined in the following chapter.

# Program Design and Developmental Theory

$C$oncern for children's safety and the desire to cultivate their intellectual abilities at a young age have engendered efforts to accelerate the learning process. Despite the good intentions behind them, these efforts may advance ideas that are beyond the developmental levels of children in the early grades. As the National Association for the Education of Young Children explains:

> Concerned adults, who want children to succeed, apply adult education standards to the curriculum for young children and pressure early childhood programs to demonstrate that children are "really learning."[1]

Exploring this problem, Elkind has written extensively about the "miseducation" of children.[2] He advocates early childhood education that is in step with young children's physical, cognitive, and emotional development. This is a sensible standard against which to assess programs that teach children how to fend off sexual assaults.

Following this standard, the question naturally arises: What is the fit between the developmental abilities of children ages 2½ to 9 years and the form and substance of prevention training? When thinking of children's development, it is well to begin by considering not what a child can learn but how a child can learn best.

## HOW DO CHILDREN LEARN?

Educational materials come across most effectively when the mode of presentation is tailored to the student's age.[3] The older the child, the greater the attention span and tolerance for didactic lessons; in contrast, younger children often ignore or resist this form of presentation. Preschool and elementary school age children learn experientially—through exploration, manipulation, repetition, and interaction.[4] Some developmental theorists might suggest that the child's primary means of development is attained through active participation in the learning process.[5] Children grasp new concepts more readily when offered an opportunity to explore ideas through expressive techniques such as role playing, drawing pictures, and talking about the experience; as a general rule, children respond with more enthusiasm when engaged in active rather than passive learning.[6]

Group size is also a significant factor in the educational process. Individual and small-group experiences are the optimal arrangements for learning in the early years. State standards for preschool funding in California, for example, require one adult educator for every eight children.[7] With this adult-to-child ratio of 1:8, a group of up to 16 children in a classroom is a manageable learning environment. These standards were set in light of various research findings on the relation between class size and children's education.[8] The teacher–child ratio recommended for the first and third grades is somewhat larger (1:10 or 1:12), accommodating classroom groups of up to 20 and 24 children with two teachers.[9]

In addition to group size and the use of active learning techniques, the duration of exposure to new information is an important variable in the process of educating young children. The retention of new concepts in the early grades requires gradual introduction and regular exposure over time. Young children do not absorb information like sponges. Cowan suggests that their learning process is more akin to a generator–transformer mechanism, where ideas are taken in and used in ways that work best for the child.[10] Through repetition and reinforcement children integrate new concepts into their cognitive structure. Few parents or teachers provide a single admonition to children and expect it to be followed; young children need to be reminded numerous times before they are trusted with new information.

In structuring prevention curricula, providers have attended to some of the special learning needs of young children. They recognize, for example, that the attention span of a 3-year-old is more limited than that of a 9-year-old. Preschoolers rarely devote themselves to an activity for longer than 15 or 20 minutes.[11] Thus, classroom presentations to preschoolers typically run for 15 minutes, whereas early elementary programs last an hour. More easily distracted than older students, primary-grade children and preschoolers are reluctant participants when bored by the task at hand.[12] Responding to this characteristic, prevention workshops for preschoolers include lively plays complete with songs, puppets, rhymes, and pictures. These assorted activities were conceived to attract and hold the transient attention of their young subjects. Some first-grade curricula also include animated modes of instruction, however, by the third grade, the rhymes and songs disappear from most programs and the instruction becomes more didactic.

Although animated modes of instruction may hold their attention, the role of personal experience in learning about the world is crucial to younger children.[13] Words do not always translate into meaning until they are experientially perceived by the child. It is possible to drill children to remember words and phrases, or to teach them rhymes and songs. But the simple repetition of words and tunes is not necessarily an indicator of comprehension. Indeed, when listening carefully to children, one sometimes hears the most delightful confusions, such as "I pledge allegiance to the flag of the United States of America and to the republic for which it stands, one nation under God, *invisible . . .*"

Language development is no small matter when it comes to helping primary-age children master new material. Children learn new concepts most quickly when they are expressed in familiar words.[14] If a new vocabulary is presented in tandem with unfamiliar concepts, children may be able to recall the words that are used, with little idea of what they mean. In testing what young children learn from prevention programs, the distinction between "parroting back" and a full understanding of the material is often difficult to draw. Elkind also cautions adults not to assume children's understanding of concepts based on their language usage.[15] In evaluating the Talking About Touching Program with 9- and 10-year-olds, for example, Downer found that 94% of her experimental sample could define assertiveness after training, but only 47% were able to give an example of an assertive reply.[16]

The issue of how well children really understand sexual abuse prevention lessons is as significant for third graders as for preschoolers. When children are given too much information, it can cause cognitive disequilibrium. The way they deal with this imbalance is to take in the material that makes sense and to either discard the extraneous information or try to make sense of it within their existing cognitive structure.[17] When information is discarded, children have only a partial understanding of the material. When trying to integrate concepts that they do not understand, children can misinterpret what is being taught,[18] a serious matter when these ideas deal with sexual molestation.

Bernstein and Cowan's work on children's understanding of sexual activity suggests that young children often distort information that adults try to communicate on this topic, and have great difficulties integrating the concepts.[19] The review of prevention concepts in Chapter 3 reveals that a good number of ideas are presented to children at every age level. Although less information is communicated to younger children, on average, each grade is faced with a relatively large amount of material to absorb in a relatively short time. Not only are there a considerable number of concepts. but many of the words used by programs to transmit the ideas are unfamiliar to children, particularly preschoolers. From age 2½ to 3½, a child's vocabulary increases from approximately 400 words to 1,000 words.[20] By age 4 it doubles again.[21] Although this is a significant advance in a short time span, the preschooler still has a very limited vocabulary. It is unlikely that preschool children learn many of the new words, such as "shin," "bribe," or "rights," over the brief course of prevention training. This is somewhat less of a problem for first and third graders. School-age children not only have a larger vocabulary, but they can also articulate the meaning of words more easily.[22] Words and concepts remain constant in their meaning, even when different individuals use them; definitions of words also become clearer and more stable in school-age children's minds.[23] Compared to preschool children, who do not initially understand the meaning of many words in prevention lessons, and thus have difficulty recalling them, older children find it easier to remember much of the information provided. In general, school-age children do not face the cognitive challenges that preschoolers must contend with regarding the substantive content of sexual abuse prevention programs. Nevertheless, how well first- and third-grade children comprehend the full array of concepts presented in an average session of prevention training remains unclear.

## COGNITIVE REQUISITES OF PREVENTION CURRICULA

In the course of their exposure to prevention curricula, children are called on to master abstractions, multidimensional constructs, symbolic representations, and practical skills. These tasks place intellectual demands on children that are not always consonant with their abilities, particularly those of the youngest participants.

### Dealing with Abstractions

Much of the material in prevention curricula involves concepts that are moderately abstract such as safe, free, secrets, bribes, intuition, and children's rights. According to Piaget, the preschool or "preoperational" child's thinking is restricted to concrete perceptions of the world in which actions are irreversible and objects indivisible.[24] Thus, the child's abstract understanding is markedly limited at this age.[25] As children develop in the primary-grade years and shift from the preoperational to the operational stage, their capacity for abstract thought increases (the process is gradual, and many children do not develop abstract thought processes until much later).[26] Whereas preschool children often physically move or handle an object before they can understand it, children of primary school age begin to manipulate objects mentally. This is a major hurdle of the early years, but the process is incremental, and does not mean that these youngsters think as adults do. Children in the primary grades can use some symbols, but they still need concrete reference points for understanding.

The development of this thought process can be seen quite clearly by examining the notion of secrets—a central concept in most prevention programs. If one were to ask a preschool child to define a secret, the child's response would focus on the description of a concrete action. That is, the child would probably say that secrets involve the act of whispering in someone's ear or cupping a hand over one's mouth; the content of the secret would be lost, especially if it had been communicated in audible tones. As children grow, they begin to comprehend the idea that a secret is more than an act of communicating words, that it involves keeping something hidden or concealed, regardless of how it is communicated. A perpetrator might tell a child of 8 or 9 in a normal voice that she should not reveal what has happened to anyone; although the message is not whispered, the 8-year-old is likely to understand that she has been told to keep a secret.

The ideological principles on which many curricula are based involve a set of fairly abstract ideas about "children's rights." These rights are typically classified as "rights to be safe, strong, and free."[27] The message that children have certain rights often is not heard in the way that well-meaning adults intend. As one child development specialist put it, "To them, the word 'right' means the opposite of 'left' or 'wrong.' "[28] Kohlberg suggests that "having a right" is equated with children's understanding of "being right."[29] The right to be "strong" is intended to communicate a sense of inner strength and psychological empowerment. This is a particularly difficult idea for children to grasp. Understanding their world through concrete activities and experiences, strength is viewed mainly in relation to its physical outcome. Thus, efforts to communicate a right to psychological empowerment may be heard as a license to use physical force. The right to be "free" is equally complicated. Does it mean free to eat ice cream or go to sleep whenever they want? Indeed, what it means to be free—freedom from (coercion) or freedom to (realize one's potential)—is a long-standing subject of philosophical debate.

## Interpreting Multidimensional Constructs

Adults have the ability to perceive multidimensional aspects of their environment. However, young children are apt to think along only one dimension at a time.[30] They do not perceive two characteristics simultaneously; nor do they allow additional experience to enhance their initial perception. Instead, they tend to fixate either on the quality or quantity of an object as it is immediately observed.[31] This creates possibilities for confusion, as prevention curricula contain many concepts that are multidimensional.

The "touch continuum," for example, combines dimensions of physical and emotional experience that may confound its meaning for young children.[32] This continuum not only categorizes the physical experience of touching but also connects that experience to one's emotions (i.e., "a good touch makes you feel good" and "a bad touch makes you feel bad").[33] The confusing touch is in the middle ground, with an equally perplexing definition. Confusing touches include either multiple emotions regarding a single event (e.g., "you feel good about it at first and then change your mind and you don't like it any more")[34] or a merging of the action with the actor (e.g., "you like what the person is doing, but you don't like the person").[35] But Cowan suggests that preschool children experience emotions serially and singularly; the blending of emotional experience is not an accurate depiction of the young child's experience.[36] The preschooler loves her new dress or hates her shoes. She loves her mommy when she's nice and hates her when she's stern. Expressions of ambivalence are rare and not well understood by young children. Therefore, the mixed-up touch, which signifies two conflicting emotions about a single experience or person, is difficult to comprehend.

Just as younger children experience emotions singularly, they also have great difficulty perceiving multiple character traits in individuals.[37] Hartley and Hartley studied children's understanding of multiple class membership and found that young children believe that traits can be attached to only one object.[38] For example, when children were asked if their mother were still a mother when she was at work, many responded negatively, saying that the mother could not have two labels because she would then be two people. This tendency to think in unidimensional terms is not well suited for prevention messages that try to convey the multiple characteristics of offenders:

> There are two kinds of people who sexually abuse children: strangers and people you know. Most of the time it is someone the child knows. When someone in a kid's family sexually abuses a child, it is called incest.[39]

In fact, most of the prevention curricula include multiple labels in their definitions of behavior:

"Secrets can be 'good' or 'bad.' "[40]

"Safe touches are caring. They don't hurt our bodies or feelings," and/or "They can be given by someone you don't want them from—regardless of how they feel."[41]

"Unsafe touches hurt our bodies or feelings," and/or "They may not hurt our bodies or feelings, but are on our private parts."[42]

"You may want [a '?' touch] at first but then change your mind." Or, "You may like the person who's doing the touching, but you may not like how the touch feels."[43]

Not only are these concepts two-dimensional, but they include temporally separate aspects as well—events that may occur at a later time. Yellow touches can turn into red touches; tickling may become sexual abuse. These temporal eventualities represent a two-dimensional shift in thinking. School-age children may be able to deal with these constructs, but preschoolers are usually perplexed by them.

Young children are similarly inept in making dispositional or temporal transitions with regard to character traits. As Kraizer observes, "Young children are unable to reconcile a 'bad' touch occurring with 'good' people, that is, people they love."[44] Rholes and Ruble have examined children's understanding of the inconsistency of character disposition and action.[45] Their work shows that preschoolers cannot anticipate the behavior of others over time. In fact, the implications of their study suggest that a young child who is abused once may not be able to predict that the same offense could occur in the future.

One of the goals of many prevention curricula is to communicate the possibility that seemingly innocuous situations may transform into threatening events. They suggest that children discern potential threats and take preventive action in case the threat becomes real. This idea is taken directly from women's self-defense training. However appropriate it may be for adults, the idea of anticipating danger is not in keeping with the capacities of young children. Coppens examined preschool children's ability to take preventive action that would stop an unsafe situation from occurring.[46] Her findings show limited anticipatory behavior; children must first know that a situation is unsafe before they will act. This study confirms Schultz and Mendelson's work, which notes that preschoolers have greater success at identifying factors that cause an effect than they have with identifying factors that prevent an event from occurring.[47] Programs that encourage children to "trust [their] funny feelings"[48] and to act on the basis of emotional cues do not fully appreciate the temporal dimensions of this task and the demand it places on children to evaluate a situation for potential danger and take preventive action.

## Translating Symbols

During the preschool years, children gradually begin to perceive material things and actions, not only objectively but also in a representational fashion.[49] They "pretend" to drink from a cup, talk on the telephone, or animate dolls as people. This has a clear connection to children's cognitive development; by internalizing observations and experiences through symbolic play, they are simultaneously assimilating their experience. Although this early symbolic thinking is a stepping-stone to more challenging cognitive tasks, not all children are capable of translating some of the more advanced forms of symbolic representation employed in prevention curricula. Returning to the touch continuum, for example, in one program, red, yellow, and green lights are used to symbolize the different types of touching.[50] Depending on their age and experience, some children may be in the process of learning the absolute meaning of "red," "yellow," or "green." Others may have advanced to the point that they can understand the symbolic meaning of colors in relation to traffic safety. Those children may be able to grasp the transformed concept:

> "When we get a green light touch, we say Go! We want it to go on and on."

> "A red light touch makes us feel bad and to a red light touch we say *stop*."

Children's symbolic thought, however, goes only as far as their experience. Specifically, the reason red, yellow, and green are considered constructive symbols for children is that it is assumed the traffic safety concepts have been mastered. Children run into problems when the symbols are beyond their personal experience. For example, one curriculum includes a "Heart," a "?," and a "No" touch.[51] The question mark touch can be an intelligible symbol of the uncertainty that may be aroused by some forms of physical contact if children have mastered reading, writing, and of course, punctuation skills. However, when used with children who have not yet learned the alphabet, the symbolic message remains incomprehensible.

## Learning Practical Skills and Their Application

Beyond the introduction of new words and concepts, the teaching of practical skills is the centerpiece of prevention programs. Saying no to unsafe touches and exerting oneself in physical self-defense are among the prevention techniques conveyed through classroom instruction. Many experts question whether young children are able to learn these skills and apply them effectively.[52] Consider, for example, training in self-defense, which is based on a model for adults used by the Women Against Rape program. Even where grown women are involved, few instructors attempt to teach self-defense in one lesson, partly out of misgivings about its inappropriate application.[53] There is also concern that training in self-defense might make some women overconfident of their abilities to combat an assailant, which could do them more harm than good.[54] In some cases, instructors believe that training in self-defense for women depends largely on psychological preparation and is only in part a matter of physical techniques.[55]

These issues take on deeper meaning when young children, rather than adult women, are the subjects of self-defense training. Children simply do not possess the physical strength to defend themselves against adults. While these lessons are highly unlikely to increase safety, the potentially negative consequences of self-defense training—inappropriate use and overconfidence—loom more prominently for children than for adults. Brief exposure to these techniques in the classroom may suggest that the use of physical force is acceptable behavior in the schoolyard. In one school, for example, at the conclusion of a CAP presentation for third graders that taught self-defense, the children immediately began to try out their newly learned techniques on each other. The teacher was left with the task of breaking up these altercations and undoing the lesson that had just been taught.

Self-defense training delivers a message to children that they may effectively exercise abilities that in reality they do not possess. In this regard, it is a message that may create an unwarranted level of confidence. There is some evidence that children interpret this message in ways that could be hazardous to their well-being. Nibert and his associates asked preschool children after exposure to a CAP program how they might react to various threatening circumstances. This study revealed that the children's primary response to one or more of the questions was to "hit or kick" a bully, a stranger, or a known abuser.[56]

## SOCIAL AND MORAL REQUISITES OF PREVENTION CURRICULA

The teaching of abstract concepts, symbolic representations, and certain practical skills places heavy demands on the cognitive abilities of young children to interpret prevention lessons and to apply them appropriately when at risk of being harmed. Beyond the constraints posed by their cognitive development, other developmental boundaries limit what young children can absorb from prevention curricula. Given their levels of social and moral development, lessons concerning, for example, guilt, bribes, rules about touching, and trust require careful examination.

## It's Never the Child's Fault

Sexual abuse prevention training curricula typically devote several minutes of instruction to telling children that they should not feel guilty if they are abused. In contrast to this message, research on the egocentrism of young children suggests that they often assign responsibility to themselves for events in which they are not involved.[57] Because of this orientation, a few minutes of classroom instruction may not be enough to convince a preschool child that she is not to blame for a sexual assault. Moreover, the child's relationship to the offender also affects his or her sentiments of guilt or shame.[58] Over 75% of sexual abuse cases involve someone known to the child.[59] Therefore, it is probable that the offender has a strong influence on the child's emotional experience of the abuse.

If the notion of assigning responsibility to others for an offense in which they are involved is difficult for children to grasp, should the lesson be discarded? Many argue no. Some providers in the field of prevention claim that although a young child may not fully comprehend the ideas of guilt and blame, the training "plants a seed of knowledge" that can be referenced in later years.[60] Whatever its long-range consequences, introducing the idea of culpability in an abbreviated lesson may be counterproductive for young children in the short term. Although sexual molestation can be physically painful, much abuse of children in the early stages is characterized by fondling, petting, or exposure, which may not necessarily be perceived as a disagreeable experience.[61] In fact, recent work with sexual abuse victims indicates that many children (perhaps even a majority) initially fail to recognize that they are being abused.[62] By associating this behavior with feelings of guilt, prevention curricula may inadvertently arouse the very emotions that they seek to relieve in young children.

## Threats and Bribes

Certain other lessons also may be problematic for children in the early phases of their moral development. According to Kohlberg, for example, young children's orientation to obedience shifts over time. He identifies six stages of moral development.[63] In the first stage, children primarily focus on punishment, obedience, and physical and material power.[64] Rules are understood in relation to the consequences of punishment by an authority figure; at this point in development very few internal mechanisms for regulating behavior have been acquired. During Stage 2, the child's orientation shifts, not so much to avoid punishment as to obtain reward from others. Kohlberg's formulation complements Piaget's groundbreaking work on the process of moral development. Piaget distinguishes two stages: the initial stage he called "heteronomous morality" and the later stage, "autonomous morality."[65] In the first stage, children are guided by externally imposed rules rather than by internalized standards or codes for regulating behavior.[66]

There is much discussion regarding the age at which children change their orientation to obedience.[67] Kohlberg finds the first stage of moral reasoning pronounced until age 7. The second stage becomes more prominent until approximately age 10; thereafter more advanced stages dominate the child's thinking. If his model is correct, then preschool morality is governed by Stage 1, first graders are approaching Stage 2 (some have reached this stage), and third graders are firmly established in Stage 2 (a few will be in transition to Stage 3).

How do these perspectives on moral development relate to sexual abuse prevention training? Prevention programs typically instruct the class about how to repel a sexual assault (say no, run away, use self-defense) and to report the incident (tell someone). Children who are developmentally in Kohlberg's first or second stages of morality, however, are strongly inclined to obey their primary caretakers (to avoid punishment, to gain rewards). Thus, bribes, threats, and strong admonitions from a closely related adult offender have an almost compelling influence on the behavior of young children. In fact, there is evidence suggesting that children's compliance with rules is strongly related to their relationship with adult figures of authority.[68] Piaget's conceptualization of the developmental process also suggests that children's initial orientation to obedience may inhibit them from repelling a sexual assault or from defying the offender's cautions to secrecy. As he explains:

> Any act that shows obedience to a rule or an adult, regardless of what he may command, is good. . . . The good, therefore, is rigidly defined by obedience. . . . This only points to [the child's] real defenselessness against his surroundings. The adult and the older child have complete power over him.[69]

Given a command not to tell by a close adult authority and a suggestion to tell in a brief presentation by a stranger in the classroom, children are likely to obey the real authority in their lives. In the early stages of development, authority is made legitimate by size, strength, and relationship.[70] Disobedience to authority is often followed by unpleasant consequences. The ability to distinguish between types of morality increases, of course, with age and development.[71] As children move from preschool to the early elementary school grades, their orientation to obedience shifts from acceptance of adult rules as absolutes to greater reliance on their own reasoning.[72]

## Safety Rules

A number of studies have been undertaken to identify the extent to which children's sense of morality is dependent on their cognitive development (from preoperational to concrete operations),[73] whether it is a learned behavior[74] or if, in fact, children conceptualize morality more broadly.[75] Damon associates children's reasoning about justice with their logical reasoning based in concrete operations.[76] But other studies show that relationships between children and authority figures are actually multi-dimensional and dependent on the environmental context.[77] It has been suggested that children as young as age 3 are able to distinguish true moral transgressions from the breaking of conventional standards.[78] Moral transgressions can be described by their intrinsic value or by the consequences of the action, such as inflicting harm or pain on people.[79] Conventional standards are based on the practice of social norms (e.g., manners, dress code). Several studies report that children tend to view moral transgressions negatively, regardless of their age. In contrast, behaviors that break conventional standards elicit a more varied pattern of response.[80] Smetana shows, for example, that in the eyes of young children conventional transgressions are permissible in the absence of a clearly defined prohibition and that such rules define the basic nature of conventional morality for children.[81]

These studies suggest that if the children perceive an act as a true moral transgression, they are more likely to understand it as "wrong" (and may be more easily influenced to say no, run away, or report the incident to an adult). If they understand the behavior only in terms of a social construct, they may be coaxed to abandon the rule when faced with persuasive arguments against its acceptability.

Young children's perception of moral transgressions and conventional morality comes into conflict when prevention programs offer contradictory rules about touching. A popular curriculum for children of all ages uses the terms "safe" and "unsafe" touches to describe its touch continuum.[82] "Unsafe touches" are first described as "touches which hurt our bodies or our feelings." The definition corresponds to the child's sense of moral transgression based on physical consequences. This curriculum also asks children to differentiate touches based on their intuition. If it "feels funny"[83] or if it is a touch "you don't like,"[84] the child is instructed to recognize the immoral act and report it. Here "unsafe touching" actually includes two definitions. The first has painful consequences and relates to a child's sense of basic morality. The second is based on conventional standards of morality as indicated in the following rule for behavior:

> Today we are going to talk about another kind of unsafe touch—a touch to which you should always say "No!" Sometimes grownups try to touch children on their private body parts, or they try to make kids touch the grownup's private body parts. It is not okay for these people to touch kids' private parts unless it is for health reasons. . . . There are some things grownups can do, but children should not.[85]

Because sexual abuse does not necessarily cause pain (it may actually feel somewhat pleasurable for a time), the child may not perceive the act as an obvious moral transgression.[86]

In regard to rules against touching children's private parts, prevention programs are trying to communicate a relative standard of conventional morality. These rules are justified not by the immediate consequences of behavior but by the prescription of adult authorities. Of course, not all touching of children's private parts involves sexual molestation. But when it does, the young victim encounters two contradictory rules of conventional morality—one prescribed by the curriculum presenter, the other prescribed by the perpetrator who insists that the behavior is not wrong. The difficulty in teaching preschoolers about the ramifications of sexual abuse and ways to prevent it become strikingly clear, as deYoung explains:

> If [children] are able to make only a moral judgment, that is, an assessment of the rightness or wrongness, the goodness or badness, of a situation on the basis of its outcomes and consequences, then in cases of "gentle" molestation in which there is nonintrusive sexual contact, verbalizations expressing love and care, and no unsettling threats, children will not perceive this type of touch as bad.[87]

Programs that depend on the concept of a "touch continuum" that is beyond the understanding of many youngsters may result more in confusion than prevention.

Social rules that censure child sexual abuse will have a stronger imprint on older subjects. As they advance through their elementary school years, children become legalistic in their orientation.[88] Conventional rules take on a new significance because they are sanctioned by the group, and group expectations play an important role in older children's lives. Prevention providers who tell older children that sexual activity with adults is wrong, clearly get their subjects' attention; these children want to conform to group standards of correct behavior. But when providers say that such sexual activity is "against the law," they may be compelling some children to make very difficult decisions about loyalties to people close to them. Children whose orientation is legalistic would naturally assume that if sexual abuse is indeed illegal, the perpetrator will be imprisoned. If abused by a close relative or family friend, the child may be torn between doing the right thing by reporting the offense and remaining silent in order to protect the offender against going to jail.

## Trust and Attachment

Forming and sustaining healthy attachments with adult caregivers is a major developmental hurdle in the preschool years[89] and crucial to a child's social development throughout childhood. When children are warned about bad things that could happen to them it is important that the message itself does not cause harm by undermining their trust in essential caregivers. In this regard, some of the messages conveyed through sexual abuse prevention workshops would seem to have negative implications. Drawn from several prevention curricula, the following statements do little to promote trust and attachment:

> "People could do things to you that make you feel uncomfortable or could even hurt you. These people can be anyone; even people you know very well or people you love."[90]

> "Sometimes, someone you know, a friend of your family, neighbor, cousin, may try to hurt or scare you by touching you in a way that is confusing or in a way which you do not like."[91]

> "We know there are two kinds of people who touch children in private parts of their bodies when they don't like it or it feels funny: strangers and people you know."[92]

Messages such as these reinforce children's sense of vulnerability in a dangerous world, a place where they are easily hurt and frightened.

Children in preschool through third grade remain highly dependent on adults for meeting their most basic needs. Although the older children may rely more on peers for social support than younger ones do, in this age range all children depend on parents and primary caregivers for food, clothing, shelter, socialization, and emotional support. In some respects, prevention programs that promote children's rights and independence are at odds with the normal conditions of dependence appropriate for young people. Children should be encouraged to seek the help of adults when they are in trouble or in a vulnerable situation. Prevention lessons that emphasize telling a trusted adult support the idea that children can depend on adults for safety and assistance. A better way to phrase this idea would probably be a suggestion to "talk about it with someone you know"; this would move children away from the possible confusion between "telling" and "tattling." Placing the emphasis on communication and mutual assistance between adult and child is an approach to prevention that sustains trust and attachment.

## FEMINIST THEORY AND CHILD DEVELOPMENT

Prevention programs based on feminist theory seek to empower children and teach them what they need to learn to protect themselves from sexual abuse. Developmental theory explains a good deal about how children learn and what they may be able to learn at different ages. These theories offer somewhat incompatible prescriptions for prevention training. What children need to learn psychologically and physically in order to protect themselves against abuse according to feminist theory is not always what they may be ready and able to learn according to developmental theory.

Developmental theory, as previously noted, underlines a number of important aspects of prevention curricula that are difficult for young children to grasp. With regard to cognitive development, the use of abstract concepts and concepts that contain more than one dimension are problematic. This is not a trivial matter because many of the basic prevention lessons involve information that is relatively abstract and multidimensional. Although ideas such as rights, secrets, and a "?" touch are no doubt self-evident to adults who design prevention curricula, they are often beyond comprehension to young children. In preschool and the early grades children may "parrot back" the words and phrases through which these ideas are conveyed without fully understanding either their meaning or the lesson to which they are attached.

In the area of moral development, the way young children interpret moral standards and their orientation toward obedience to adults suggest they would have a very difficult time putting into practice lessons about bribes and rules about touching. Programs that provide children with simple prescriptions for their safety do not take into account the complexity of abuse, nor the subtlety of judgments involved in a child's response to potentially harmful situations. Finally, children's early attachments to caregivers are essential to their later social development. From the point of view of empowerment and learning to protect themselves, it may be helpful to inform children that parents, relatives, and other adult figures in their lives could sexually molest them. In regard to the social needs to develop trust and feelings of security, these lessons are counterproductive.

Although developmental theory has important implications for the design of preventive curricula, this perspective has had relatively little influence on the prevention movement, particularly in children's programs. In our discussion of developmental theory, the reader may have noticed a certain lack of precision when it comes to identifying the exact age or grade at which children may be ready to absorb prevention lessons of varying complexity. We have referred to developmental implications for children—young children, preschool children, and children in the early and later grades. In dealing with young children, a few years makes a tremendous difference. The developmental literature suggests that all of the aspects of prevention programs noted as difficult for children to grasp would apply to 4-year-old preschoolers, but as we move up to third graders, who are twice this age, the ability to learn these lessons increases. (It is important to bear in mind that being able to learn a prevention lesson is not the same as being able to put it into practice when faced with a threatening situation.) How much this ability increases and precisely what concepts and lessons are appropriate at the different levels between preschool and third grade, however, are not clear. This issue is explored in Chapter 5, which examines the learning of prevention concepts among program participants in the first and third grades.

C·H·A·P·T·E·R 5

# Age and Learning: Analysis of the Early Grades

T he developmental issues raised in the last chapter suggest how a few years in age can make an important difference when assessing prevention programs for young children. As noted earlier (in Chapter 3), the sexual abuse prevention training curricula are fairly uniform in their content across the early grades. Although developmental theory and empirical evidence indicate that much of this material is beyond the social and intellectual grasp of 3- and 4-year-old preschoolers, it may be within the compass of 6- or 8-year-olds.

The issue of age and learning in prevention programs will be examined in light of findings from a study of first- and third-grade participants in the eight California programs previously described. This study used a quasi-experimental pretest–posttest design. Although this design cannot account for the extent to which findings are influenced by history and maturation, a posttest-only group was included to control for the possible effects of testing. Data about what students learned from the programs were gathered through the administration of questionnaires and an interview schedule. These in-struments were pilot-tested with 36 first-grade and 35 third-grade children and reviewed by administrators from the prevention programs involved in the study. In the final sample of participants, interviews were conducted with 334 students, of whom 305 also completed the written questionnaire, which was read aloud to all the students. (For a more detailed explanation of the research methods, see Appendix B.)

## PREVENTION LESSONS: WHAT WOULD YOU DO?

The study questionnaire utilized a three-item multiple choice format accompanied by a small drawing that represented each of the response categories. Composed of 14 questions (see Table 5.1), this instrument covers a range of basic concepts used in the major lessons of prevention training. These lessons involve telling, secrets, stranger danger, physical abuse, intuition, guilt/blame, perpetrators, touching, and assertiveness. Some of the lessons, such as those that deal with telling and touching, were examined from several different perspectives.

An item-by-item analysis (see Appendix A, Table A.4) of the pre- and posttest responses reveals that the overall sample of children registered gains in knowledge on all but one question. That question (no. 11) asked: When would it be all right for someone you know to touch you. On this issue, prevention programs generally try to portray the concept of touching along a continuum from positive to negative. To touch is a neutral action; only when an adjective is added (i.e ., good touches, bad touches) do the programs distinguish the type of touch given. Yet many of the children in this sample reacted to the word "touch" negatively. Although Question 11 makes no reference to a bad touch, or a touch to the private parts, after the children's participation in the program, this question was interpreted with an increasingly prohibitive connotation. Before the program, 36% of the total sample stated that a touch would "never be all right." At posttest, this category of response increased to 43%. The largest change came from first-grade children whose incorrect responses increased by 10%. The posttest was conducted 6 months after the program was given, so the results capture a level of knowledge that remained with the children over this period.[1]

In general, children were more likely to see a range of adult figures as potential helpers in times of distress rather than relying solely on family members as their source of support. They were more likely to say that they would assert themselves in uncomfortable situations, and they were less likely to say that they would keep a secret about touching. On 5 of the 14 questions, changes in the patterns of response were statistically significant for the total sample; within the two groups, first graders evidenced statistically significant differences on four questions; third graders, on three questions.

Some responses reveal interesting differences between first- and third-grade students. For example, on Question 7 a large percentage of the sample answered that only strangers might "try to touch you in a way you do not like." Approximately half of the first graders held this belief on pretest and, more important, maintained this belief on posttest. Although 34% of third graders responded with "only strangers" on pretest, most changed their answer to the correct category of "anybody" after the program. This wariness of strangers was also revealed in first-grade children's answers to Question 12. Here, first graders were again more likely than the older group to respond that they would say no only if the

TABLE 5.1. Study Questionnaire

---

1. Who could help you if you had a problem?

   **A. Could grown-ups you like help you?**[a]
   B. Could only people in your family help you?
   C. Could no one help you?

2. What would you do if a big person tried to do something to you that you did not like?

   A. Would you hit or kick the big person?
   **B. Would you tell a grown-up you know?**
   C. Would you let the bigger person do it?

3. What would do if a big person told you to keep a secret about touching?

   A. Would you tell your friend?
   B. Would you keep the secret?
   **C. Would you tell a grown-up you know?**

4. When would it be okay for a grown-up you know to spank you?

   **A. Would it be okay if it were just a little spank?**
   **B. Would it never be okay?**
   C. Would it be okay if it left a bruise?

5. What would you do if you got a funny feeling inside you when a big person touched you?

   **A. Would you tell the big person to stop?**
   B. Would you keep your feelings a secret?
   C. Would you tell the big person it feels funny?

6. What if a big person touched you in a way that you did not like, whose fault would it be?

   **A. Would it be the big person's fault?**
   B. Would it not be anyone's fault?
   C. Would it be your fault?

7. Who might try to touch you in a way that you did not like?

   A. Would only strangers?
   B. Would only people you know?
   **C. Would anybody?**

8. What would you do if your friend told you that a bigger person touched his or her private parts?

   **A. Would you help your friend to find a grown-up to tell?**
   B. Would you tell your friend to keep it a secret?
   C. Would you tell your friend you feel sorry for him or her?

*(continued)*

TABLE 5.1. *(continued)*

9. What would you do if a grown-up wanted you to do something that you did not think was okay?

   A. Would you do what the grown-up told you to do?
   **B. Would you not do what the grown-up told you to do because your feelings are right?**
   C. Would you wonder what to do?

10. What would you do if you told a grown-up something that bothered you and the grown-up did not believe you?

    A. Would you forget about it?
    **B. Would you find someone else to tell?**
    C. Would you not know what to do?

11. When would it be all right for someone you know to touch you?

    A. Would it be all right if the other person liked it?
    B. Would it never be all right?
    **C. Would it be all right if you liked it?**

12. What would you do if a big person did something to you that you did not like?

    **A. Would you say no?**
    B. Would you say no only if it were a stranger?
    C. Would you let the big person do it?

13. What would you do if a big person tried to touch you in a way you did not like?

    A. Would you not tell anyone about it?
    **B. Would you tell a grown-up about it?**
    C. Would you tell your friend?

14. What would you do if someone you did not know wanted to give you something?

    **A. Would you say no?**
    B. Would you take it?
    **C. Would you ask your mom if you could have it?**

---

[a]Correct responses were affirmative answers to questions shown in **bold**.

offender were a stranger. Although the percentage decreased slightly after their participation in the program, on the posttest more than 50% of the first grade children still held to this response.

Third-grade children had a good understanding of how to deal with "secrets about touching," as evidenced by their high rate (over 90%) of correct responses to Question 3 even before they experienced prevention training. First graders showed less knowledge on pretest, but a substantial increase on posttest.

Moving beyond the analysis of individual items, a summary score was developed to investigate children's overall grasp of the material. Based on the number of correct responses to the questionnaire, the highest score possible was 14. As Table 5.2 indicates, the mean score for the total sample was 10.12 on pretest, increasing to 11.24 on the posttest.

First-grade children achieved a mean score of 9.39 on the pretest and 10.66 on the posttest. Viewed in terms of proportions, on the pretest they answered 67% of the questions correctly, which increased to 76% after participating in prevention training. Although the difference between the pre- and posttest scores was statistically significant, the absolute change in score of only 1⅓ points was not high. Because the total score range is narrow (0–14), a gain of 1 point translates into a 7% increase in the proportion correct.

Third-grade children did better on the pretest than did first-grade children. Their mean pretest score of 11.31 was almost 2 points higher than that of the first graders' pretest and two-thirds of a point higher than the first-grade posttest scores. Thus, third graders scored better before going into the prevention programs than first graders scored after receiving the training. Increasing by close to 1 point on the posttest, the

TABLE 5.2. Summary Analysis of Questionnaire Results

| Score | Total sample | Third grade | First grade |
|---|---|---|---|
| Mean pretest score | 10.12 ($n = 231$) | 11.31 ($n = 88$) | 9.39 ($n = 143$) |
| Standard deviation | 2.16 | 1.63 | 2.13 |
| Percentage correct | 72% | 81% | 67% |
| Mean posttest score | 11.24* | 12.19** | 10.66*** |
| Standard deviation | 1.89 | 1.58 | 1.82 |
| Percentage correct | 80% | 87% | 76% |
| Percentage change | + 8% | + 6% | + 9% |
| Posttest-only score | 11.05 ($n = 74$) | 12.11 ($n = 36$) | 10.08 ($n = 38$) |
| Standard deviation | 2.26 | 1.90 | 2.20 |
| Percentage correct | 79% | 87% | 72% |

*$t = 5.94$, $p < .0001$
**$t = 3.66$, $p < .0001$
***$t = 5.39$, $p < .0001$

difference in third-grade children's scores before and after the program was also statistically significant. Overall, third graders responded correctly 80% of the time on pretest, demonstrating a high degree of knowledge before the program began; after participation in prevention training their level of correct response rose slightly, to 87% of the questions.[2]

In addition to the sample of students tested before and after participation, a second sample of 36 third graders and 38 first graders was tested only after the program. This posttest-only group allows us to examine the extent to which prior exposure to the questionnaire might influence the children's ability to perform on the posttest. However, the very small differences in scores between the posttest and posttest-only groups were not statistically significant (see Table 5.2). As such, it is unlikely that the demonstrated gains in knowledge can be attributed to the pretest experience.

## Program Outcomes

Although the analysis in Chapter 3 suggests that there are few substantive differences in concepts and lessons taught by the eight California programs, the form in which these materials are presented varies. In order to explore the extent to which the different forms of presentation may have influenced learning, children's pre- and posttest scores were examined by program site. In conducting this analysis, concepts drawn from the written questionnaire were compared to concepts found on the School-Age Program Concepts (Table 3.4, p. 44). Some of the programs explicitly cover all of the concepts included on the questionnaire, but others may not. Therefore, in analyzing student outcomes by program site, each program's mean score and percentage correct is compared to the total possible for that program as indicated by the concepts chart. (A detailed breakdown of pre- and posttest scores for each of the programs is shown in Appendix A, Table A.5).[3]

In general, the outcome scores did not vary a great deal among first- and third-grade programs. The largest gain in knowledge among the third graders was registered by children in the Touch Program and among first graders by those in the Child Abuse—Recognize and Eliminate (CARE) program. The smallest gains occurred in the Talking About Touching (TAT) program for third graders and the first-grade Child Assault Prevention program (CAP).

The absence of any gain in knowledge (actually, a small decrease in the posttest mean) among the third-grade participants in the TAT program is of particular interest because this program, delivered in 12 lessons, is considerably longer than the other three at that grade level. As already noted, third graders come into these programs knowing more of the material that will be presented to them than do first graders. By the third grade, children appear to be so familiar with these ideas that longer and more extensive presentations of the material (as in the TAT program) may not have an appreciable influence on learning. This is further suggested by the finding that whereas both first and third graders tended to show an increase on the posttest, in three of the four third-grade programs, changes in scores were not statistically significant—in contrast to the first grade, where in three out of four cases the changes were significant.

## Telling

Five of the 14 questions addressed aspects of children's "telling responses" in several situations.[4] A separate analysis of these questions was conducted to explore changes in this area. First-grade children had a pretest score of 3.69 (out of a total of 5), or 74% correct, to questions about who and when they would tell if faced with a potentially abusive situation (see Appendix A, Table A.6). Their posttest score increased to 4.29, or 86% correct; the difference between pre- and posttest scores was statistically significant. This was not the case for third-grade children, who started out with a very high pretest score of 4.42, or 88%, which did not leave much room for change. Although their posttest scores increased slightly, the difference was not statistically significant.[5]

Examined by program site, a few differences stood out among first grade programs (for details, see Appendix A, Table A.7). The greatest increase between pre- and posttest scores was found in the CLASS program. A significant change was also evidenced by the first grade CARE program. The weakest results were experienced in the first-grade CAP and third-grade TAT programs.[6]

In assessing the questionnaire results, several points should be kept in mind. Taking responses to all of the questions as a whole, it appears that the programs had only a limited impact on children's knowledge. Examining responses in different domains, the strongest impact was on first-grade children's telling responses. Third graders had higher scores but showed smaller gains in most instances because they began with more advanced knowledge of prevention-related behaviors. Children in first and third grades started out with correct scores on two-thirds and four-fifths of the prevention ideas before exposure to these materials. It is important to remember that by chance alone they could have guessed correctly on about one-third of the multiple-choice questions. On average, children learned only one additional concept after prevention training. According to statistical tests, this change was significant; that is, it was unlikely to occur on the basis of chance alone.

There is, however, an important distinction to be drawn between statistical significance and substantive significance. Statistical significance is a statement of probability. The fact that the very limited gains were unlikely to occur by chance does not imbue the results with substantive meaning for sexual abuse prevention. Does a change in 1 point on a 14-point scale actually make any difference in a child's prevention-related skills and behaviors? Although this question perplexes researchers and program providers alike, it is difficult to imagine that so small a gain in knowledge would have much of an effect on behavior.

## TOUCHING AND FEELING

Distinctions between different types of touches—those that make children feel good, mixed-up, and bad; those that are safe and unsafe; those they do not like and those that make them feel funny—form the cornerstone of many prevention curricula. Children are expected to understand that there is a connection between the physical act of being touched and the emotions it may generate. Earlier findings from the Family Welfare Research Group's California preschool study revealed that many children of preschool age had difficulty making this connection, which is so basic to much of the prevention curricula.[7] To explore how well first and third graders understand this and other aspects of training, pre- and posttest interviews were conducted using a picture book and wooden figurines. The picture book included four sketches of interactions frequently encountered between adults and children that involve touching. These sketches depicted adults hugging, tickling, tucking children into bed, and spanking them. In the interviews, first and third graders were asked to describe how they thought the children in these pictures felt (happy, mixed-up, or sad), why, what might make them change their feelings, and whom the adult represented.

The responses to the hugging picture were positive and maintained a high degree of stability, with 83.5% of the students, on both the pretest and posttest, describing the child as feeling happy.[8] Among those who did change, most (9.3%) moved appropriately toward a positive response on the posttest. When a sample of preschool children was asked a similar question in the earlier study, they demonstrated neither the degree of positive response nor the stability expressed by the elementary school sample. Only 58% of the preschoolers thought the child was happy on both the pre- and posttest. Those who changed tended to move in a positive direction. Overall, however, 75.6% of preschoolers perceived the child as happy on the posttest, compared to 92.8% of the elementary school sample.

Addressing a somewhat ambiguous situation, the interview responses to the tickling picture were less stable and more diverse.[9] Almost one-third of the students altered their views from pretest to posttest, yet these changes did not vary in a particular direction. Thus, on both pretest and posttest a total of about 60% of respondents described the child being tickled as happy, and close to 23% said that the child was confused. There is an interesting difference between these findings and the pattern of responses that emerged in the study of preschool children. After their participation in prevention training, there was a slight decrease (from 20% to 17%) in the proportion of first and third graders who thought the child being tickled would feel sad. In contrast, preschool children's responses moved decidedly toward a more negative interpretation, with the proportion who viewed the child as sad doubling from 16.5% to 34.1%.[10] These findings raised a question of whether prevention programs may have sensitized preschool children to the negative possibilities of some types of physical contact that appear on the surface as friendly or ambiguous. The different patterns of response between preschoolers and elementary school children suggest that this concern would not apply to the older children, an implication reinforced by their reactions to the tucking-in-bed picture. Although the tucking-in-bed picture was also presented as a somewhat ambiguous situation, on the pretest it was seen as generating happy feelings by 78% of the elementary school sample, a proportion that increased to 83% after participation in the prevention programs.

In both the pre- and posttest interviews the vast majority (96%) of students thought the child in the spanking picture was unhappy. Their assessment of the emotions connected to this physical interaction was stable and unambiguous. Preschool children had a similar reaction: those describing the child as sad increased from 68% on pretest to 87% on posttest. As in the other comparable pictures, the preschoolers' pattern of response to connections between touching and emotion was neither as stable nor as appropriate as that of the elementary school sample.

After describing the emotions attributed to the children in each picture, the students were asked why they thought the children felt this way. The objective here was to assess the extent to which students could make a logical connection between experiencing a touch and feeling an emotion related to that physical interaction. Findings from the preschool study indicated that after the prevention program half of the preschoolers were unable to provide a logical explanation for the responses they gave to all of the pictures, which casts some doubts on how firmly they grasped the relation between touching and feelings. In contrast, first- and third-grade students were able to give an example that corresponded to the emotion they had observed in almost every case.

The students were next asked to imagine conditions under which one's emotional response to touching might change (i.e., those who initially observed a child in one of the pictures as happy were asked, "What might make this child sad?"). This question sought to determine how well students understood that a temporal shift in emotions might occur as physical interactions changed. Prevention curricula attempt to communicate the idea that what begins as seemingly benign physical contact could turn into sexual abuse—a good touch turns into a bad touch. Most preschoolers were unable to imagine a range of situations that might cause feelings to change from one state to another. Their unidimensional thinking tends to ground them in the here and now, making it difficult to conceive of hypothetical futures. Although preschoolers had a hard time with this question, between 93% and 98% of the first- and third-grade students could formulate logical examples of how the situation might change.

The findings noted above deal with the students' responses to a set of pictures in which they were presented with different kinds of physical contact and asked to describe affective reactions associated with these contacts. This sequence was reversed in a second set of pictures, which showed children in an emotional state and asked the students to describe the kind of touch that might have made them feel this way. ("Somebody touched this girl and she feels mixed-up about the touch. What do you think happened to her?") On this question, results from the preschool study indicated that young children had a better ability to explain what might have happened to cause the mixed-up feelings.[11] The elementary school sample scored considerably higher in this area than did preschoolers, and those able to offer an appropriate reason for the mixed-up emotion increased from 76% on pretest to 84% on posttest (see Appendix A, Table A.8). Within the elementary school sample there was a substantial difference between the two groups, with 98% of the third graders able to give an appropriate response on the posttest compared to 73% of the first graders. Thus, the ability to grasp the fairly complex idea of a confused or mixed-up emotion appears to increase at a high rate up through the early elementary grades.

When the elementary school sample was asked who might have touched the mixed-up boy (or girl), over half of the students replied that it was someone the child did not know (i.e., a stranger). Third graders maintained a stable pattern of response to this question, with a little over 70% suggesting, on both the pre- and posttest, that it was a stranger. The first graders' pattern of response showed a 17% increase ($p < .003$) in the number of students who responded on the posttest that the child was touched by a stranger.

Along the same line as their answers to the questionnaire, both first and third graders indicated a tendency to associate sexual abuse with strangers. When shown the picture of a child with a sad face, the students were specifically told: "Someone touched this boy (girl) on his (her) private parts and he (she) feels sad about this." In response to the question of who touched this child, on the posttest 60% of the sample identified the offender as a stranger and only 21% said it was someone known to the child (see Appendix A, Table A.9). This result corroborates findings from Wurtele and Miller's study, in which children from kindergarten through first grade and from fifth through sixth grade were told about a hypothetical incident of sexual abuse and were then asked a number of general questions to determine their perception of the incident.[12] Neither the abuser nor the victim in the story was given a name, gender, or age. When asked who the offender was, 75% of the younger children said a "stranger," whereas 71% of the older children thought it was someone the child knew. Again, younger children have difficulties reconciling the fact that good people sometimes do bad things to children.

In a final question on the pictures, students were asked what the boy (or girl) should do if given a mixed-up touch. On the pretest a majority responded that the child should "tell." After their participation in the prevention programs, the number of students offering this response increased by more than 20%. Corresponding to results from the questionnaire, first-grade children registered a larger gain from pre- to posttest (27%) than did third graders (12%).

Similarly, when asked what the "sad child" might do if she were touched on her private parts, most students (81% on pretest and 88% on posttest) answered that the child should "tell." Some students also suggested other prevention-related behaviors, such as the child should "run" or "say no." Two percent of respondents offered self-defense strategies. Less than 10% of the students were unable to suggest prevention-related behaviors. Given children's attachments to parents and other care providers, as well as their natural dependence on adults for protection, it is not surprising that of the prevention lessons taught in prevention programs, "telling" is one that they assimilate best.

## SECRETS AND STRANGERS

In the last part of the interview three vignettes were acted out between the student and the interviewer using wooden figurines. The first vignette involved a young child who needed to speak with her friend about a problem. The interviewer's figurine spoke to the child's:

"I have something I want to talk to you about. Last night a friend of our family's was over. Mom and Dad had to go to the store for some milk and . . . well . . . this guy, um, he tried to touch me on my private parts. It was hard to know what to do. What would you do if something like that happened to you?"

Students spontaneously play-acted their responses to the friend, giving a variety of prevention-related answers. The majority of children (67% on pretest and 71% on posttest) said that they would tell:

*I'd tell mom or dad or who was there.*

*When my mother gets back I'd tell her he's touched me. She should call the police or dial 911.*

Some of the students took the story of the "friend of the family" and reconceptualized it as a stranger story. Here we see a child making sense of the story in the way that works best for her:

*I'd tell him to get out and close the door and never come back and when my mom comes back tell her a stranger came and touched you in the private parts and you didn't want to.*

As the vignette continued, children were informed that the incident was supposed to be kept secret:

"He told me never to tell my parents—or anyone else. It has to be our secret. He said if I keep it a secret he'll take me to the toy store and get me whatever I want. But you know, I feel funny about this. What do you think I should have done? . . . What about the toy store? He said he'd take me after school today. Why do you think he promised me that?"

Most students thought that the molester was lying or trying to bribe the child. Among those who felt that the molester's offer was innocent, first graders were in the majority. Their comments suggested benign intentions:

*Because you were nice to him.*

*Because he liked you and he wanted to buy you toys.*

*Because he wants you to have fun.*

Although 25% of first-grade children expressed views such as this on the pretest and 15% maintained this perception on posttest, only 2% of the third graders thought the molester's intentions were innocent. Those who questioned the intentions generally gave responses such as the following:

*He'll take me to do it again.*

*Because he doesn't want to get in trouble. He doesn't want to go to jail.*

*Maybe he would have took me away.*

*Because he didn't want nobody to know.*

Finally, the scenario touched on the issue of guilt and blame. Students were told:

I was just watching TV when he started to try to touch me, but I feel like maybe it was my fault. Do you think it was my fault?"

On pretest, 14% of the elementary school sample said that the incident was the child's fault, and 6% continued to hold this view on the posttest. The difference was statistically significant, suggesting that about 8% of the students learned that sexual abuse is not the child's fault. It appears, however, that this idea was largely understood by most children before they entered the program.

The second vignette brought a child (wooden figurine) walking home into contact with an adult stranger. The adult was identified as a "person you don't know" rather than a stranger because the label "stranger" might have biased the responses. The adult figurine approached the child and said:

"Hello, how are you? I just baked these cookies for my friends who live in that house across the street. Would you like one?"

Eighty-three percent refused the cookie on the pretest, increasing to 90% on the posttest. Asked to explain their behavior, those who refused commented that they would not accept the cookie because the person was a stranger, because something bad might happen, or because the ingredients might be harmful:

*No, because there might be something in them like drugs.*

*They might be poisoned or have a pin inside.*

Almost one-third of the respondents offered the stranger an excuse, many of them quite polite:

*No thank you. I'm not hungry.*

*No thank you, I already had some.*

*I'm allergic to cookies.*

*Mama said I can't have cookies before dinner.*

In response to a refusal, the stranger claimed to know the child's mother and indicated that "she said it was okay." Twelve percent of children accepted the cookie with this inducement on the pretest, but only 6% did so on the posttest. Overall, elementary school age children showed a consistent response to the stranger, maintaining a high level of avoidance on pre- and posttest.

The last vignette involved a discussion in which the students played a "big kid" who is being asked to explain prevention concepts such as strangers, secrets, and touching, to the interviewer's little child figurine. The little child begins by asking: "What's a stranger?" Children are obsessed with the notion of strangers, the bogeymen of the 1980s. Some of the students had a fairly accurate perception of strangers, and others only imagined them under the worst possible circumstances. For example, most third-grade children (72%) observed on both the pre- and posttest that a stranger is "someone you don't know. " Sixteen percent of third graders, who on pretest defined a stranger as a bad person, changed to a neutral response after the program. In contrast, only 42% of first graders gave an accurate definition of strangers, and many described them as bad or evil people:

*Someone who can kill me or hurt me.*

*Somebody that touches you in your private parts.*

*They grab you and take you.*

Although a number of first graders changed their responses from "bad" to "neutral" on posttest (18%), almost an equal number of children changed their response from "neutral" to "bad" (14%) as well. Overall, about one-quarter of first graders gave a negative response both on pre- and posttest.

A high proportion of first graders answered the question "What's a stranger?" in terms of imputed behavior rather than simply as someone unknown. Later in the discussion all of the students were asked, "What do strangers do?" This question evoked an even stronger negative response from first graders, with 77% indicating on posttest that strangers do harm. While fewer third graders expressed this view, in contrast to their initial definitions, more than half (52%) responded with negative comments. This may indicate that third graders have memorized the correct definition of a stranger but have not entirely freed themselves of stereotypes regarding strangers' behavior. First-grade responses revealed both the prevalence of negative stereotypes and the unidimensional tendency in their thinking—strangers can only be bad; if they are good, they are no longer strangers.

First graders' jaundiced vision of strangers again comes through in the kinds of responses given to the question, "What do they look like?" Many responses conveyed an image of the stranger as robber or kidnapper.

> *They have masks over their heads.*
>
> *They wear masks and they hide.*
>
> *Like an ugly looking face and they look big . . . they can't be little.*

The concept of secrets, also crucial to sexual abuse prevention training, seems to be misunderstood by a large proportion of children. When preschoolers were asked about secrets in the earlier study, results indicated that only 11% of the sample could explain this concept on the pretest, a figure that remained virtually constant on the posttest. The elementary school sample showed much better comprehension on the pretest, with 65% giving a correct, neutral response to the question "What's a secret?"

> *It's when somebody tells somebody else something and they don't want anyone else to know.*
>
> *A secret is something that you keep that nobody else is supposed to know except the two people.*

Yet about one-third of the sample was still unable to define a secret accurately. This proportion remained about the same after participation in the programs.

Finally, the students were asked, "What's a touch?" A touch refers to making physical contact with objects and people. Although in conventional usage the term "touch" has no negative connotation, some children, particularly first graders, appear to pick up the idea from prevention programs that touching is usually a harmful act:

> *A touch is somewhere on your private parts.*
>
> *When a stranger touches you in a private spot.*
>
> *When somebody hits you.*
>
> *In your private parts where you don't like to be touched.*

Before prevention training 22% of first graders described a touch in these negative terms. After the program, there was a significant change in the pattern of response, as those expressing a negative definition of the term increased to 35.7%. This may reflect the way younger students hear and learn the language of prevention curricula. "Good touches," such as hugging and kissing, have particular words associated with the behavior that defines the act. These words are familiar to young children. "Bad touches" involve *touching* a child's private parts. Here "to touch" is an integral part of the definition of sexual abuse.

## IMPLICATIONS FOR PREVENTION PROGRAMS

While elementary school age children appear to have made some knowledge gains after exposure to prevention programs, the meaning of these results must be carefully appraised. One of the more interesting features of the study results is the amount of information offered in prevention training that students possessed prior to taking the programs.

What accounts for this knowledge? The answer is unclear, yet one important factor appears to be the high degree of parental education in the home (which will be discussed in more detail in Chapter 6). Other contributing factors may include television, which provides a variety of prevention messages throughout the day. Alongside smoking prevention and "just say no" advertisements, McGruff and other fanciful characters remind children how to keep themselves safe. The prevention movement itself must also be given a measure of credit for increasing public awareness of child sexual abuse. As a result of the program providers' steady efforts to bring the issue to the fore, child sexual abuse is now more commonly discussed, and certainly more widely publicized, than in the past. Some might even speculate that the high levels of knowledge initially demonstrated by first and third graders are a direct result of earlier exposure to classroom prevention programs going back to pre-school training. Even though preschoolers did not grasp many of the prevention concepts, it might be argued that a "seed" of knowledge and insight had been planted somewhere in their subconscious, which bloomed several years later. There is, however, no empirical evidence of this "sleeper effect." On the contrary, there is some evidence of an erosion of learning. Several studies indicate that students register a decline in the amount of knowledge from prevention training retained over time.[13] Although the possibility of a sleeper effect cannot be dismissed, it seems more likely that the relatively high scores on the pretest questionnaires derive from a combination of parental education, media messages, generally heightened public awareness, and exposure to other children who have received prevention training. This also explains to some extent the relatively high amount of information about prevention lessons registered on the pretest questionnaire and in response to some of the interview questions.

Beyond their pretest knowledge, how much of the prevention material did students learn? It is important to bear in mind that responses to the questionnaire and interview in the classroom setting do not tell us whether students acquired skills and behaviors that would actually be used to protect themselves in threatening situations. The issue under consideration is simply the extent to which their knowledge increased. Based on results from the questionnaire and interview, it appears that first and third graders learned and retained a small amount of prevention knowledge. In most areas changes were quite limited; on the questionnaire, for example, their average scores increased by about 1 point on a 14-point scale, or less than 10%.

These findings are supported by a growing body of evidence confirming that students in the early elementary school grades register relatively small gains in knowledge from sexual abuse prevention training programs. Outlined in Table A.10 (Appendix A), this body of research includes 14 evaluations of various programs around the country that reported the scoring system and results of experimental and quasi-experimental research designs.[14] The first six studies listed involve comparisons between pre- and posttest of experimental and control groups in which student scores increased by 10% or less after prevention training on scales ranging from 5 to 50 items. Among this group, the study by Woods and Dean compared the TAT program with the special edition of the *Spiderman* comic book that was produced in cooperation with the National Committee for Prevention of Child Abuse. After reading the *Spiderman* book, students' scores increased by two thirds of a point on a 15-point scale, a gain of about 4%; those exposed to the TAT program increased their average scores by 2.1 points on the same scale, for a gain of about 13%. It is interesting to note that the differences were remarkably small relative to the time and effort involved in these two approaches. The TAT program requires about 4 hours of classroom instruction, whereas *Spiderman* is a 16-page comic book that takes no longer than 20 minutes to read.

The findings reported in the other eight studies show gains somewhat higher than 10%, but still rather limited in different respects. For example, in the study by Wurtele et al., the control group responded correctly to 75% of the items without any prevention training. The two studies by Kraizer and her colleagues show significant increases in students' role-play responses (from 27% to 67% correct and from 31% to 59% correct), but in neither case were the final averages very high. The gains reported by Fryer et al.,[15] deal with students' responses to stranger/

danger simulations, the usefulness of which is widely questioned (see the discussion in Chapter 1, pp. 13). And although there was a significant increase in knowledge among students who received training in the study by Conte et al.,[16] on the average their posttest scores indicate that students understood only about 50% of the concepts taught by the program.

Although the overall gains in knowledge among first and third graders in the California study were relatively small, results were stronger in some areas of learning than in others. In considering the different areas of learning, a word about strangers is necessary. Although most prevention programs do not exaggerate the threat of abuse by strangers, something in their message seems to get distorted by young children. At the same time that programs appear to have a moderating influence on the way third graders view strangers, they seem to exacerbate the fear of strangers among first graders, as reflected in their responses to many of the questions on posttest.

This problem may be difficult to resolve. At their current stage of development, first graders are inclined to follow a unidimensional mode of thinking in which individuals are characterized by singular traits. In the young child's mind, a person who does "bad" things is a stranger, and a stranger must *only* do "bad" things. With age and development, children begin to assign more than one character trait to an individual. As they grow out of their preoperational constructs, children will be able to understand that strangers may possess a range of characteristics. Until then, programs will have a hard time explaining to young children that while some strangers are bad, others are indeed good.

In another area, as suggested earlier, programs may be creating some confusion about "touching." Although many programs try to communicate that touching falls along a continuum from good to bad, it is the bad that students seem to identify most readily with the idea of a touch. Providers might look more critically at the way this message is delivered. Perhaps other words could be used to define the act of sexual abuse.

Finally, among the lessons best learned were those that taught children to tell adults about uncomfortable or abusive situations. First graders increased their correct scores on "telling" responses even more than did third graders, who started off with a fairly high degree of knowledge in this area. Similar findings are reported by Kraizer and Fryer, who note that before training less than 50% of their experimental group gave the right answer to two items concerned with telling adults about threatening incidents; after training 100% of the group responded correctly to both items.[17] Of course, preparing the responsible adults in their lives to respond to children's disclosures is a critical link in assuring the effectiveness of this lesson. Foremost among the responsible adults in young children's lives are their parents and teachers. The following chapters examine how parents and teachers view prevention programs.

# Private Responsibility: Is Parental Consent Informed?

$S$exual abuse prevention programs place importance on training children to recognize bad or unsafe touches from friends and relatives as well as strangers, empowering them to say no, yell, and even fight back and advising them to tell adults when sexually abusive behavior occurs. To a large extent the lessons of empowerment and assertiveness are designed to help children protect themselves. This perspective is not entirely in accord with the normative view that parents have a basic responsibility to care for, supervise, and protect their children. The question then arises: What is the role of parents and how do they perceive prevention training?

Relatively little is known about how the subject of child sexual abuse is handled in the home or how protective measures taken by parents in this area are influenced by abuse prevention programs. Are parents familiar with what is being taught to their children in these programs? Are these prevention lessons reinforced by parents in the home? Do parents view the programs as desirable and effective? To what extent do they observe intended and unintended program consequences in their children's behavior?

The parental role in protecting children and their views of prevention programs are examined in a 1988 survey conducted with 115 parents of third grade students participating in the eight California programs previously described. This group of parents was interviewed 1 week before and 1 month after their children received the sexual abuse prevention training course. In interpreting the results from these interviews one must bear in mind that the sample, although representing a broad range of groups, consisted of parents with both the time and interest to participate voluntarily in the study;[1] most of the parents also permitted their children to serve as subjects. One might assume that, for whatever reasons, these parents were more attentive to the prevention programs than the average parent.

Some of the questions posed in the third-grade parents' interview are similar to those asked in the Family Welfare Research Group's (FWRG) 1986 survey of 116 parents of preschool children in California programs and to Nibert, Cooper, and Ford's questionnaire survey of 223 parents of preschool children receiving the Child Assault Prevention program in Columbus, Ohio.[2] Several of these questions also were examined in an earlier study by Finkelhor, which focused on 521 parents-at-large in Boston.[3] Based on a random sample of parents with children aged 6 to 14, Finkelhor's 1981 survey was conducted at a time when child sexual abuse was just beginning to emerge as a public issue. Separated by time and distance, alternative methodologies (interviews and questionnaires), different auspices (Nibert, Cooper, and Ford were staff members for the program they studied; the FWRG survey was conducted by an independent university-based group), and demographic differences (e.g., Finkelhor's subjects were predominantly white and Catholic), the results of these and several other studies that examine the way parents assess prevention programs can be, at best, roughly compared with those from the current survey of parents of third graders in the eight California programs. Recognizing these limitations, it is nevertheless useful to compare the results of these studies in an effort to gain a broad view of parental behavior and attitudes in this area. Thus, where relevant, comparative findings will be noted.

## TALKING TO CHILDREN IN THE HOME

The subject of sexual abuse prevention is much in the air. An increasing number of books and pamphlets are becoming available that describe how parents may broach this subject with their children.[4] Moreover, television programs frequently relay messages about prevention directly into the living room. It is not entirely surprising, then, that 81% of the parents of third graders indicated they had discussed the topic of sexual abuse with their children when they were interviewed before their children's participation in the California prevention programs. There were no significant differences between the likelihood of raising the subject with daughters or sons, but respondents indicated a greater degree of comfort in talking about it with daughters. As already noted, these parents may have been somewhat more attentive to sexual abuse prevention training than the average parent. The high rate of interaction on this topic may also reflect the fact that during this period Californians were regularly assailed by chilling reports on the McMartin Preschool trial (see Chapter 2, p. 22).

The California findings on the extent of parental communication with children about child sexual abuse are to some degree corroborated by responses to the Nibert, Cooper, and Ford study of CAP program families in Columbus, Ohio. Of the 223 parents surveyed in this study, 64% indicated that they had talked to their preschool-age children about sexual abuse prior to participation in the CAP program.[5] The higher degree (81%) of parental communication in California may reflect differences in the ages of the children in these studies; that is, parents may be generally more inclined to discuss this sensitive topic with 9-year-olds. Although parents in the California sample who favored teaching children about sexual abuse prevention thought that 5 years old, on the average, was an appropriate age to introduce the subject, this average decreased to 4 years old among the 9% of parents in the sample who indicated that they had been abused as children.

In sharp contrast to the experiences in California and Ohio, Finkelhor's survey of parents in Boston found only 29% of the sample reporting that they had discussed the subject of sexual abuse with their children.[6] Most of the parents in this sample believed it to be inappropriate to discuss this topic with children younger than 9 years.

Several explanations may account for the differences between the results of Finkelhor's study and more recent surveys in California and Ohio. The sample for the Boston survey was drawn from parents in the population-at-large, while the California and Ohio studies focused on a pool of subjects who were, perhaps, more attuned to the issues of child sexual abuse because their children were about to participate in prevention programs. In terms of demographic characteristics, the Boston sample was 89% white, the average age was 38, and 72% of the respondents were employed. In comparison, the California sample was 61% white, the average age was 37, and 51% of the mothers were employed. It is not clear, however, why these demographic characteristics might produce differences in the directions found.

The different findings may be more a result of history than of alternative sampling frames and demographic characteristics; that is, they may reflect real changes in behavior over time, stimulated in part by greater awareness of the problem. Indications of such increased awareness can be detected in parents' views on the magnitude of the problem and its sources. When asked about the prevalence of sexual abuse in the United States, 51% of the parents in the California sample estimated that one-quarter of all children suffered from this offense; a startling 36% believed that over half of all children are abused (a figure slightly higher than the 29% of parents reporting the same estimate in the California preschool study). These responses from California suggest that some parents, in becoming more aware of the problem, may have developed a rather inflated view of its dimensions. Although estimates by professionals in the field vary widely on this matter, incidence figures of 20% to 25% for females and less than half that rate for males are often cited as authoritative (see Chapter 1 for a discussion of measurement problems). Compared to the California findings, Finkelhor's earlier survey of parents in Boston registered much lower estimates of abuse rates; 19% said one quarter of girls were abused, 30% thought that 1 in 10 girls was abused, and 30% believed it happened to about only 1% of girls.

As for the sources of this problem, only 10% of the parents in California believed that strangers are the main perpetrators of abuse, a fairly accurate perception according to research. Revealing greater sensitivity to the problem, the California findings again differ considerably from those of the earlier Boston survey, in which parents identified strangers as offenders in 50% of the cases. Since 1981, when the Boston survey was conducted, there has been considerable change in the social climate surrounding issues of child sexual abuse. Indeed, in 1988, it would have been almost impossible to draw a sample of parents in the population-at-large in California whose children either had not participated in prevention programs or were not about to do so. Public awareness and political responsiveness have increased (as noted in Chapter 1) as the sexual abuse prevention movement gained momentum. If the considerably higher degree of parental communication reported in the more recent studies is truly the product of heightened social awareness, the credit for this noteworthy development must be attributed mainly to the vigorous efforts of the sexual abuse prevention movement.

Although comparative data are not available, findings from the California surveys suggest the important role that the media has come to play in drawing public attention to the problem of abuse. Responding to the question of how family discussions about child sexual abuse were initiated, about 31% of the third-grade parents indicated that they had raised the subject, and 22% reported that it was raised by their children. However, the highest proportion, 40% of the sample, noted that television programs provided the initial stimulus for family conversations on this subject. In recent years, television has produced a number of documentaries, movies, and public service announcements dealing with child sexual abuse. Even the popular nursery programs such as "Sesame Street" and "Romper Room" have conveyed messages about preventing this problem. In the California survey of preschool parents, 61% of the respondents noted that their children had been exposed to prevention concepts through viewing television.[7]

An increasing amount of family discussion about how to prevent sexual abuse would seem generally beneficial, but the question remains, what do parents actually say to their children? Are these discussions characterized by oblique references or straight talk? In the California study this subject was approached from various perspectives. Many parents were relatively direct and graphic. In contrast to the experience in California, Finkelhor's earlier survey of parents in Boston showed not only less parent–child communication on this subject, but also a much narrower realm of discourse, which focused primarily on the threat of strangers. Few of the respondents in the Boston survey were as explicit as those in the California sample in discussing how abuse involved touching the private parts of their children's bodies.[8]

In the California study, the majority of parents were very direct in their treatment of the subject. Instructing their children to say no or to tell if they are touched inappropriately, parents offered advice and rules such as:

> *People shouldn't touch your private parts.*
>
> *Nobody should touch your body.*
>
> *I say, if somebody touches your boobs, or puts their hand in your panties, you tell mom.*
>
> *I tell her about touches and to tell someone she trusts if someone touches her and she's uncomfortable with it.*
>
> *Don't let anybody touch you if they're being more than just friendly.*

About 4% reported that they would point to their children's private parts or name them and give straightforward instructions about touching. Some parents (3%) reported playing "what if" games with their children, using hypothetical situations as a way to teach them protective rules. Others (5%) questioned their children about whether anyone had ever touched their private parts. "Stranger danger" was often discussed; sometimes (13%) it was the only topic parents covered. In several cases, the family discussions were vague and indirect, with subjects reporting that they told their child "how it happens to other children" or "to be careful wearing dresses."

Survey findings reveal that before participating in sexual abuse prevention programs, most parents in the California (81%) and Ohio (64%) samples had talked to their children about this subject. After their children had participated in these programs, one might expect the expressed interest in this area to have carried over and stimulated as high, if not higher, a level of exchange about the prevention programs and what their children had learned in them. However, in both cases only about two-thirds the number of families that had previously conversed about child sexual abuse indicated talking about the program after their children received the training. In the Ohio study, 42% of the children had discussed the prevention training program with their parents.[9] And in California, 57% of the sample reported having family discussions about these programs. In revealing a moderate degree of parent–child communication about the content of sexual abuse prevention programs, these findings would suggest that parent perceptions of the programs could have been informed to some extent by the information gained in these discussions.

## FAVORABLE PERCEPTIONS: ARE THEY WELL INFORMED?

There is no question that most parents have a highly favorable perception of sexual abuse prevention programs. Among the parents of third graders in the California survey, 84% thought that their children needed the program prior to participation. After participation, 90% of the parents viewed the program as useful to their children. While only 11% of the total sample indicated any concerns about their children's exposure to the program, 20% of those who participated in the prevention training meetings for parents expressed reservations about their children's involvement in these programs. These results were fairly consistent across the program sites. Similar findings were reported in the California survey of preschool parents, where only 8% expressed concern about their children's participation in the programs, a figure that increased to 15% among those who attended the parent workshop.[10] In general, then, parents held the programs in high esteem, regardless of the curriculum being taught.

There is a question, however, concerning the empirical grounds for these perceptions. Are they based on well-informed views of program content or on insights and evidence from other sources? Regarding information about educational content, all of the prevention programs had parent components, participation in which offered an opportunity to learn about the children's curriculum. But only 13% of the study sample attended these parent meetings, a poor showing and even lower than the 34% attendance rate reported among preschool parents.[11] As indicated earlier, it should be remembered that the parents in this sample were a self-selected group, whose voluntary participation in the study suggests that they had both more time and greater inclination to participate in prevention-related activities than the average third-grade parent has.

It is possible that the parents learned of the program's content from their children. As previously noted, 57% of the parents reported discussing the prevention programs with their children after the training. When probed about the content of these discussions, however, it turned out that only 20% had addressed subjects emphasized in the training curricula (such as telling secrets and touching), 12% had discussed stranger danger, and 25% had talked about the child's participation in the research project. Given the low rates of attendance at parent meetings and the limited degree of substantive communication about program content with their children, knowledge from these sources cannot account for the high proportion of parents with favorable perceptions of prevention programs.

Knowledge about program content could have been obtained from reading materials and other sources, but this does not appear to be the case. When asked to specify what information and skills their children might have gained from the programs, almost one-half (48%) of the parents indicated that they had no idea what their children might have learned. In the next most common response to this question, 29% of the parents stated that their children had learned nothing much beyond information already presented in the home or on television. Only 4% of the parents reported that their children might have learned that they could be sexually abused by adults who are among their family and friends, a piece of information emphasized by many of the prevention programs.

This last point is of interest because there is some evidence from other research that children can absorb lessons concerning the possibility of intrafamilial sexual assault. A study of 63 grade school children conducted in Kansas by Swan, Press, and Briggs found that after exposure to prevention training, the largest and most significant difference among twelve measures of change in knowledge was registered on the question of whether violent sexual assault could be inflicted by a family member. The proportion of affirmative responses to this item more than doubled, from 39% to 88%; the second largest gain appeared on the question of whether sexual abuse might be inflicted by a family member through gentle methods, to which the rate of affirmative response increased from 64% to 93%. Similar to the California findings, a large majority of the 40 parents surveyed in the Kansas study reported positive feelings (75%) about their children's exposure to prevention training, none indicated negative feelings, and 25% reported uncertainty. It did not appear, however, that these parents were aware of the fact that one of the main results of their children's training was to heighten their awareness of the possibility of being sexually abused by a family member.[12]

Although the parents in the California survey had only vague ideas about the specific content of the programs to which their children were exposed, they had fairly clear and highly positive beliefs about various self-protective skills that their children brought to these programs. When asked to assess their children's potential responses to abuse in four areas of behavior typically addressed in prevention programs, most parents judged the coping skills in these areas quite favorably for both sons and daughters. Before experiencing the prevention programs, the vast majority of parents thought their children would behave appropriately in each of the four areas. The most positive responses were to questions concerning whether their children would yell if grabbed by an adult and would tell if an adult touched them in ways that felt uncomfortable; more than 85% of the parents believed that the correct behavioral response would be forthcoming in both cases. Parents were less sure about whether children would think it was their own fault if they were sexually molested. These generally positive views of their children's coping abilities (for a detailed breakdown see Appendix A, Table A.11) were reinforced by participation in the prevention programs. When asked to assess how the children might respond to abuse after having received the prevention training, in each area parents expressed even further assurance concerning their coping abilities.

Most parents believed their children were well equipped with self-protective skills before they underwent prevention training. The findings also suggest that even more parents came to hold these beliefs after training. To some extent these findings parallel the fairly high mean score (81%) on the questionnaire concerning knowledge about these behaviors that third graders registered prior to participation in the program and the small increase in this score (87%) noted after participation. It is important to recognize, however, that neither the parent's beliefs about how their children might behave nor the children's knowledge of the appropriate response in abusive situations offer any guarantees that children would be able to act effectively to protect themselves if faced with threatening or seductive advances by an adult. Even adults often are unable to respond effectively to social interactions that are frightening or confusing.

These data from the California survey suggest (a) that parents are not well informed about the range of substantive information and ideas their children are exposed to in sexual abuse prevention training programs and (b) that parents believe their children possess a fairly high degree of coping skills prior to prevention training. What, then, accounts for the favorable perceptions of prevention programs by such a high proportion of respondents? The data cannot answer this question. Perhaps parents really have greater knowledge about the curricula than the data infer. There is also a reasonable possibility that parental judgments in this instance are influenced by both the positive goal of sexual abuse prevention training and faith that the public institutions supporting these programs have good evidence that this purpose is being met. Parents may simply find it difficult to imagine, for example, that the state of California would spend more than $10 million a year to introduce prevention curricula into the public schools without knowing its effects, even if these effects are not evident to the parents. Or parents may believe that, at the very least, no harm and some good might come from these efforts.

From a broader perspective, the high proportion of parental satisfaction with sexual abuse prevention programs found in the California survey coincides with a body of evidence from program-satisfaction surveys that reveals a general tendency for consumers to respond with favorable assessments of social services. This pattern of response is variously attributed to politeness, gratitude at receiving free services, and a natural inclination to rationalize one's involvement in a program as a worthwhile activity.[13] Whatever the reasons, it is difficult to conclude that the positive views of the third-grade parents derive from a clear understanding of either the substantive content or behavioral effects of prevention programs. Indeed, regarding the programs' behavioral effects, parental observations point to some matters of potential concern.

## UNINTENDED CONSEQUENCES: PARENTAL OBSERVATIONS

It appears that the parents' generally favorable view of sexual abuse prevention programs is influenced by the programs' good intentions. But good intentions do not always produce positive effects. Many professionals have expressed concerns about unintended consequences for both parents and children that might result from these programs. For parents the unintended consequence is essentially that of cultivating a false sense of security.[14] Told by providers that these programs will teach children how to protect themselves from sexual abuse, parents have little reason to question whether these good intentions can be realized. Why else would the schools allow these programs to be given? Few parents are aware that the research on this matter reveals a distinct lack of evidence of program effectiveness, nor are they cognizant of the fact that there is considerable disagreement among professionals concerning the value of these programs. Absent this knowledge, it is psychologically comforting for parents to think that prevention training has been well tested and really works. If the programs are effective, there should be less need to worry about the child's safety. To the extent that parents believe that these programs provide a blanket of protection for children, their concern and vigilance are likely to diminish. With parents thus lulled by a false sense of security, the overall level of family protection for young children might well decline.

With regard to children, questions have been raised as to whether the programs might increase their anxiety, make them less comfortable with family intimacy, contribute to their forming an excessive fear of strangers, and interfere with their normal development of sexuality.[15]

Seeking to appraise the behavioral manifestations of both intended and unintended consequences from the parent's perspective, the California survey posed a number of questions about any changes observed in their children's behavior after exposure to prevention programs.

Most parents of children in the third grade reported no noticeable changes in their children's behavior. Of those who did observe change, considerably more identified behaviors that might be characterized as intended or positive than unintended or negative. Specifically, with regard to unintended effects, the extent to which program participation may have heightened anxiety was reflected in parent's responses to four questions dealing with (1) changes in their children's sleeping patterns, (2) communication of "what if" concerns, (3) reaction to strangers, and (4) indication that children appeared to have been frightened by any aspect of the training. Altogether, 18% of the parents reported negative effects in one or more of these areas.

This finding is considerably below the level of negative change observed by parents of younger children in the California preschool study. In response to questions addressing their children's reactions to strangers, sleeping patterns, and communication of "what if" concerns after prevention training, 22% of the 116 parents in the preschool survey identified negative effects in one or more of these areas. As expressed by some of the third graders' parents, the kinds of concerns noted involved, for example:

> *When he just received the program he had nightmares about somebody chasing him, but now everything seems to be fine.*

> *Not recently, but during the first week after the presentation, my son had difficulties falling asleep. He was afraid that a stranger was in his room.*

> *She asked, 'What happens if I get kidnapped?'*

With regard to intended consequences, parents were asked about behaviors that reflect two types of program objectives: (1) efforts to increase children's general awareness of ideas conveyed in prevention training such as physical contact and body parts, and (2) attempts to promote their empowerment. Four questions were posed addressing the extent to which parents observed their children's increased awareness of program ideas. These questions dealt with whether parents had found their children more communicative about touching, about their bodies, and about other topics related to the training curricula and whether they had heard them repeating phrases and songs from the programs. Twenty-six percent of the parents expressed positive responses in one or more of these areas.

Empowerment of children is one of the prevention programs' central objectives. Following this emphasis, the strongest intended consequences observed by parents were in response to two questions dealing with empowerment. Here parents were asked if they had noticed a greater or lesser sense of independence in their children and whether the children had become more or less assertive since participation in the program. Twenty-one percent of the parents reported increases in one or both of these areas.

It should be noted, however, that although empowerment and assertiveness are intended consequences of prevention training, these qualities do not always manifest themselves in desirable behavior among young children. One parent in the California survey reported, for example, that after participation in the training program:

> *My child has realized that this is a potential weapon. She told her brother that she would tell the police that he touched her where he shouldn't if she couldn't see a particular TV program one night.*

Reppucci and Haugaard relate another example of how children may misinterpret and misuse what they absorb from lessons to enhance their power and assertiveness:[16]

> A first grade child interpreted the message that she had a right to say 'no' as generalizing to all realms of behavior. For several weeks following the prevention program she frequently told her parents that she had the right to say "no" to any request that she did not like or that made her feel uncomfortable. The parents reported much anguish and frustration on their part about this behavior and about the fact that they had to punish her in order to convince her that she did not have the right to disobey them whenever she wanted to.

While differing somewhat in the exact proportions of positive and negative response, several other studies that have examined the way parents perceive their children's behavior after prevention training show a general pattern of results that is similar to those of the California survey—that is, a high proportion of parents reporting no changes in behavior, with those who did observe changes noticing more positive than negative effects. In the Ohio survey of 223 parents of preschool children, for example, Nibert, Cooper, and Ford found that almost two-thirds of the respondents saw no change in behavior after their children participated in the CAP workshops, 26% observed what they characterized as "good" behavioral changes, and 7% noticed behavioral changes that they characterized as "bad."[17] Along the same lines, findings from the

Kansas survey by Swan, Press, and Briggs indicate only 5% of the parents reporting negative reactions such as loss of sleep or appetite, nightmares, or expressions of fear.[18] A somewhat larger observation of adverse effects is reported in Kleemeier and Webb's survey of 20 parents in a study of prevention efforts in Atlanta. Responding to a questionnaire with multiple outcome measures, 35% of these parents observed that their children showed signs of a negative emotional reaction, and 20% noted negative changes in their behavior after participating in the program.[19]

In contrast to the findings noted above, there are a few studies that report that parents detect no adverse changes in their children's behavior. Wurtele and Miller-Perrin's 1987 research on children of kindergarten age to sixth grade in a small community in Washington, for example, showed no statistically significant differences in parents' ratings of their children's behavior before and after participation in prevention training.[20] Similarly, Binder and McNiel's study of children 5 to 12 years old in a suburban community in a western state found no increase between pretest and posttest ratings of emotional distress. Indeed, this study reports a minimal but statistically significant decrease in children's emotional distress scores based on parent assessments.[21]

None of the surveys of parental observations is without flaws. Both of the studies that found no adverse changes had relatively small, nonrandom samples—in each case, fewer than 45 parents. Moreover, the emotional distress rating scale employed by Binder and McNiel allowed for a narrow range of responses—"hardly ever," "sometimes," and "often"—that focused not on changes observed in children's behavior but on the parent's general assessment of behavior. This approach may be somewhat insensitive to measuring immediate adverse effects of prevention training on behavior. For example, how would a parent rate an 8-year-old who rarely had nightmares but experienced several in the week right after participation in a prevention training program? This immediate experience might not influence a parent's general assessment of the child as "hardly ever" having nightmares. Questions focused on any changes in the child's behavior observed soon after prevention training would be more likely to register these adverse effects.

Just as weaknesses are evident in the studies that found no adverse effects of prevention training, there are serious limitations in the studies that reported from 5% to 35% of the parents observing immediate negative reactions, such as heightened anxiety, in their children's behavior. The Atlanta study in which the highest percentage of respondents noted signs of negative reactions involved a very small sample of only 20 parents. One methodological problem is that since four of the studies lacked nontreatment control groups, we cannot say with certainty that the observed effects resulted from the children's participation in prevention programs. It is possible that in the normal course of events, some number of children in the study sample would have displayed, for example, increased anxiety during the research period due to other incidents in their lives. Thus, the absence of nontreatment control groups would lead one probably to overestimate negative program effects.

Another problem is that parents were not asked beforehand to observe systematically for any negative behavioral effects following their children's involvement in the programs but rather to recall any reactions that came to mind after the fact. The favorable view of prevention training expressed by many parents before it occurred may have influenced both perceptions of their children's behavior after the program and their recall of that behavior in the direction of underestimating negative effects. Finally, the number and type of questions asked may influence the rate of negative effects reported. Thus, using one general question about "good" and "bad" changes in children's behavior, the Ohio survey found 7% of parents of preschool children indicating negative effects. By comparison, using four questions dealing with more specific behaviors, the California preschool parent survey revealed 22% of respondents observing negative effects. In another context, assessing how the number and type of questions asked affect studies of sexual abuse prevalence rates, Finkelhor and associates suggest that multiple specific questions may work better because they deliver more cues that assist in recall, provide more time for respondents to consider the topic, and avoid general labels (e.g., "bad" changes) that respondents may be disinclined to apply.[22]

## INFORMED CONSENT: WEIGHING RISKS AND BENEFITS

The adverse behavior reported by parents cannot be attributed unequivocally to their children's participation in prevention programs. But the research findings contribute to misgivings about the potential for negative effects. Although not conclusive, the weight of the evidence points to small but perceptible negative effects related to prevention training. Is this something parents should view as an appreciable matter of concern or a negligible cost for the prevention of sexual abuse? The answer depends on several considerations regarding evidence of program effectiveness and the nature of informed parental consent.

Some program providers would dismiss the potentially negative effects as inconsequential. Thus, Alice Ray-Keil, former director of the Seattle Committee for Children (which markets the Talking About Touching curriculum nationwide), points out that although children have some adverse reactions to prevention programs, they also may suffer anxiety from fire drills, tornado drills, and other sorts of training that are deemed necessary for their well-being.[23] Nibert, Cooper, and Ford (executives and staff of the National Assault Prevention Center, which developed the CAP Program) conclude that with only 7% of parents reporting "bad changes" in their children's behavior, the principal finding of the Ohio study reflects a general absence of adverse program effects observed by parents. They suggest that this finding should help to ameliorate fears about sexual abuse prevention training for young children.[24]

There are, of course, other ways to interpret these findings. How might a typical parent respond, for example, if informed that the Ohio study found that prevention training had no observable impact on two-thirds of the children but that "bad changes" were noticed in the behavior of a little more than one out of five cases among the 33% who did show some immediate effects? Expressing the results this way underlines an important consideration from the parents' perspective. That is, in prevention programs the practical weight given to risks of unintended negative consequences is ultimately a function of the extent to which the programs' positive objectives are likely to be achieved. Program providers may see the small probabilities of adverse reactions as a trivial matter where other people's children are concerned. But whether the probabilities are 5%, 7%, or 20% that children will have nightmares, wet their beds, and experience other psychological discomfort after receiving sexual abuse prevention training, most parents would ask, "Why take the risk?" If, on the one hand, these programs had no influence on preventing sexual abuse of children, the risks would appear a matter of serious concern and thoroughly unwarranted. On the other hand, if the programs served to inoculate children against abuse, as the providers claim, then the risks would be considered no more serious than the soreness and physical discomfort sometimes following a smallpox vaccine and equally acceptable.

The problem is that no one knows how effective this training is in preventing abuse, and (as noted in Chapter 1) it remains a matter extremely difficult to test through social experimentation. Providers' claims, beliefs, and good intentions aside, as Reppucci and Haugaard declare: "There is no evidence, not even one published case example, that primary prevention has ever been achieved."[25] Although the lack of evidence on this point is not proof of ineffectiveness, it does confound evaluations of risk.

Whatever the consequences for primary prevention, some program advocates assert that children's training is valuable because it leads to disclosures of abuse. According to this view, program goals include a form of secondary prevention that involves the interruption of ongoing abuse as well as curtailing maltreatment before it begins. Again, however, there is no systematic evidence that shows these programs to be effective instruments of secondary prevention. In the California preschool study, two children (out of 116 interviewed) disclosed abusive incidents; however, they made these disclosures only to the research staff during their interviews, not to their teachers or program presenters.

Two months after the presentations no disclosures had been reported in any of the programs studied. The program providers indicated that they generally experienced few disclosures from children at the preschool level.[26] Other studies that examine the effectiveness of educational training report no evidence of a significant disclosure rate.

But is evidence really necessary? Are not some things self-evident, as Ray-Keil's comparison to fire drills implies? The fire drill is a deceptive analogy because, indeed, some preventive measures are reasonably manifest. Everyone agrees about what constitutes a fire; that getting out of a building on fire is a good idea; that what is required is an ability to walk, which children possess at an early age; and that to facilitate such exit, one should be shown the way out and practice an orderly departure in case of fire. If this creates some anxiety, so be it. Schools do not ask parental consent for their children to participate in fire drills, and there is no commercial marketing of fire drill curricula and an array of related educational paraphernalia.

Sexual abuse prevention training is another matter. There is lack of agreement about the range of behaviors that constitute abusive acts. As noted in Chapter 1, surveys on the incidence of sexual abuse vary widely in their estimates, depending in large measure on their definitions of the problem, which may include behaviors ranging from noncontact abuse (propositions and exhibitionists) to fondling to physical penetration.[27] It is not at all clear that some of the central lessons of prevention training— teaching young children that their parents and relatives could sexually molest them, trying to heighten their awareness of good and bad touches, and showing them how to fight against adults—are appropriate or effective measures to prevent abuse.[28] Thus, for example, after analyzing the curricula and reviewing the research findings on a variety of prevention programs, six psychologists, writing in *School Psychology Review*, recommend that schools should not adopt programs "based on empowering children to trust their feelings, to say no, and to be assertive."[29] Similar recommendations were put forth by the blue-ribbon task force on preschool curricula in California (see Chapter 2). Finally, whether or not these lessons are appropriate, there is much uncertainty (as noted in Chapter 4) about the extent to which young children are able to absorb the ideas and make practical use of them in real-life situations.

In the absence of clarity and agreement on prevention program benefits, the immediate risks of children experiencing even brief episodes of emotional distress and other negative reactions to this training cannot be quickly dismissed by an analogy to the side effects of fire drills. Beyond the risk of immediate and transitory negative effects looms the possibility that sexual abuse prevention training may have long-term unintended consequences of a more lasting and serious nature. One of the concerns increasingly voiced by professionals about these programs is that in providing the first lesson about sexual behavior (good and bad, safe and unsafe touches) for many children they may convey a lasting impression that sexuality and physical intimacy are unwholesome or essentially dangerous.[30] As Finkelhor and Strapko put it:[31]

> If children have already had peer sexual experiences (playing doctor, etc.) what sense do they make of it after all the discussion about good and bad touching? Are they apt to feel guilty or confused, especially since the programs are unlikely to give such sex play specific endorsement? How many children exposed to these programs get the idea that sexual touching is always or almost always bad or dangerous or exploitive? . . . These are important issues that have not been considered very thoroughly by the educators themselves, not to mention researchers.

Professionals disagree about the benefits and express much uncertainty about the risks of sexual abuse prevention programs. Advocates and critics of prevention training weigh these risks and benefits according to their own lights. But the question of whether the potentially negative effects should be of serious concern to parents cannot be affirmed or dismissed at this stage by the existing evidence from social science. It is a matter that remains for parents to judge for themselves. Indeed, many schools require parental consent before children are allowed to participate in prevention training programs. However, this consent is often a pro forma request on a slip of paper asking parents to check whether they agree to have their children participate. In California, for example, most schools ask for only "passive" consent. Under this procedure, if permission forms are not returned with an explicit refusal, it is assumed that parents agree to their children's participation in the program. A typical consent form offers the following information:

> Once again we will be having a special program for the children sponsored by the San Luis Obispo Child/Teen Abuse Prevention Program. The "Touch Program" will help children deal effectively with uncomfortable situations. This program was developed within the framework of several exemplary programs in the United States, and has been presented annually to San Luis Obispo County Public Schools since 1982. The prevention program is funded and monitored by the Office of Child Abuse Prevention, State Department of Social Services.
>   The concept of good touch, bad touch, learning touch (simple spanking) and confusing touch (Sexual Abuse) is simple and helps

children differentiate between types of touching. Please note that no words which may be considered offensive (such as genitalia terms) are used in the program. Their use is left to your discretion. Assertiveness is taught as a preventative technique and is demonstrated through stories. The last point "Whom do you tell?" allows the children to explore the people in their lives who can help them.

The attached permission slip must be signed and returned to school *only if* you *do not* wish your child to attend.

Another form, after describing the program, concludes by telling parents:

We feel that this instruction is essential for the self-protection of all students. Should you prefer that your child *not* participate, please notify us. Your child will be provided this instruction unless you tell us you do not want your child to participate in this child abuse personal safety lesson.

As they are currently written, parent consent forms for sexual abuse prevention training convey neither the experimental nature of these activities nor the potential risks of participation. By this omission, they lend an implicit legitimacy to these programs, suggesting a degree of professional consensus about the harmlessness and effectiveness of prevention training for which there is little evidence. It is a well-accepted principle in research and experimentation that people should not be exposed to risks without their knowledge or against their will. In order for parents to exercise informed consent, they need to be made aware of the tentative nature of these programs, along with what is known and unknown about the potential risks and benefits to their children. Given the uncertainty and professional disagreement that surrounds prevention training, parents would be well served by schools that adopt the standard procedures for informed consent used by institutional review committees for the protection of human subjects. These procedures require that people be given a forthright description of the possible risks and benefits of their involvement in the activity for which permission is being sought.

# Public Responsibility:
# Teachers as Guardians

Y oung children spend a large part of their waking hours in school. Thus, it comes as no surprise that problems of abuse are often identified by teachers in the classroom setting. A study by the Carnegie Foundation, for example, estimates that 89% of teachers see abused or neglected children in their schools.[1] A recent report released by the National Committee for Prevention of Child Abuse (NCPCA) also noted that 100% of the principals surveyed in their study indicated that they saw at least one case of suspected abuse or neglect every year.[2] Almost half of these principals saw between 5 and 15 cases annually. Obviously, teachers are in a position to play a pivotal role in sexual abuse prevention efforts. Underlining this point, Riggs calls for a more vigorous investment in the teacher's role as protector of young children who may be victims of incest, noting: "School personnel have both a moral and legal obligation to help students experiencing problems and/or manifesting behaviors indicative of being traumatized."[3] Henke makes a similar plea, pressing teachers to take a more active stance because those who abide by "the principle 'never get involved' permit human tragedies to develop and perpetuate themselves."[4]

As the only professionals who work with children every day, in the normal course of events teachers are, after parents, probably the most important adults in their students' lives. Recognizing this unique position of school personnel, all states mandate that teachers report suspected cases of child abuse.[5] The child abuse reporting law in California, for instance, was instituted in 1963, with teachers included as mandated reporters in the 1981 revisions.[6] Many other professionals whose work brings them into regular contact with children such as medical practitioners and social workers, as well as commercial film processors, are also mandated reporters. While some would like to see educators take a more

97

active role in the investigation and treatment of child abuse,[7] as in most states, the California law does not require them to gather evidence or to have firm proof that abuse has occurred for reporting purposes. All that is asked for is "reasonable cause" to suspect that a child has been abused. Thus, teachers and other professionals are charged to act as a screening mechanism that sets the investigative process in motion, with child welfare agencies called in to examine suspected cases more carefully.

## CLASSROOM REPORTING: WHY TEACHERS HESITATE

How do these professionals exercise their mandated responsibility to inform the proper authorities about potential cases of abuse? A 1981 study of the reporting patterns of various professionals found teachers to be one of the groups most likely to meet their reporting obligation. Given a hypothetical vignette, school personnel more often indicated that they would report a suspected case of child abuse to the local child welfare agency than did criminal justice professionals, mental health workers, or other social service workers. Yet the study revealed that teachers, along with other mandated reporters, made a decision *not* to report more often than was warranted.[8]

It is difficult to know exactly the extent to which suspected cases of child abuse go unreported. Several studies have examined the reporting behaviors of medical and mental health professionals.[9] One of the largest surveys on the incidence of child abuse estimates that professionals failed to report 40% of the sexually abused children they saw in 1986.[10] Focusing on school personnel, the National Committee for the Prevention of Child Abuse (NCPCA) surveyed a nationwide sample of teachers on their knowledge, attitudes, and beliefs concerning child abuse. Findings from this 1989 survey indicate that close to 90% of the teachers who knew of a case reported it to someone, most often to other school personnel. However, the majority of teachers declared a lack of knowledge about how to detect cases of abuse and had little or no training on the subject. Indeed, more than one-third of the teachers surveyed were unaware of their school district's policies and procedures for identifying and reporting abuse.[11] An earlier study by the American Humane Association draws an even less encouraging picture of teachers' reporting behavior. Their 1980 data show school personnel nationwide reporting suspected incidents of abuse in only 18% of the cases.[12]

Teachers' attitudes and behaviors in regard to reporting were examined as part of the California study of sexual abuse prevention programs in the early grades. Interviews were conducted with 22 teachers whose classes received prevention training under the four third-grade programs in the California sample. They were a seasoned group of professionals who had worked as educators for an average of 16.9 years.[13] Sixty-four percent of the teachers recalled having received some type of training in child abuse detection and reporting, but their experiences were highly variable. For example, two of the teachers underwent two hours of training, every year, by the local police, several others remembered some training in college and discussions at staff meetings, and one teacher went to a training session sponsored by a child abuse prevention program.

Given two hypothetical situations, these third-grade teachers were asked what they would do if a child in their class told them (1) that he or she had been sexually abused by a stranger or (2) that he or she had been sexually abused by a parent. In both cases, by far the most common response was that they would report the disclosure to the principal (see Appendix A, Table A.12). Among the several other responses, it is interesting to note that more teachers would call the local child protective service (CPS) agency in the case of parent abuse (36%) than for stranger abuse (27%), in which case they would be more likely to call the child's parent and the police. In either instance of abuse, 14% of the teachers indicated that they would want to check the accusation in some way, even though verification of abuse is clearly outside their formal purview of responsibility. This response reflects the skepticism with which some teachers view children's disclosures. In general, these findings suggest that teachers stand ready to report incidents of abuse in the face of an explicit disclosure by their students.

Whether due to embarrassment or fear, however, many sexually abused children do not come forward and report their mistreatment.[14] In most cases teachers must rely on their observations and impressions. Moving from hypothetical situations of explicit disclosure to their actual behavior under the more typical conditions of uncertainty, the California teachers were asked if they had ever made any reports in suspected cases of abuse. Thirty-six percent of the sample indicated that they had filed a child abuse report at some time in their careers. But had they ever suspected a student of being abused on whom they did *not* file a report? With a surprising degree of candor, an even larger proportion of teachers responded affirmatively to this question. Seventy-three percent of the teachers said that they had suspected instances of neglect and let them go unreported, 64% had noted physical abuse, and 46% had believed children were sexually abused, yet reports were not filed on behalf of the children. With regard to suspected incidents of sexual abuse, teachers explained this response in several ways:

*A friend's uncle was fondling her. I told the child not to go to the friend's house because I didn't know what to do.*

*I spoke with the child's parents about her behavior.*

*I worried about what I would do if she brought it up in class.
What would I say?*

The findings from several studies suggest that teachers tend to underreport suspected cases of abuse. Various factors help to explain this tendency. Some teachers are reluctant to report their suspicions because of the possible effects on their rapport with children and families. A study of Head Start personnel, for example, suggests that teachers' reporting behavior is influenced by their relationship with the family;[15] teachers are concerned about interfering with private family matters and child-rearing practices.[16] Picking up on these points, Trudell and Whatley criticize the mandated reporting laws for putting teachers in the awkward position of screening possible incidents of abuse for public authorities while they work to build trusting relationships with the classroom families.[17] Seeking to identify why teachers might be hesitant to file child abuse reports, Barvolek's study of school personnel in Wisconsin found that 40% of the respondents did not report suspected cases for fear of getting involved in the situation.[18] Many teachers fear that reporting abuse will result in some form of retaliation by parents.[19] Along these lines, the NCPCA survey found that 63% of teachers were afraid of legal problems that might arise in the event of false allegations. They evidently were not aware that states provide legal immunity for mandated reporters.[20]

Some of the underreporting by teachers may be attributed to a reluctance to interfere in family matters and fear of retribution, yet much of this behavior may also be explained as a lack of training in the sensitive process of identifying and reporting abuse. In the Barvolek study, 56% of respondents noted that they had never received training in the area of child abuse and neglect.[21] According to the Education Commission of the States, the amount of training received in child abuse when teachers studied for their credential averaged less than three hours, and many educational programs offered no training in this area.[22] Students in teachers' colleges verify the Education Commission's findings. One study reveals that whereas 80% of the students enrolled in teaching programs knew that they would probably encounter an abused child during their career, fewer than 50% felt equipped to handle the situation adequately.[23] A similar study by Gliszczinski found that student teachers, who knew that they would have a legal responsibility to report once they were credentialed, were not certain about the normal procedures for making such reports.[24]

The recent National Survey of Principals pointed out the discrepancy between principals' and teachers' perceptions of the adequacy of training in detecting and reporting child abuse.[25] That survey found that whereas only 28% of elementary school principals reported dissatisfaction with their school's training on the topic of child abuse, more than two-thirds of classroom teachers felt that the training was inadequate to meet their needs.

Before reports are made, of course, teachers must be able to identify children in trouble. Examining the extent of their knowledge about the symptoms of sexual abuse, Levin's research reveals that teachers were most aware of the possible indicators of physical abuse and neglect, and least able to identify signs of sexual abuse.[26] These responses paralleled those of the third-grade teachers in the California survey. Although a few of these teachers noted "flirtatious comments" or a child's "unusual knowledge about sex" as possible clues, most had little idea of what to look for and thought sexually abused children would be extremely difficult to detect.

## TEACHER IMPRESSIONS OF PREVENTION PROGRAMS

When asked to give their impressions of sexual abuse prevention training programs, a number of studies indicate that teachers tend to be rather positive in their ratings.[27] In this regard the California sample was no exception. Among this group, 91% of teachers thought that the prevention workshop was useful to children in their third-grade classes. They believed that the content and vocabulary were age-appropriate for third graders, and two-thirds responded that the programs were sensitive to the students' ethnic backgrounds. More than half (57%) of the teachers also expressed approval of the prevention training staff who presented the programs in their classrooms.

Although teachers generally held the programs in high regard, 19% revealed that they were bothered by one or another aspect of the prevention training. Their concerns were voiced in comments such as:

> I was brought up in a different era and time. The idea of putting these thoughts in their heads is uncomfortable.

> I don't want it to make them fearful of their relatives. Will they be sexually hung up forever?

Even in the face of doubts as profound as this one, however, teachers still expressed few reservations about having the children in their classrooms participate in the program. For some teachers it seems their beliefs in or hopes for the program objectives overshadowed their personal concerns about program content.

After the program, about two-thirds of the teachers reinforced the prevention lessons by discussing related issues in the class:

*We were talking about Hansel and Gretel, and I said that they were being abused by the stepmother, who wasn't taking care of them.*

*I put the phone number up on the wall and pointed it out.*

Of the teachers who did not review prevention material after the program, many expressed either discomfort with the topic or a sense of other classroom priorities. As they explained:

*It's not a subject I talk about much. I'm not sure how to talk about it.*

*No, I haven't discussed it. That's not my job. That's their [the prevention agency's] job.*

After the program, teachers did not notice any particular changes in behavior among their students. But one-quarter of them reported that students appeared confused by the presentations. Others said that students showed discomfort when the topics of molestation and private parts were discussed. There was wide agreement that students found the role-playing sequences the most engaging aspect of prevention training.

Following their participation in the programs, students initiated relatively little discussion about prevention lessons. But when they did raise the topic, teachers indicated that it was almost always in relation to the threat of abduction by strangers. As noted in Chapter 6, a number of parents also observed children expressing these concerns. Despite the programs' efforts not to exaggerate this danger, discussions of strangers and kidnapping make a strong impression on young children.

From the teachers' perspective, sexual abuse prevention training did not appear to have an appreciable effect on their students' classroom behavior. The growing attention afforded this problem both in school and through the media, however, seems to have had some impact on the teachers' attitudes and conduct. Half of the third-grade teachers said that increasing public concern about child sexual abuse had heightened their sense of vulnerability. Some indicated a conscious change in their classroom behavior, saying they had become more cautious about the physical affection they shared with children (18%) and the way they responded to children's remarks that expressed normal sexual curiosity (18%).

The California sample is not alone in its increasing sense of vulnerability. In 1986 the Superintendent of the Waukegan, Illinois, school district issued a memorandum to the district's 700 teachers advising them to avoid all physical contact with students.[28] The Superintendent's concern was that a hug or a pat on the back might be misinterpreted by young students who are being taught to evaluate physical contact; prevention lessons based on the empowerment model inform children that touches they do not like, are not in the mood for, that feel too tight or funny or wrong are "bad" and should be resisted. Although at first glance it may appear hypersensitive, the Superintendent's advice takes on a degree of prudence when reconsidered after a careful reading of many good touch/ bad touch curricula.

Although teacher approval of good touch/bad touch programs is high, as the curricula come under closer scrutiny, school personnel may find it fitting to assign one or two individuals to play the critical role of the gatekeeper, reviewing their school's selected approach to classroom-based prevention education. This role would include reviewing available curricula for their content, cultural sensitivity, and probable acceptance by other school staff and community members. The gatekeeper ensures quality control—disallowing the presentation of inappropriate materials, insisting on experienced presenters, and ensuring that outside presenters make more than a token effort to involve parents[29] and train teachers. Examining programs with a critical eye, the gatekeeper may be especially important in choosing a classroom-based curriculum.

## STRENGTHENING THE TEACHER'S PROTECTIVE ROLE

Classroom teachers in the early grades might play a more effective role in sexual abuse prevention efforts if they were less apprehensive and more knowledgeable about this problem and their reporting obligations. The approach to prevention training that relies mainly on students' exposure to program providers from outside the school does little to reduce the teachers' apprehension or to increase their knowledge.

There is growing sentiment among some educators that teachers need to be better prepared to deal with this problem. Molnar and Gliszczinski suggest, for example, that such preparation involve a uniform program of pre- and in-service training for all teachers, which addresses the legal and ethical aspects of reporting.[30] Ten Bensel and Berdie concur, offering a somewhat broader view of teacher training that includes topics such as "identification, reporting dynamics, medical evidence, implications for physical, mental, and psychological development, treatment and follow-up, legal issues, and the role of the schools."[31]

McCaffrey and Tewey go a step further, proposing that the teachers' role be integrated with the activities of other community professionals who deal with abused children.[32] They emphasize training school personnel in how to talk comfortably with maltreated children and their parents, how to set reasonable and appropriate behavioral and academic expectations for maltreated children and how to provide follow-up activities that are helpful to a child once a report has been made.

A variety of written materials have been developed to educate teachers about child abuse and to encourage discussion of this topic in the classroom.[33] These booklets and manuals include definitions of abuse, indicators of abuse, reporting procedures, songs and activities for children, and lists of community resources. Although written materials of this sort are useful supplements for school personnel, they do not substitute for a strong, interactive training program, which can educate teachers about the problem and help mitigate some of the social and psychological factors that constrain their actions on behalf of children.

Models of child abuse prevention training programs for teachers vary in length from several hours to several days. The Los Angeles Unified School District, for example, conducts an intensive 32-hour training program over a period of 4 days.[34] Covering the largest school district in California, this program is delivered to teachers, administrators, and other school personnel. During the program, participants review, discuss, role-play and work through a variety of issues related to the sexual, physical, and emotional abuse of children. The information conveyed in these sessions takes into account the status of children from a historical perspective; social–psychological factors contributing to abuse; family dynamics prevalent when abuse occurs; behavioral and physical indicators of abuse; and strategies for dealing with abused children in their classes. This training emphasizes that the central responsibility for protecting children lies squarely with the responsible adults in their lives.

The study of California's elementary school prevention efforts included an exploratory survey of participants in the Los Angeles program to glean a rough measure of how much school personnel learn from prevention training. A 40-item test of topics covered by the program was administered to school personnel before and after they received prevention training. Eighteen participants completed these tests; 12 were teachers, and the other 6 included school principals, nurses, and counselors. On the pretest, participants registered a mean score of 21.94 for a correct response rate of 55%. After the 32 hours of training, their mean posttest score increased significantly ($t = 7.41$, $p < .001$) to 32.39 for a correct response rate of 81%. These positive results, of course, are at best suggestive and call for cautious interpretation because of the small size of the sample, the lack of a control group, and the single assessment instrument used. In a more elaborate effort to evaluate a briefer model of teacher training, two studies of a 6-hour program also reveal that teachers made significant gains.[35] They showed an increase in knowledge about abuse and in their empathy for abusive parents.

As previously noted in regard to the programs for children, a gain in knowledge does not necessarily translate into behavioral changes. With regard to mature adults, it does imply that in confronting the problems of child abuse such knowledge will bring greater insight, better anticipation, and perhaps more confidence to act. Although one might expect that a serious effort in prevention training for teachers would strengthen their protective role in the classroom, the outcome remains to be demonstrated. On this point a word of caution is in order. Information is available that may help increase a teacher's ability to detect sexual abuse. However, this information is far from precise. Based on the knowledge currently available in this area, even well-trained teachers would still find the accurate detection of sexual abuse a very difficult matter.

Teachers require more than training to become active participants in the prevention of child abuse. They also need to form a conviction about the importance of their role in protecting children from various sources of social harm. Felner and Felner suggest that "drop-out rates, teen pregnancy, substance abuse, youth suicide, emotional and behavioral problems, and, not least, academic failure, are but a few of the prevention targets schools are being asked to address."[36] Teachers are caught in the middle of these often conflicting demands.

With resources relatively fixed and many social problems on the school agenda, the current approach of devoting a workshop to each problem may not be the optimal model for prevention education. An alternative approach has been suggested, under which schools become actively engaged in the prevention effort rather than serving as passive recipients of prepackaged programs.[37] Barth and Derezotes describe a model that is teacher-delivered and school-centered rather than visitor-delivered and classroom-centered. The intent of this approach is to modify the school ecology by involving school staff and administrators, parents, community members, and children. Blending academic coursework with fundamental primary prevention concepts, the objective is to create an environment that supports children's help-seeking behavior, their concern for others, independent thinking, communication, and their own self-protection. The model is broad-based, integrating concepts relevant to a variety of prevention concerns, and requires less diversion of resources from other tasks required by the schools.

School personnel can also work in conjunction with other professionals to develop protocols for handling child abuse reports and follow-up, as well as developing services within the school and community that promote children's well-being.[38] For example, through regular contact with the local child welfare agency and the police department, school personnel can facilitate procedures to make investigations of sexual abuse more child-oriented and more responsive to the needs of the school. Beyond reporting and investigation procedures, efforts can be made by the schools to help children suffering from abuse. Findings from the National Principal's Survey are encouraging on this note: 82% of elementary-school principals report that they refer children suspected of abuse or neglect to counseling services within their schools or communities.[39]

As these efforts suggest, school personnel can play a more central role in the development of alternative approaches to preventing child abuse. To do this requires increased collaboration with the child welfare system and the assumption of greater responsibility for prevention training within the schools.

# Prevention Policy: Constraints and Alternatives

Policies designed to prevent social problems have gained considerable attention in recent years. This growing appeal of primary prevention policies comes as no surprise. Instead of treating symptoms, they hold out the promise of putting a halt to poverty, delinquency, drug addiction, child sexual abuse, and other seemingly intractable ills of modern society. Between the rising hopes for primary prevention policies and their practical application, however, there remain certain limiting conditions that constrain the scope of public action.

Primary prevention (as noted in Chapter 1) involves policy that aims to keep a problem from happening, as distinguished from secondary prevention efforts which seek to minimize the immediate impact and duration of the problem through early diagnosis and treatment, and tertiary prevention, which involves procedures to keep the problem from getting worse over time.[1] There is an important temporal distinction between the primary and the secondary/tertiary levels of prevention. Primary prevention takes place before the problem has struck or at least at some incipient stage during which its symptoms are barely discernible.[2] The *main objective* of secondary/tertiary prevention is usually to treat the existing problem, not to deal with its aftermath.

Because of its advanced timing, primary prevention of social problems offers the potential to alleviate a great deal of human suffering. But, in order to realize this potential, there are at least three constraints to prevention measures that often need to be addressed. These constraints involve identification of the appropriate target, normative definition of the problem, and unintended consequences of social intervention.

107

## SOCIAL CONSTRAINTS: TARGETS, CONSEQUENCES, AND NORMS

The advanced timing of primary prevention creates a special issue, that of identifying the appropriate target of intervention. Before the problem is clearly evident, how are policymakers to determine who should receive prevention services? This issue is less pressing with regard to secondary and tertiary prevention. In these cases, the problem has surfaced and services are designed to treat and rehabilitate people already identified as in need of help. But, to attack the problem before it has been identified, policymakers must decide who is at risk and aim the prevention services in their direction.

Generally, the targets of intervention may be defined in terms of entire populations or, more narrowly, according to selective criteria. The selective approach involves the identification of "high risk" groups as the targets for preventive services. Thus, for example, the National Institute of Mental Health Office of Prevention has identified children of divorced or separated parents as a special high-risk population in regard to mental health problems.[3] In Hawaii, a state program recently has been established to evaluate all new parents to determine whether they were abused as children, whether they lack self-esteem, whether they have difficulty getting along with children, and other danger signs which suggest that they might be prone to commit child abuse. Parents identified as high risk according to these criteria are offered counseling and home visits for up to 5 years.[4]

The trouble with these selective efforts is that many social problems such as delinquency, mental illness, and child abuse attach both stigma and, in the public eye, some degree of individual responsibility to people who are experiencing the problems or who are judged to be at risk of getting them. It would embarrass almost anyone to be identified as a potential child abuser, and it is difficult to imagine that parents and children would not experience some level of discomfort when children are assessed as potential delinquents by public programs. Because the ability to predict exactly who will suffer these problems is imprecise, in the normal course of events many people labeled as high-risk would not experience the problem. The crux of this issue is how the targets of primary prevention programs can be identified without doing some harm—creating stigma, negative self-image, or just plain psychological discomfort among the designated high-risk population. The extent to which labeling results in a self-fulfilling prophecy is an issue long debated in social science.[5]

How does this constraint operate in child sexual abuse prevention policy? There is a reasonable amount of evidence that might assist policymakers to identify those at greater than average risk of becoming either perpetrators or victims. Among the risk factors frequently cited, for example, girls are at higher risk than boys of being sexually abused, stepfathers are more likely to abuse children than are natural fathers, girls who are abused are more likely to have mothers employed outside the home, and adults who were sexually abused as children are more likely to become abusers than those who were not. For each of these factors, however, the rate of predictability is not high. Most girls are not abused, most stepfathers do not abuse their children, most children of working mothers are not victims of sexual abuse, and most adults who were sexually abused as children do not become perpetrators (indeed, while the victims of child sexual abuse are mainly girls, the adult perpetrators tend to be overwhelmingly male).[6] For purposes of public intervention it is difficult to identify any of these groups as at high risk of becoming sexual abusers or victims without attaching negative labels to many people who will commit or suffer no offense.

Rather than focusing on high-risk groups as the target of intervention, the child sexual abuse prevention movement has instead taken a universal approach. All children are seen as potential victims, and prevention programs have been designed to strengthen their resistance against sexual abuse. Prevention training is seen as providing young children with an "inoculation" that injects knowledge and skills that empower children to effectively ward off sexual molestation.

Taking a universal approach to sexual abuse prevention through classroom training programs mitigates some of the negative aspects of labeling more narrowly targeted high-risk groups. If all children are at risk, none have been singled out as having particularly harmful parents or living conditions. Of course, to deliver these programs to all schoolchildren is considerably more expensive than to focus preventive efforts more narrowly on those most at risk. Considerations of cost aside, while the universal approach to sexual abuse prevention training avoids one set of problems, two critical issues remain when the training is applied to children in preschool and the early elementary grades.

First, are 3- to 9-year-olds an appropriate target for interventions that seek to empower potential victims? A survey of 2,464 parents reveals that 94% believe that 5- to 6-year-old children cannot reliably cross the street alone; and almost a third of these respondents perceive even 10-year-olds as insufficiently skilled to cross streets alone.[7] If they are not thought capable enough to manage the relatively simple business of waiting for a green light and looking both ways before walking a short distance, do parents really imagine that children in the early elementary grades can possibly defend themselves against the social and psychological manipulations of adult authority that are involved in cases of sexual abuse? Adults frequently cannot distinguish between a friendly pat, an affectionate hug, and a sexual advance. Efforts to empower young children by trying to teach them to make these often subtle distinctions, to challenge adult authority, and, if necessary, to physically defend themselves implicitly shift much of the responsibility for their protection from the adult community to the children themselves. Many people would not judge this an entirely desirable situation.

The second issue associated with a universal approach to prevention training concerns the implications of conveying to young children that they are potential victims of sexual abuse. Programs that identify children as the target of intervention need to educate their subjects about the nature of the danger and where it may come from. Because parents are among the major perpetrators of sexual abuse, these training programs usually contain lessons informing young children that they could be sexually molested by parents and other relatives. For example, the Talking About Touching curriculum shows a picture of a father tucking his daughter into bed and asks what the child should do if the father sometimes puts his hand under her pajamas and touches her private parts. The curriculum indicates that the possibility that a parent could abuse his child is a message that clearly needs to be delivered—but in a sensitive way that will not overly concern children to whom this message is conveyed.[8] Although the universal approach does not single out a high-risk group whose parents are presumed to have a tendency for pedophilia, it creates a much wider, if somewhat vaguer web of suspicions. All children are told that parents could sexually abuse them, an idea that few 4-year-olds would imagine on their own. No matter how sensitively it is presented, this is a disturbing message delivered at a time in children's lives when it is important to have a sense of trust that parents and caregivers will nurture and protect them.

The psychological discomfort that may be aroused when children are identified as the subjects for prevention training reveals another constraint on preventive programs. This constraint arises from the unanticipated consequences of social intervention. Proposals for preventive programs are frequently based upon plausible theory or popular ideas, but scientific knowledge about how to prevent social problems is at best tenuous. There are a number of cases in which prevention efforts based on plausible theory, popular ideas, and good intentions have produced results that were unexpected and not entirely desirable. Teenage driver education courses, for example, aim to prevent accidents by teaching teenagers safe driving techniques. It is unclear how well these courses succeed in making teenagers safer drivers, but they do make it easier for teenagers to get their licenses. Although the evidence is not decisive, a study of 10 towns in Connecticut that eliminated courses showed a substantial decrease in the number of 16- and 17-year-old drivers and a concurrent decline in the number of serious auto accidents.[9]

Turning to child sexual abuse prevention training, three kinds of unintended consequences have been identified. In terms of immediate results, questions have been raised as to whether the programs might increase children's anxiety and contribute to their forming an excessive fear of strangers. Regarding these concerns several studies (reviewed in Chapter 6) have documented parental observations of some degree of negative side effects in their children's behavior. Although a few studies also report parents detecting no adverse changes, the weight of the evidence suggests a small but perceptible level of immediate negative effects. In addition to the risk of immediate, though limited, negative side effects, there is the possibility that sexual abuse prevention training may have more harmful long-term consequences with regard to the way children come to experience sexuality and physical intimacy.[10]

Beyond their impact on children, sexual abuse prevention programs also may result in unintended consequences for parents. Here, the main concern is that of cultivating a false sense of security. Because these programs are sponsored by the schools, parents have little reason to question how well they work and tend to believe that they are effective. To the extent that parents think these programs can actually help children to prevent sexual abuse, their watchfulness is likely to decrease. Indeed, if the programs are effective, there should be less need to worry about the child's safety. Finally, from a broader perspective, an unanticipated consequence of these programs may be to inhibit the involvement of men in child care activities. There is a certain irony here. Just as men are being encouraged to assume warmer more nurturing roles as fathers and caretakers, children are being taught to report kisses and touches that might feel funny.

All social interventions—both those of an ameliorative nature and those designed to prevent problems—may have unanticipated consequences. The unexpected negative consequences of preventive measures, however, are of special concern because these interventions take place before the problem has struck—before people are suffering from it. Thus, they have the potential to do harm to individuals who otherwise might experience no difficulties. How serious are the risks associated with sexual abuse prevention training? The answer depends to a large extent on how effective the programs are in achieving their main objective. However, as noted throughout this book, there is a distinct lack of evidence supporting the effectiveness of prevention training for young children and considerable disagreement among professionals about the value of these efforts. In the absence of clearly positive results, the experience of even relatively small negative consequences multiplies in significance.

The third constraint reflects the fact that there is not always normative agreement about what constitutes a social problem. How many drinks make one an alcoholic? Do high divorce rates indicate a problem of marital instability or a desirable condition of individual freedom and personal choice? In the case of child sexual abuse, there is a core of behavior, such as having intercourse with a child, that reasonable people would agree is abusive and many other behaviors that fall into a large realm of uncertainty (e.g., are some of Mapplethorpe's photographs child pornography?).

The lack of normative agreement about the full range of behaviors that constitute child sexual abuse is reflected in the vastly disparate results of 15 surveys conducted since 1976, which seek to estimate the prevalence of this problem. As noted in Chapter 1, these surveys report the proportion of females sexually abused as children as ranging from 6% to 62% of the population; for males the estimates range from 3% to 31%. The discrepancies among these findings are accounted for mostly by the researcher's operational definitions of sexual abuse, which involve a combination of behaviors and experiences, including sexual propositions, exposure to an exhibitionist, posing for nude photographs, unwanted touches, kisses, fondling, sexual intercourse, and other physical contact.[11]

Programs that train young children to prevent sexual abuse must, of course, inform them about the nature of this problem. The typical approach is to identify the child's private parts (parts of the body covered by bathing suits) and to explain that it is bad or dangerous for anybody, even parents, to touch these private parts except when the child is being bathed or examined by a doctor. The "bad" or "dangerous" touch should be resisted and reported to an adult. (Some programs try to avoid discussion of private parts and simply tell the child that a bad touch is any touch that makes them feel bad or uncomfortable. This approach denies the possibility that sometimes a child might experience a sexual touch as enjoyable.) In attempting to define conventional morality for children, prevention programs must formulate simple rules of physical contact that they can understand. These rules establish narrow boundaries for children's responses to physical intimacy in family life.[12] It is hard to set criteria governing physical intimacy between parents and children because this behavior is intensely private and very diverse.

The diversity exists not only among individual families but among cultural groups. In a survey of 358 Californians drawn from several cultural groups, for example, people were asked if it was acceptable for a grandfather to touch his 3-year-old grandson's genitals with pride; over

90% of black, white, and Hispanic respondents said no, while 43% of the Asian respondents thought it was all right. For many Asians, the grandfather's show of affection and pride associated with touching his grandson has no seductive or abusive connotations. When asked if it was acceptable for a father and mother to kiss in front of their 12-year-old son, over 95% of black, white, and Hispanic respondents said yes, while 57% of the Asian subjects gave a negative response. Kissing was perceived by many Asians as a form of sexual foreplay to be conducted in private.[13]

The lessons of child sexual abuse prevention training set normative boundaries that do not reflect the diverse patterns of physical intimacy in American family life. A mother touching her 4-year-old daughter's chest and a father patting his son on the behind violate the rules against bad touching most often conveyed to young children by these programs. Beyond advancing normative views of conventional morality and appropriate family interactions that represent a very narrow band of professional opinion about the nature of the problem, these programs also convey a normative message about the nature of the solution to this problem—that is, that young children are expected to take charge of their lives, to be empowered to protect themselves against the dangerous outside world. It is a normative message that downplays the responsibility of family and community for the protection of their youngest and weakest members.

To raise these issues concerning the target of intervention, unanticipated consequences, and normative implications of preventive efforts is not to diminish the importance of these efforts, but to caution that prevention policy be designed and tested with a critical eye. Careful experimentation is required to assure that these efforts are not oversold or prematurely institutionalized. Until firm evidence is established concerning the potential effects, both positive and negative, of prevention training, parents have a right to be informed about the experimental nature of these programs. At the same time, there are alternatives to be explored that might prove less problematic than the current focus on empowering children. In this regard, new insights from research on both offenders and victims suggest some ways that resources now invested in empowerment models of prevention training might be used more constructively.

## OFFENDERS AND VICTIMS: RECENT INSIGHTS

Prevention programs for preschoolers and primary-grade children have been designed with little attention to theories of child development and hardly any systematic knowledge of how offenders and victims interact in the process of child molestation. They are based instead on providers' "best guess"[14] about the kinds of information young children need to empower themselves. Recently available data on the behavior of offenders and victims and their perceptions of prevention efforts offer new insights into the design of an age-appropriate curriculum.

On the process of child sexual abuse, Finkelhor suggests that there are four preconditions that must exist for the act to take place.[15] The model is speculative but nevertheless somewhat instructive in providing a macro-perspective on the abuse process. First, an individual must be psychologically motivated to abuse a child. The individual must then suppress internal inhibitors prohibiting the act and surmount external inhibitors and obstacles. Finally, the offender must overcome the child's resistance to the offense.

As can be seen from this model, sexual abuse prevention training focuses on the fourth precondition of abuse. By shoring up the child's resistance, it is believed that an offender will be deterred from completing the act. This approach does not take into account the tremendous psychological (and sometimes physical) effort the perpetrator has made to overcome the first three inhibitors; the final stage in the process may be the least daunting. The more that is known about offenders, the better we understand the challenge of prevention. Some studies have begun to tell us about the nature of offenders,[16] and clinical work is providing a glimpse into why they prey on children.[17] But little has been done to illuminate a micro-perspective that examines the "how" of child sexual abuse. How do perpetrators select their victims? How do they engage the child? And how do they maintain their secrecy?

Conte and associates' ground-breaking study on these issues offers some initial insights into the engagement process: how offenders entice the child and keep him or her from resisting the offender's actions.[18] This study focused on 20 male perpetrators actively involved in treatment. The offenders were interviewed individually using a semistructured interview guide. Topics covered included how the offender selected the child, how the victim was engaged, and whether or not coercion was used.

The results indicate that offenders look for "friendly," "trusting," and "vulnerable" children. As the fear of being apprehended appears to be their greatest concern, perpetrators select their victims with an eye to the child's continued silence:

> First you would groom your victim by heavy handedness promoting fear . . . then isolate the victim so that no one else would be around. The next step would involve making the child think that everything is okay so they wouldn't run and tell. You could convince them there is nothing wrong with it or pressure a child not to tell . . . using force or coercion.[19]

Another study, conducted by Budin and Johnson, questioned 72 prison inmates who were convicted of sexual crimes against children.[20] The authors of this study found that over 20% of perpetrators had used intimidation to gain the child's cooperation and more than one-quarter had used threats to prevent the children from telling an adult. Each of these studies point to the offender's fear of being detected. Perpetrators were less concerned about children being empowered to resist sexual assaults. If a child were to say no, offenders said that they would continue to coerce the child until he or she acquiesced.[21] Self-defense techniques also would do little to discourage a perpetrator from his or her intent. Rather, the most powerful deterrent appears to be the child's warning that he or she would disclose the incident.

These findings are corroborated by accounts from the victim's perspective as well. Berliner and Conte's exploratory study with 23 sexually abused children aged 10 to 18 reveals the prominence of the relationship in the process of victimization. About three-fourths of the children had known the offender for at least one year before the abuse began. In a gradual process of grooming their victims, the offenders often developed a friendly connection with them, first meeting emotional needs for warmth and affirmation before the physical relationship began. In the course of enticing the child into sexual contact, the offender used various measures such as bribery and games as well as threats of abandonment, rejection, and physical harm. Berliner and Conte indicated that one of the best-accepted preventive strategies (i.e., saying no) would not be particularly effective:

> Few of the children we interviewed felt that if they had said no, the abuse would have stopped. Many expressed a belief that it would have continued or that they would have been further harmed."[22]

The implications of these initial studies are significant for prevention programs. The studies point to the elaborate efforts by which perpetrators find and seduce their victims. They highlight the degree of coercion involved in engaging the child and maintaining the child's silence, and they show how an insidious process of grooming leads to physical contact with the child and the sexualization of that contact. Child sexual abuse is not a simple course of action that can be avoided by learning to say no, run, fight, or yell. As Conte explains:

> It is clear that the struggle between sexual offender and potential victim, is one in which most factors are weighted on the side of the adult. Superior knowledge, strength, and skill will not easily be overcome by children. This fact should serve both to revitalize prevention efforts, but also alert prevention professionals of the complexity of the

task. . . . It should be no surprise to prevention professionals just how complex the prevention task really is.[23]

Exposing young children to a long list of prevention strategies does little to reduce the superior knowledge, strength, and skill of adult offenders. Finkelhor suggests that prevention programs may not be as effective in teaching children useful strategies as they are in deterring potential offenders from following through with the abuse.[24] What is it about prevention training that might have a deterrent effect? Offenders will not be put off by a program that directs little children to say no and stomp on their foot or scrape down the shin, but they are keenly aware of the power of disclosure. If they believe that programs effectively teach children to tell, abusers might be more reluctant to act.

## FROM EMPOWERMENT TO PROTECTION: AN ALTERNATIVE APPROACH

The empowerment model of sexual abuse prevention training for young children has been brought into question on several accounts: the limited amount of classroom learning that takes place, the lack of evidence that classroom learning translates into behavior that can prevent abuse, the insufficient consideration of developmental factors, the appropriateness of exposing young children to the idea that they must be able to defend themselves against potential abuse from relatives and other adults, un-intended consequences, and the normative implications of good touch/ bad touch curricula. Enough issues have been raised by different scholars in this field to warrant serious consideration of alternative approaches to the prevailing model of prevention training.

One way to think about these alternatives is along a continuum from what might be viewed as the "hard option" to the "soft option." The empowerment model represents the hard option, which involves sensitiz-ing children to the dangers of sexual abuse from strangers and relatives, and teaching them to be assertive—to run, to say no, to fight, to yell—in the face of such danger. This approach seeks to convey a fairly large number of ideas in a short time. In contrast, the soft option is based on a model of protection, which emphasizes adult responsibility for young children and teaches general communication skills along with lessons about body awareness and secret touching that are integrated into the ongoing process of education by classroom teachers. A brief review of the four basic elements of this model—body awareness, communication skills, secret touching, and adult responsibility—is offered as a guidepost toward an alternative direction for prevention training.

## Body Awareness

Body awareness includes a general knowledge of all of the parts of the body as well as a healthy respect for keeping one's own body and others' safe. This requires children to know the correct names of all of their body parts so that they have a language for describing themselves to others. Fostering respect for one's body and for others includes general discussions regarding health and safety. Education about the human form, if it is done within a context that is relevant to the child, does not necessarily lead to discussions of sex education, a subject that parents are wary of and many primary-grade teachers find uncomfortable. The heightening of physical awareness helps to normalize discussions about the body and provides an acceptable vocabulary for children to use in speaking up about sexual abuse.

This is not to say that child sexual abuse prevention education should necessarily be separate from sex education. Schools usually initiate sex education in the upper grades, and this could be integrated with sexual abuse prevention materials. As children develop an understanding of the healthy aspects of sexuality, they can then be made aware of harmful practices as well. This would relieve many of the concerns that have been raised about the potential impact of sexual abuse training in the early grades on children's sexual development. Some have suggested that if children's earliest exposure to sex is provided in a negative light (through sexual abuse prevention, AIDS education, and education regarding sexually transmitted diseases), this may have adverse effects on ordinary childhood sexual play and the development of later sexual relationships.[25]

For younger children, the development of body awareness is quite distinct from the language of "body rights." Potential confusion regarding concepts such as body ownership, property, and rights is avoided, and children gain an understanding of the special nature of their own bodies. In the upper grades, as their sense of morality develops, children are better able to employ the concept of body rights. Setting limits to their body space becomes more practical for older children as they are generally touched less and require less assistance from adults in bathing and grooming.

## Communication

Prevention programs focus on teaching children that they can tell an adult if someone touches their private parts. Yet this is not the only kind of interaction around which children might be encouraged to express themselves. Rather, they can be taught that it is acceptable and appropriate to communicate with adults about their displeasure or discomfort with many situations involving their body, their personal feelings, and the feelings or safety of others.

Teachers play an especially important role in developing communication skills among children. They can structure opportunities to stimulate the development of prosocial behavior allowing children to experience cooperation, helping, negotiating, and talking with others to solve interpersonal problems. Garbarino and Kostelny suggest that "in cases of child maltreatment occurring in the context of dangerous environments, communities must usually carry things to the next step—i.e., stimulating higher order moral development."[26] Teachers are in a pivotal position to develop this higher order morality with both abused and nonabused children in the classroom.

Although it may be feasible to teach children to resolve conflicts with one another (with the occasional assistance of an adult caretaker), it is not practical to suggest that children can effectively assert themselves and negotiate with adults who are seeking to prey on them.[27] Therefore, children must be given a reliable line of defense for all of their associations with other people. They need to know that trusted adults are there to assist them in times of need and confusion. To this end, teachers and other adult caregivers should encourage children's reliance on them as helpers.

The emphasis on communication moves away from an empowerment model that is usually unrealistic for young children. The protective approach fosters trust and healthy attachments between children and their caregivers. Most adults do not sexually abuse children, and most children are not sexually abused. Messages conveying the idea that trusted adults might do serious harm to children can undermine their confidence in relationships with adults and foster insecurity. Children who are being abused also need to be assured that there are trustworthy adults in this world who mean them no harm, and whose primary interest is in their well-being. They need to feel that trusted adults will listen to them if they come forth with a problem.

But what about this approach is specific to child sexual abuse? How would a child be able to distinguish if he or she were being sexually abused? In the early years, there may be no useful way to teach children how to distinguish between types of touches. An approach that focuses on telling about all types of difficult, confusing, or bothersome situations may be the best that we can do in terms of delivering a general abuse prevention lesson to young children. Yet this approach also delivers a warning that might deter potential offenders. With other adults in the community becoming more alert, listening to and cultivating discourse with children, the offender's secret is not safe. As children are encouraged to trust and communicate more actively with teachers and caregivers, those being abused or "groomed" for abuse are at any time more likely to reveal their situation.

## Secret Touching

Beyond the general approach of facilitating communication, there is a specific lesson that can be taught. By the time they enter first grade, children have a fairly clear understanding of secrets. They are no longer entirely bound by concrete actions and have incorporated abstract thought to the degree that they can talk about secrets and keep secrets with their peers and family members. Because of this newly developed ability, the lesson of "secret touching" can be introduced at this age. In this lesson children are taught that if they are ever told to keep a secret about touching, something wrong is going on, which they should report to a trusted adult. The approach is specific and does not ask children to make fine distinctions between abstract ideas. In contrast, when they are taught about "good" and "bad" secrets, children are required to make an assessment of the content of the secret as well as the potential outcome if the secret is or is not told (i.e., "a good secret will make you feel good when you tell it"[28]). Those in the upper grades are able to make distinctions of this kind, but younger children usually cannot. Therefore, relying on the simple concept of "secret touching" is more age appropriate for first and third graders.

In certain cultures, as already noted, parents and other relatives will sometimes touch their children's breasts or their genitals as a show of affection and pride.[29] The intent is not sexual seduction, and the behavior is viewed as acceptable within the culture. If children are taught that it is "secret touching" that is wrong, they will not be confused if touched openly and without shame in the company of parents and relatives.

What if children are threatened that terrible harm will come to them or their loved ones if they reveal a "secret touch"? There are surely instances in which no amount of assurance by teachers and other adults will alleviate the fear that abusers may instill in their young victims. Teaching children to reveal "secret touching" cannot be expected to have much influence on those being terrorized by their abusers. In these cases, careful observation by other adults in the child's immediate environment may be the only means of uncovering abuse.

## Adult Responsibility

The protection model relies heavily on the support of adults. As the natural guardians of young children, parents and teachers play an essential role in this model. Children who have been sexually abused often display a number of emotional or behavioral indicators.[30] To intervene effectively on behalf of children, parents and teachers need to be made aware of these signals and the appropriate responses. Although information about indicators of abuse, as previously noted, is not at all definitive, training in the prudent interpretation of these signs can help adults to exercise their protective role. Child sexual abuse, as indicated in Chapter 7, is an emotional and difficult subject for many adults. Pushing past this psychological aversion is the first step toward assuming responsibility for the prevention of abuse. This step involves teaching adults how to listen and respond to children's needs. Adults who are not open to hearing disclosures of abuse can do little to aid or comfort children in need of protection.

Another important area of training involves teaching adults to assist children in resolving their conflicts and expressing their emotions. The preschool and primary-grade years are a time of developing social skills; using words to resolve difficulties does not come naturally. Teachers and parents who encourage children to communicate and who respond to their words will foster a trustful relationship.

Finally, focusing on Finkelhor's third precondition of abuse (external inhibitors), parents need to be made aware of the way abusers operate, particularly the grooming process through which they select and gain control over their young victims. At the same time parents should be encouraged to exercise greater vigilance in regard to children's whereabouts and the company they keep. Women, in particular, need to be taught about the process of abuse, what to look for in the way their children behave, and how to respond. This is not to say that women should assume the full responsibility for protecting their children, but the role they play in inhibiting the actions of offenders has been found to be an especially important factor in the prevention of abuse.[31]

For a variety of reasons, the taboo that prohibits sexual relations with children is not as strong as it should be. According to Finkelhor's preconditions for abuse, the maintenance of this taboo is an effective inhibitor against the perpetrator's actions.[32] Cohn suggests that child sexual abuse is not intentionally promoted in our society but may be tacitly "*allowed* by the lack of strongly voiced taboos . . . saying it is *not* ok to molest kids."[33] For example, a study of book titles in pornography stores revealed that from one-quarter to one-third of the titles referred to sex with underage children or incestuous sex.[34] Other authors have found the widespread use of children as sexual objects in the popular media and advertising.[35] This sexualization of children does little to disinhibit offenders who might be inclined to sexually abuse a child. The message that such behavior is intolerable should be reinforced and disseminated widely, primarily through media campaigns but also through parent education programs.

## Empowerment versus Protection

To be empowered, individuals need to experience control and to have a realistic sense that they can change their environment. The empowerment ideology of the rape prevention movement may be appropriate for adult women, who, it presumes, can take charge of much of their surroundings; any deficit in their power is attributed more to socialization than to gender. But for children it is a different matter. As Smith explains in her manual for women's self-defense:

> Children are relatively powerless to change their life circumstances and do not understand the forces which dominate their lives until much later. As adults we can understand, we can change our internal values and fight for our rights.[36]

Compared to the empowerment model, the protective approach distills the number of concepts down from the 20 or more taught to children in current programs to a few central ideas: body awareness (including the correct names of one's genitalia), communicating to peers and adults about one's feelings, seeking help (in the form of telling, getting help, or talking to a trusted adult), and secret touching. Many of the difficult and questionable aspects of the empowerment model are avoided, such as following safety rules that have confusing and unclear exceptions; determining a "safe" distance to stand from a stranger; the mastery of a particular type of safety yell; the teaching of physical self-defense techniques; saying no to adults, who may respond with an escalation of force; distinguishing between ideas that have no clear dividing lines (i.e., good and bad secrets or good and bad touches[37]); and interpreting recondite language such as "children's rights," "empowerment," and "body ownership." The protective approach places no burden on young children to perceive, evaluate, and act in instances that are unclear, emotionally charged, and very confusing. Finally, this approach does not confront children with the possibility of abuse from someone they know. This idea is difficult for children to comprehend and does little to foster the sense of trust and security necessary to enlist adult assistance when needed.

Social movements go through various transformations. They may grow, decay, and change, depending in part on the ebb and flow of public sentiments and success or failure in attaining their goals.[38] At one level, the child sexual abuse prevention movement has achieved a remarkable degree of success: it has stimulated a significant increase in public awareness of the problem. At another level, however, the predominant model of prevention training devised to address this problem has shown limited results and comes under growing criticism. Serious questions about the effectiveness of the empowerment model are raised by development theory about what children are capable of learning and doing, by recent insights into the elaborate and cunning methods employed by offenders, by findings on the limited gains in knowledge registered by students after prevention training, and by unintended consequences of this training. Whether based on the protection model described above or on some other approach, an alternative method for safeguarding young children warrants testing. The empowerment model, however, represents more than simply a means to achieve the movement's prevention objectives. It is an integral part of the movement's ideology about the kind of normative change that should take place, one that emphasizes the responsibility of children to care for themselves. The child sexual abuse prevention movement is at a crossroads. It may evolve in response to the theoretical insights and empirical findings that discommend the empowerment model, or it may ignore these issues and continue along the current track. The direction that will be taken depends on whether it is more firmly committed to the ideology of having children care for themselves or to the larger social objective of caring for children.

# Epilogue

Facing a budget deficit of several billion dollars in 1990, the state of California was forced to reduce spending on social programs. The Governor's initial budget for fiscal year 1990–1991 included a proposal to eliminate funding for the Child Abuse Prevention and Training Act Program. In a report to the legislature prepared for the budget hearings on this proposal the Legislative Analyst's Office concluded that

> "it is, in general, unclear whether the knowledge imparted by the program helps children to change their behavior and thereby prevents abuse. Moreover, researchers and experts disagree over how to interpret the information gains that the program has demonstrated. Finally, a large body of evidence, summarized in the department's own task force report, indicates that much of the preschool curricula is beyond the cognitive ability of preschoolers.

Allowing, however, for the possibility that the knowledge gains registered by older children still might have some beneficial effects in the prevention of abuse, the report offered two alternatives for the legislature to consider instead of terminating the program. On the preschool level, it suggested that they might "refocus the program from direct instruction of students to training of parents and teachers." Regarding K–12 programs, "an option to outright elimination would be to significantly scale back the program" and then require an in-depth longitudinal study to determine if the program actually helped children to protect themselves.

In the end, another option was adopted. When the final state budget passed in the fall of 1990, responsibility for the funding and delivery of services under California's Child Abuse Prevention Training Act was transferred from the State Office of Child Abuse Prevention (OCAP) to the Department of Education. However, this transfer of responsibility was not accompanied by the $10.4 million previously allocated to OCAP for the annual support of this program. The schools are expected to finance prevention efforts through general-purpose and staff-development funds currently at their disposal. Whether this shift will mark the demise of comprehensive child sexual abuse prevention training in California or the birth of an alternative approach carried forward by professional educators remains to be seen.

# Notes

*Chapter 1. Empowering Children to Prevent Sexual Abuse*

1. C. C. Tower, *Understanding Child Abuse and Neglect* (Boston: Allyn and Bacon, 1989), pp. 4–5.

2. B. Knox, "Los Olividados," *New York Review of Books*, 29 June 1989, pp. 9–12.

3. Tower, *Understanding Child Abuse*, pp. 9–10.

4. R. Hunter, *Poverty: Social Conscience in the Progressive Era*, ed. P. d'A. Jones (New York: Harper & Row, 1965), pp. 253–254.

5. H. C. Kempe, F. Silverman, B. Steele, W. Droegemueller, and H. Silver, "The Battered Child Syndrome," *Journal of the American Medical Association*, 181(17) (1962): 17–24.

6. D. Martin, *Battered Wives* (San Francisco: Glide Publications, 1976).

7. L. Lederer, ed., *Take Back the Night: Women on Pornography* (New York: Morrow, 1980).

8. See M. Angelou, *I Know Why the Caged Bird Sings* (New York: Random House, 1969); J. Barr, *Within a Dark Wood: The Personal Story of a Rape Victim* (Garden City, NY: Doubleday, 1979); R. L. McCunn, *Thousand Pieces of Gold: A Biographical Novel* (San Francisco: Design Enterprises of San Francisco, 1981); K. Millett, *Flying* (New York: Knopf, 1974); T. Morrison, *The Bluest Eye* (New York: Simon and Schuster, 1970); J. Russ, *On Strike against God* (Brooklyn, NY: Out & Out Books, 1980); J. Swallow, ed., *Out from Under: Sober Dykes and Our Friends* (San Francisco: Spinsters, Inc., 1983).

9. D. Finkelhor, "Sexual Abuse of Boys," *Victimology*, 6(1981): 71–84; D. E. H. Russell, "The Incidence and Prevalence of Intrafamilial and Extrafamilial Sexual Abuse of Female Children," *Child Abuse and Neglect*, 7(2) (1983): 133–146. For

other studies estimating the national rates of abuse and neglect, see American Humane Association, *Child Abuse and Neglect Reporting Study* (Washington, DC, 1980); *National Study of the Incidence and Severity of Child Abuse and Neglect* (Washington, DC: U.S. Department of Health and Human Services, 1980).

10. A. C. Kinsey, W. B. Pomeroy, C. E. Martin, and P. H. Gebhard, *Sexual Behavior in the Human Female* (Philadelphia: W. B. Saunders, 1953).

11. PL 93–247, Child Abuse Prevention and Treatment Act, 1974.

12. E. Hoffman, "Policy and Politics: The Child Abuse Prevention and Treatment Act," *Public Policy*, 26(1) (Winter 1978): 71–88.

13. D. Besharov, "Doing Something about Child Abuse: The Need to Narrow the Grounds for State Intervention," *Harvard Journal of Law and Public Policy*, 8 (Summer 1985): 539–589.

14. *Study of National Incidence and Prevalance of Child Abuse and Neglect: 1988* (Washington, DC: U.S. Department of Health and Human Services, 1988).

15. D. Finkelhor and Associates, *A Sourcebook on Child Sexual Abuse* (Beverly Hills, CA: Sage Publications, 1986).

16. H. Miller, *The Social Ecology of Child Abuse* (Berkeley, CA: University of California at Berkeley, Family Welfare Research Group, 1988).

17. Finkelhor and Associates, *Sourcebook*.

18. J. J. Haugaard and N. D. Reppucci, *The Sexual Abuse of Children* (San Francisco: Jossey-Bass, 1988).

19. See, for example, D. Finkelhor, *Sexually Victimized Children* (New York: Free Press, 1979); M. E. Fromuth, "The Relationship of Childhood Sexual Abuse with Later Psychological and Sexual Adjustment in a Sample of College Women," *Child Abuse and Neglect*, 10 (1986): 5–15; and G. S. Fritz, K. Stoll, and N. N. Wagner, "A Comparison of Males and Females Who Were Sexually Molested as Children," *Journal of Sex and Marital Therapy*, 10 (1981): 54–59.

20. D. E. H. Russell, *Sexual Exploitation, Rape, Child Sexual Abuse and Work Place Harassment* (Beverly Hills, CA: Sage, 1984); G. E. Wyatt, "The Sexual Abuse of Afro-American and White-American Women in Childhood," *Child Abuse and Neglect*, 9 (1985): 507–519.

21. J. J. Haugaard and R. E. Emery, "Methodological Issues in Child Sexual Abuse Research," *Child Abuse and Neglect*, 13 (1989): 89–100.

22. Haugaard and Reppucci, *Sexual Abuse of Children*.

23. G. E. Wyatt, "Sexual Abuse of Women in Childhood."

24. D. Finkelhor, *Sexually Victimized Children*.

25. J. Landis, "Experiences of 500 Children with Adult Sexual Deviants," *Psy-*

*chiatric Quarterly Supplement*, 30 (1956): 91–109; D. E. H. Russell, *Sexual Exploitation;* M. Tsai, S. Feldman-Summers, and M. Edgar, "Childhood Molestation: Variables Related to Differential Impacts on Psychosexual Functioning in Adult Women," *Journal of Abnormal Psychology*, 88 (1979): 407–417.

26. C. Adams-Tucker, "Proximate Effects of Sexual Abuse in Childhood: A Report on Twenty-Eight Children," *American Journal of Psychiatry*, 139 (1982): 1252–1256; L. O. Ruch and S. M. Chandler, "The Crisis Impact of Sexual Assault on Three Victim Groups: Adult Rape Victims, Child Rape Victims, and Incest Victims," *Journal of Social Service Research*, 5 (1982): 83–100; D. E. H. Russell, *Sexual Exploitation*.

27. G. E. Wyatt, "The Relationship Between the Cumulative Impact of a Range of Child Sexual Abuse Experiences and Women's Psychological Well-Being," *Victimology* (in press); J. Herman, D. E. H. Russell, and K. Trocki, "Long Term Effects of Incestuous Abuse in Childhood," *American Journal of Psychiatry*, 143 (1986): 1293–1296.

28. T. G. Sandfort, "Sex in Pedophiliac Relationships: An Empirical Investigation among a Nonrepresentative Group of Boys," *Journal of Sex Research*, 20 (1984): 123–142; A. Yorukoglu and J. P. Kemph, "Children Not Severely Damaged by Incest with a Parent," *Journal of the American Academy of Child Psychiatry*, 5 (1966): 111–124.

29. J. P. Byrne and E. V. Valdiserri, "Victims of Childhood Sexual Abuse: A Follow-up Study of a Non-compliant Population," *Hospital and Community Psychiatry*, 33 (1982): 938–940; B. M. Cormier, M. Kennedy, and J. Sangowicz, "Psychodynamics of Father–Daughter Incest," *Canadian Psychiatric Association Journal*, 7 (1962): 203–217; M. Fischer, "Adolescent Adjustment after Incest," *School Psychology International*, 4 (1983): 217–222; D. J. Gelinas, "The Persisting Negative Effects of Incest," *Psychiatry*, 46 (1983), 312–332; H. A. Giaretto, "A Comprehensive Child Sexual Abuse Treatment Program," in P. B. Mrazek and C. H. Kempe, eds., *Sexually Abused Children and Their Families* (Elmsford, NY: Pergamon Press, 1981); D. Lubell and S. Soong, "Group Therapy with Sexually Abused Adolescents," *Canadian Journal of Psychiatry*, 27 (1982): 311–315; C. Rogers and T. Terry, "Clinical Intervention with Boy Victims of Sexual Abuse," in I. R. Stuart and J. G. Greer, eds., *Victims of Sexual Aggression: Treatment of Children, Women, and Men* (New York: Van Nostrand Reinhold, 1984); K. Sturkie, "Structured Group Treatment for Sexually Abused Children," *Health and Social Work*, 4 (1983): 299–309; R. C. Summit, "The Child Sexual Abuse Accommodation Syndrome," *Child Abuse and Neglect*, 7 (1983): 177–193.

30. Adams-Tucker, "Proximate Effects of Sexual Abuse"; Byrne and Valdiserri, "Victims of Childhood Sexual Abuse"; Gelinas, "Persisting Negative Effects."

31. K. N. Dixon, E. L. Arnold, and K. Calestro, "Father–Son Incest: Underreported Psychiatric Problem?" *American Journal of Psychiatry*, 135 (1978): 835–838; Fischer, "Adolescent Adjustment after Incest," pp. 217–222; Gelinas, "Persisting Negative Effects"; Lubell and Soong, "Group Therapy"; Sturkie, "Structured Group Treatment."

32. K. L. James, "Incest: The Teenager's Perspective," *Psychotherapy: Therapy, Research, and Practice,* 14 (1977): 146–155; Lubell and Soong, "Group Therapy."

33. Rogers and Terry, "Boy Victims of Sexual Abuse."

34. Adams-Tucker, "Proximate Effects of Sexual Abuse"; B. E. Bess and Y. Janssen, "Incest: A Pilot Study," *Hillside Journal of Clinical Psychiatry,* 4 (1982): 39–52; K. N. Dixon, E. L. Arnold, and K. Calestro, "Father–Son Indext," pp. 835–838; J. Goodwin, ed., *Sexual Abuse: Incest Victims and Their Families* (Boston: John Wright, 1982); J. Herman, *Father–Daughter Incest* (Cambridge, MA: Harvard University Press, 1981).

35. L. S. Anderson, "Notes on the Linkage Between the Sexually Abused Child and the Suicidal Adolescent," *Journal of Adolescence,* 4 (1981): 157–162; F. H. Lindberg and L. J. Distad, "Survival Responses to Incest: Adolescents in Crisis," *Child Abuse and Neglect,* 9 (1985): 521–526; S. Shapiro, "Self-Mutilation and Self-Blame in Incest Victims," *American Journal of Psychotherapy,* 41 (1987): 46–54.

36. M. deYoung, "Counterphobic Behaviors in Multiply Molested Children," *Child Welfare,* 68 (1984): 333–339; B. James and M. N. Nasjleti, *Treating Sexually Abused Children and Their Families* (Palo Alto, CA: Consulting Psychologists Press, 1983); R. Borgman, "Problems of Sexually Abused Girls and Their Treatment," *Social Casework,* 665 (1984): 182–186; M. J. Kohan, P. Pothier, and J. S. Norbeck, "Hospitalized Children with a History of Sexual Abuse: Incidence and Care Issues," *American Journal of Orthopsychiatry,* 57 (1987): 258–264; Fischer, "Adolescent Adjustment after Incest," 217–222; A. Y. Yates, "Children Eroticized by Incest," *American Journal of Psychiatry,* 139 (1982): 482–485.

37. Bess and Janssen, "Incest: A Pilot Study"; R. H. Gundlach, "Sexual Molestation and Rape Reported by Heterosexual and Homosexual Women," *Journal of Homosexuality,* 2 (1977): 367–384; Rogers and Terry, "Boy Victims of Sexual Abuse."

38. D. Daro, *Confronting Child Abuse: Research for Effective Program Design* (New York: Free Press, 1988).

39. Finkelhor and Associates, *Sourcebook.*

40. Ibid., p. 163.

41. M. Kessler and G. Albee, "Primary Prevention," *Annual Review of Psychology,* 26 (1975): 557–591. Also see H. R. Lamb and J. Zusman, "Primary Prevention in Perspective," *American Journal of Psychiatry* 136(1) (1979): 12–17; A. S. Mariner, "Benevolent Gambling: A Critique of Primary Prevention Programs in Mental Health," *Psychiatry* 43 (1980): 95–105.

42. See, for example, R. E. Helfer, "A Review of the Literature on Prevention of Child Abuse and Neglect," *Child Abuse and Neglect* 6 (1982): 251–261; and *Attorney Generals' Commission on the Enforcement of Child Abuse Laws* (Sacramento, CA: State of California, Office of the Attorney General, 1983).

43. Much of the following discussion of the history of the child abuse prevention movement is taken from a detailed account found in the introductory chapter of M. Nelson and K. Clark, *The Educator's Guide to Preventing Child Sexual Abuse* (Santa Cruz, CA: ETR Network Publications, 1986).

44. The Illusion Theatre, *Sexual Abuse Prevention Project,* Unpublished material (available from author, 304 Washington Avenue North, Minneapolis, MN 55401).

45. M. Olson, *Personal Safety,* Unpublished material (available from Council on Child Sexual Abuse, P.O. Box 1357, Tacoma, WA 98401).

46. G. Crisci, *Personal Safety Program.* Unpublished material (available from author, P.O. Box 763, Hadley, MA 01035).

47. Bridgework Theatre, Inc., Unpublished material (available from author, 113 East Lincoln Ave., Suite 3, Goshen, IN 46526).

48. S. K. Kraizer, *Children Need to Know Personal Safety Program* (New York: Health Education Systems, 1980) (available from publisher, P.O. Box 1235, New York, NY 10116).

49. National Committee for the Prevention of Child Abuse, *Teachers Confront Child Abuse: A National Survey of Teachers* (Chicago: Author, 1989).

50. W. C. King, *Social Movements in the United States* (New York: Random House, 1956), p. 27.

51. W. B. Cameron, *Modern Social Movements* (New York: Random House, 1966), p. 78.

52. S. Brownmiller, *Against Our Will: Men, Women, and Rape* (New York: Simon and Schuster, 1975).

53. S. Griffin, *Rape: The Power of Consciousness* (New York: Harper and Row, 1979).

54. J. L. Herman, *Briefing Paper* (Paper presented at the Wingspread Symposium, Cincinnati, OH, December, 1987).

55. M. Daly, *Gyn-Ecology: The Metaethics of Radical Feminism* (Boston: Beacon Press, 1978).

56. G. Groves, "Preface: He Turned and Ran Away," in D. Caignon and G. Groves, eds., *Her Wits about Her* (New York: Harper and Row, 1987).

57. Cited in *Preschool Project Training Manual* (Berkeley, CA: Child Abuse Prevention Training Center of Northern California, 1983), p. 8.

58. Ibid., p. 4.

59. J. Wilson, *Introduction to Social Movements* (New York: Basic Books, 1973), pp. 27–29.

60. C. Plummer, "Prevention Education in Perspective," in M. Nelson and K.

Clark, eds., *The Educator's Guide to Preventing Child Sexual Abuse* (Santa Cruz, CA: ETR Network Publications, 1986).

61. K. Beland, *Talking about Touching* (Seattle, WA: Committee for Children, 1985) (available from publisher, 172 20th Avenue, Seattle, WA 98122).

62. S. Patterson, *Preschool Curriculum* (unpublished manuscript, Marin County, CA: Touch Safety Program, 1986).

63. G. Fryer, S. Kraizer, and T. Miyoshi, "Measuring Actual Reduction of Risk to Child Abuse: A New Approach," *Child Abuse and Neglect,* 11 (1987): 173–180.

64. C. Poche, P. Yoder, and R. Miltenberger, "Teaching Self-Protection to Children," *Journal of Applied Behavioral Analysis,* 14 (1988): 159–176.

65. G. Melton, "The Improbability of Prevention of Sexual Abuse," in D. Willis, E. Holder, and M. Rosenberg, eds., *Child Abuse Prevention* (New York: John Wiley, in press).

66. S. K. Kraizer, "Rethinking Prevention," *Child Abuse and Neglect,* 10 (1986): 259–261; J. M. Leventhal, "Programs to Prevent Sexual Abuse: What Outcomes Should Be Measured?" *Child Abuse and Neglect,* 11 (1987): 169–171.

67. J. Conte, "Ethical Issues in Evaluation of Prevention Programs," *Child Abuse and Neglect,* 11 (1987): 172.

68. A detailed analysis of the findings from the Family Welfare Research Group's preschool study is reported in N. Gilbert, J. Duerr Berrick, N. Le Prohn, and N. Nyman, *Protecting Young Children from Sexual Abuse: Does Preschool Training Work?* (Lexington MA: Lexington Books, 1989).

## Chapter 2. Age and Effectiveness

1. C. Gorney, "The Baffling Case of the McMartin Preschool," *San Francisco Examiner, This World,* 26 June 1988, pp. 10–14.

2. H. Miller, *The Social Ecology of Child Abuse: Final Report* (Berkeley, CA: University of California, School of Social Welfare, 1988).

3. For a detailed description of the process by which the bill passed, see A. Zippay, "California's Commitment to Prevention: From Idea to Statute," in N. Gilbert, J. Duerr Berrick, N. LeProhn, and N. Nyman, eds., *Protecting Young Children from Sexual Abuse: Does Preschool Training Work?* (Lexington , MA: Lexington Books, 1989), pp. 1–14.

4. Ibid.

5. A survey of California prevention providers found that 25% voluntarily disclosed their own childhood victimization. The majority of providers were familiar with the problem of child abuse because of their previous exposure to abused children through family, friends, or earlier work settings. E. Vanderschmidt, "An

Examination of CAPTA Providers: Study Results" Berkeley, CA: University of California, Berkeley, 1989, Mimeographed).

6. See, for example, Y. Dror, C. Lindblom, R. W. Jones, M. McCleery, and W. Heydebrand, "Governmental Decision Making," *Public Administration Review,* 24 (1964): 153–165; and N. Gilbert and H. Specht, *Planning for Social Welfare* (Englewood Cliffs, NJ: Prentice Hall, 1977).

7. D. Braybrooke and C. Lindblom, *A Strategy of Decision: Policy Evaluation as a Social Process* (New York: The Free Press, 1963); and Y. Dror, *Public Policy Making Reexamined* (San Francisco: Chandler, 1968).

8. A. Etzioni, "Mixed-Scanning: A 'Third' Approach to Decision-Making," *Public Administration Review,* 27 (December 1967): 385–392.

9. R. P. Nathan and J. L. Palmer, "Comprehensive Reform vs. Incremental-ism—an Exchange of Views," *The Journal of the Institute for Socioeconomic Studies* (Spring 1977): 1–9.

10. C. E. Lindblom, "The Science of 'Muddling Through,' " *Public Administration Review,* 19 (Spring 1959): 79–88.

11. D. Braybrooke and C. Lindblom, *A Strategy of Decision*.

12. P. R. Schulman, "Nonincremental Policy Making: Toward an Alternative Paradigm," *The American Political Science Review,* 69(4) (December 1975): 1354–1370.

13. M. J. Dluhy, "Introduction," in J. E. Tropman, M. J. Dluhy, and R. M. Lind, eds., *New Strategic Perspectives in Social Policy* (New York: Pergamon Press, 1981).

14. J. J. Bailey and R. J. O'Connor, "Operationalizing Incrementalism: Measuring the Muddles," *Public Administration Review* (January/February 1975): 60–66.

15. Much of the information on the implementation of the Prevention Act bill was obtained through interviews given over the course of the spring and summer months of 1988. Those interviewed include the following from the Office of Child Abuse Prevention in the Department of Social Services: Beth Hardesty Fife, chief; Bob Green, manager; Gary Matthies, project monitor; Rhoda Katz, monitor; also Hershel Swinger and Glovielle Rowland from the Southern California Training Center.

16. J. L. Pressman and A. Wildavsky, *Implementation: How Great Expectations in Washington Are Dashed in Oakland* (3rd ed.) (Berkeley, CA: University of California Press, 1984); P. Berman, "Thinking about Programmed and Adaptive Implementation: Matching Strategies to Situations," in H. M. Ingram and D. E. Mann, eds., *Why Policies Succeed or Fail* (Beverly Hills, CA: Sage, 1980); G. D. Brewer and P. DeLeon, *The Foundations of Policy Analysis* (Homewood, IL: Dorsey Press, 1983).

17. AB 147, Welfare and Institutions Code Section (1985), Chapter 12.

18. Gorney, "Baffling Case of McMartin Preschool."

19. See L. Coleman, "Therapists Are the Real Culprits in Many Child Sexual Abuse Cases," *Augustus*, 9(6) (1986): 7–9; P. Eberle and S. Eberle, *The Politics of Child Abuse* (Secaucus, NJ: Lyle Stuart, 1986); C. Gordon, "False Allegations of Abuse in Child Custody Disputes," *Minnesota Family Law Journal*, 2(14) (July/August 1985): 225–228; E. White, "Psychologist Cites Fantasy in Boys," *Detroit News* (March 1985), p. B2, quoting R. Underwager.

20. Eberle and Eberle, *Politics of Child Abuse;* Scott County Investigations (St. Paul, MN: Office of Minnesota Attorney General Hubert H. Humphrey III, November, 1984, Mimeographed).

21. L. Wimberley, *Child Abuse: A VOCAL Viewpoint* (Sacramento, CA, 1984, Mimeographed).

22. See D. Besharov, *The Vulnerable Social Worker* (Springfield, MA: NASW Publications, 1986); D. Besharov, "Unfounded Allegations: A New Child Abuse Problem," *The Public Interest* (Spring 1986): 18–33.

23. Results from the preschool study will be discussed in further detail in Chapter 5.

24. N. Gilbert, J. Duerr Berrick, N. LeProhn, and N. Nyman, *Protecting Young Children*.

25. J. Borkin and L. Frank, "Sexual Abuse Prevention for Preschoolers: A Pilot Program," *Child Welfare*, 65(1) (January/February 1986): 75–81.

26. T. Liddell, B. Young, and M. Yamagishi, *Implementation and Evaluation of a Preschool Sexual Abuse Prevention Resource* (Seattle, WA: Department of Human Resources, 1988; unpublished manuscript).

27. J. R. Conte, C. Rosen, L. Saperstein, and R. Shermack, "An Evaluation of a Program to Prevent the Sexual Victimization of Young Children," *Child Abuse and Neglect*, 9 (1985): 319–328.

28. See Chapter 4 for a more detailed description of the developmental literature.

29. Gilbert, Duerr Berrick, LeProhn, and Nyman, *Protecting Young Children*.

30. Department of Social Services, Office of Child Abuse Prevention, April 14, 1988, memo sent to all prevention providers).

31. Preschool Curricula Task Force, *First Steps: A Report to the Office of Child Abuse Prevention* (November 1989).

## Chapter 3. Ideology and Curricula

1. The Illusion Theatre, Sexual Abuse Prevention Project, 304 Washington Avenue North, Minneapolis, MN, 55401 (1980).

2. Bridgework Theatre, Inc., 113 East Lincoln Avenue, Suite 3, Goshen, IN, 46526.

3. Gene Mackey, *Bubbylonian Encounters* (Topeka, KS: Kansas Committee for the Prevention of Child Abuse, 1983).

4. For a review of a number of audiovisual materials, see G. Dietrich, "Audiovisual Materials with Critique," in P. B. Mrazek and C. H. Kempe, eds., *Sexually Abused Children and Their Families* (New York: Pergamon, 1981). Some of the more popular prevention films include the following:

*Better Safe than Sorry I, II, and III*, Filmfair Communications, 10900 Ventura Boulevard, Studio City, CA 91604.

*Bubbylonian Encounter: A Film for Children about the Sense of Touch*, Kansas Committee for Prevention of Child Abuse, 435 S. Kansas, 2nd Floor, Topeka, KS 66603.

*It's OK to Say No!*, Migima Designs, P.O. Box 70064, Eugene, OR 97401.

*Little Bear*, The Bridgework Theatre, Inc., 113 East Lincoln Avenue, Suite 3, Goshen, IN 46526.

*No Easy Answers*, Indiana University Audio Visual Center, Bloomington, IN 57405.

*Some Secrets Should Be Told*, Motorola Teleprograms, Inc., Simon and Schuster, 108 Wilmot Road, Deerfield, IL 60015.

*Strong Kids, Safe Kids*, Paramount Studios, 5555 Melrose Avenue, Hollywood, CA 90038.

*Touch*, Motorola Teleprograms, Inc., Simon and Schuster, 108 Wilmot Road, Deerfield, IL 60015.

*What Tadoo*, Motorola Teleprograms, Inc., Simon and Schuster, 108 Wilmot Road, Deerfield, IL 60015.

5. J. Salicrup, *Spiderman and Power Pack*, produced in cooperation with the National Committee for Prevention of Child Abuse (New York: Marvel Comics Group, 1984); L. Simonson, *Spiderman*, produced in cooperation with the National Committee for the Prevention of Chld Abuse (New York: Marvel Comics, 1987).

6. J. Williams, *Red Flag/Green Flag People* (Fargo, ND: Rape and Abuse Crisis Center, 1980); J. Stowell and M. Dietzel, *My Very Own Book About Me* (Spokane, WA: Lutheran Social Services of Washington, 1985) (available from publisher, 1226 Howard Street, Spokane, WA 99201).

7. For example, see: *Talking About Touching: A Personal Safety Curriculum* (Seattle, WA: Seattle Institute for Child Advocacy, Committee for Children, 1985) (available from the publisher, 172 20th Avenue, Seattle, WA 98122).

8. For example, see *Child Assault Prevention Training Center of Northern California Elementary Curriculum*, 1727 Martin Luther King Jr. Way, Suite 108, Oakland, CA 94612 (1983); *Touch Program*, P.O. Box 52, San Luis Obispo, CA 93406 (1987).

9. S. K. Wurtele, D. A. Saslawsky, C. L. Miller, S. R. Marrs, and J. C.

Britcher, "Teaching Personal Safety Skills for Potential Prevention of Sexual Abuse: A Comparison of Treatments," *Journal of Consulting and Clinical Psychology*, 54 (1986): 688–692; S. K. Wurtele, S. R. Marrs, and C. L. Miller-Perrin, "Practice Makes Perfect? The Role of Participant Modeling in Sexual Abuse Prevention Programs," *Journal of Consulting and Clinical Psychology*, 55 (1987): 559–602.

10. *Child Assault Prevention Training Center of Northern California Elementary Curriculum*; interview with CLASS curriculum designer Sherri Paterson, Family Service Agency, San Rafael, CA (1988); *Chldren's Self-Help Project*, Elementary School Curriculum, 3368 22nd, San Francisco, CA, 94110 (1983).

11. See, for example, *CARE Curriculum Description*, Los Angeles Unified School District Elementary Curriculum, 1320 W. 3rd Street, Los Angeles, CA, 90015 (1988); *Talking About Touching: A Personal Safety Curriculum*, 1985, 1987.

12. D. J. Tharinger, J. J. Krivacska, M. Laye-McDonough, L. Jamison, G. G. Vincent, and A. D. Hedlund, "Prevention of Child Sexual Abuse: An Analysis of Issues, Educational Programs, and Research Findings," *School Psychology Review*, 17(4) (1988):614-634.

13. C. Plummer, "Prevention Education in Perspective," in M. Nelson and K. Clark, eds., *The Educator's Guide to Preventing Child Sexual Abuse* (Santa Cruz, CA: ETR Network Publications, 1988).

14. Although in many states, interested schools must pay a fee for a prevention program, California programs for public schools are entirely funded by state monies.

15. *Talking about Touching Teacher's Guide* (Seattle, WA: Seattle Institute for Child Advocacy, Committee for Children, 1985), p. 1.

16. C. Anderson, "A History of the Touch Continuum," in M. Nelson and K. Clark, *The Educator's Guide to Preventing Child Sexual Abuse* (Santa Cruz, CA: ETR Network Publications, 1986).

17. *CAPP-Auburn Program*, Elementary Curriculum (tape recording), P.O. Box 5462, Auburn, CA 95604 (1988); *Talking About Touching*, 1987; *Touch Program*.

18. *Touch Program*, p. 1.

19. *Talking About Touching*, 1987, pp. 18, 22, 38.

20. *CLASS* interview.

21. *CAPP-Auburn Program*.

22. *Children's Self-Help Project*, p. IV. b-8.

23. *Touch Program*, p. 2.

24. *Talking About Touching*, 1985.

25. Ibid., 1987.

26. *CARE Curriculum Description*.

27. *Talking About Touching*, 1985.

28. *CAPP-Auburn Program*.

29. *Children's Self-Help Project*, p. IV. b-7.

30. CAP presentation observed at a local school, fall 1987; *Child Assault Prevention Training Center of Northern California Elementary Curriculum*.

31. *Child Assault Prevention Training Center of Northern California Elementary Curriculum*, Workshop information (available from Adult Workshop Information, 1727 Martin Luther King Jr. Way, Suite 108, Oakland, CA, 94612).

32. *Talking About Touching*, 1985, Lesson 5; CLASS interview; *Touch Program*, p. 2.

33. *CARE Curriculum Description*.

34. *Children's Self-Help Project*. p. IV. b-5.

35. *Talking About Touching*, 1985, p. 41.

36. *Child Assault Prevention Training Center of Northern California Elementary Curriculum*, p. 151.

37. *Children's Self-Help Project*, p. IV. b-7.

38. *Touch Program*, p. 3.

39. *Children's Self-Help Project*, p. IV. b-13.

40. *Talking About Touching*, 1985, p. 88.

41. *Touch Program*, p. 4.

42. *CAPP-Auburn Program*.

43. *Touch Program*.

44. *Child Assault Prevention Training Center of Northern California Elementary Curriculum*, p. 164.

45. *Children's Self-Help Project*, p. IV. b-17.

46. *Child Assault Prevention Training Center of Northern California Elementary Curriculum*, p. 163.

47. *Touch Program*.

48. *CLASS* interview

49. *CARE Curriculum Description*.

50. Ibid.

51. J. R. Conte, "An Evaluation of a Program to Prevent the Sexual Victimization of Young Children," *Child Abuse and Neglect*, 9 (1985): 319–328.


*Chapter 4. Program Design and Developmental Theory*

1. National Association for the Education of Young Children, "Position Statement on Developmentally Appropriate Practice in Programs for 4- and 5-year-olds," *Young Children*, September 1986, p. 20.

2. D. Elkind, *Miseducation: Preschoolers at Risk* (New York: Knopf, 1987); D. Elkind, "Formal Education and Early Childhood: An Essential Difference," *Phi Delta Kappan*, 67(9) (1986): 631–636; D. Elkind, "In Defense of Early Childhood Education," *Principal*, 65(5) (1986): 6–9; D. Elkind, *The Hurried Child: Growing Up Too Fast Too Soon* (Reading, MA: Addison-Wesley, 1981). See also J. M. Gallagher and J. Coche, "Hothousing: The Clinical and Educational Concerns over Pressuring Young Children," *Early Childhood Research Quarterly*, 2(3) (1987): 203–210; T. W. Hills, "Children in the Fast Lane: Implications for Early Childhood Policy and Practice," *Early Childhood Research Quarterly*, 2(3) (1987): 265–274.

3. N. Diamond, "Cognitive Theory," in B. B. Wolman, ed., *Handbook of Developmental Psychology* (Englewood Cliffs, NJ: Prentice-Hall, 1982); National Association for the Education of Young Children, *NAEYC Position Statement on Developmentally Appropriate Practice in Early Childhood Programs Serving Children from Birth through Age 8* (Washington, DC: Author, 1989); School Readiness Task Force, *Here They Come: Ready or Not* (Sacramento, CA: State Department of Education, 1988).

4. S. Bredekamp, ed., *Developmentally Appropriate Practice in Early Childhood Programs Serving Children from Birth through Age 8* (Washington, DC: National Association for the Education of Young Children, 1987); C. Kamii, "Leading Primary Education toward Excellence: Beyond Worksheets and Drill," *Young Children*, 40(6) (1985): 3–6; L. Kohlberg and R. Mayer, "Development as the Aim of Education," *Harvard Educational Review*, 42(4) (1972): 449–497.

5. A. Bandura, *Social Learning Theory* (Englewood Cliffs, NJ: Prentice-Hall, 1977); B. F. Skinner, "The Origins of Cognitive Thought," *American Psychologist*, 44 (1989): 13–18.

6. L. Katz and S. Chard, *Engaging Children's Minds: The Project Approach* (Norwood, NJ: Ablex, 1989).

7. This ratio meets the standards set by the National Association for the Education of Young Children accreditation process as well. See S. Bredekamp, ed., *Accreditation Criteria and Procedures of the National Academy of Early Childhood Programs* (Washington, DC: National Association for the Education of Young Children, 1989).

8. J. Berrueta-Clement, L. Schweinhart, W. S. Barnett, A. Epstein, and D. Weikart, "Changed Lives: The Effects of the Perry Preschool Program on Youths through Age 19," *Monographs of the High/Scope Educational Research Foundation,* 8 (Ypsilanti, MI: High/Scope Press, 1984); S. Bredekamp, *Developmentally Appropriate Practice;* Center for the Study of Public Policies for Young Children, High/Scope Educational Research Foundation, *The Cost-effectiveness of High Quality Early Childhood Programs: A Report for the 1982 Southern Governors' Conference* (Washington, DC: Author, 1982); A. Clarke-Stewart, "In Search of Consistencies in Child Care Research," in D. Phillips, ed., *Quality in Child Care: What Does Research Tell Us?* (Washington, DC: National Association for the Education of Young Children, Research Monograph 1, 1987); D. Phillips, K. McCartney, and S. Scarr, "Child Care Quality and Children's Social Development," *Developmental Psychology,* 23 (1987): 537–543; D. Phillips, S. Scarr, and K. McCartney, "Dimensions and Effects of Child Care Quality: The Bermuda Study," in D. Phillips, ed., *Quality Child Care: What Does Research Tell Us?* (Washington, DC: National Association for the Education of Young Children, Research Monograph 1, 1987).

9. Bredekamp, *Accreditation Criteria.*

10. P. Cowan, *Piaget: With Feeling* (New York: Holt, Rinehart & Winston, 1978).

11. Bredekamp, *Accreditation Criteria.*

12. D. Elkind, *Child Development and Education: A Piagetian Perspective* (New York: Oxford University Press, 1976).

13. D. Elkind, *Child Development and Education;* H. Maier, *Three Theories of Child Development* (New York: Harper and Row, 1969).

14. D. Bellum, *First Steps: A Report to the Office of Child Abuse Prevention* (Sacramento, CA: Office of Child Abuse Prevention, 1989), pp. 11–13.

15. D. Elkind, "Recent Research in Cognitive and Language Development," in L. T. Benjamin, Jr., ed., *The G. Stanley Hall Lecture Series,* vol. 1 (Washington, DC: American Psychological Association, 1981).

16. A. Downer, *Evaluation of Talking About Touching: Summary Report* (Seattle, WA: Committee for Children, 1984, unpublished manuscript).

17. Cowan, *Piaget;* A. C. Bernstein and P. A. Cowan, "Children's Conceptions of How People Get Babies," *Child Development,* 46 (1975): 77–91.

18. N. Diamond, "Cognitive Theory."

19. A. C. Bernstein and P. A. Cowan, "Children's Conceptions of How People Get Babies."

20. H. Gardner, *Developmental Psychology* (Toronto: Little, Brown, 1982).

21. Bellum, *First Steps,* p. 20.

22. P. H. Mussen, J. J. Conger, and J. Kagan, *Essentials of Child Development and Personality* (New York: Harper and Row, 1980).

23. Ibid.

24. J. Piaget, *Six Psychological Studies* (New York: Random House, 1967).

25. M. Donaldson, *Children's Minds* (New York: W. W. Norton, 1979); J. Garbarino, F. M. Stott, and the Faculty of the Erickson Institute, *What Children Can Tell Us* (San Francisco: Jossey-Bass, 1989).

26. J. Piaget, *The Child's Conception of Number* (London: Routledge & Kegan Paul, 1952); J. Piaget and B. Inhelder, *The Psychology of the Child* (New York: Basic, 1969).

27. *Child Assault Prevention Training Center of Northern California Preschool Curriculum,* Workshop information (available from Adult Workshop Information, 1727 Martin Luther King Jr. Way, Suite 108, Oakland, CA 94612).

28. Bellum, *First Steps*.

29. L. Kohlberg, "The Development of Children's Orientations toward a Moral Order," *Vita Humana,* 6 (1963): 14.

30. F. E. Abound, "Children's Application of Attribution Principles to Social Comparisons," *Child Development,* 56(3) (1985): 682–688; Cowan, *Piaget*.

31. K. Elkind, J. Anagnostopoulou, and S. Malone, "Determinants of Part-Whole Perception in Children," *Child Development,* 41 (1970): 391–397; L. Smith, "Perceptual Development and Category Generalization," *Child Development,* 50 (1979): 705–715.

32. M. deYoung, "The Good Touch/Bad Touch Dilemma," *Child Welfare,* 67(1) (1988): 60–68.

33. *Children's Self-Help Project,* Elementary School Curriculum, 3368 22nd, San Francisco, CA 94110 (1983); *Touch Program,* P.O. Box 52, San Luis Obispo, CA 93406 (1987).

34. *Children's Self-Help Project; Touch Safety Program* (San Rafael, CA: Family Services Agency, 1983) (available from publisher, 1005 A Street, San Rafael, CA 94601); *Talking About Touching: A Personal Safety Curriculum* (Seattle, WA: Seattle Institute for Child Advocacy, Committee for Children, 1985, 1987) (available from publisher, 172 20th Avenue, Seattle, WA 98122.

35. *Children's Self-Help Project; Touch Program*.

36. Cowan, *Piaget,* p. 137.

37. Ibid.; Abound, "Children's Application."

38. E. L. Hartley and R. E. Hartley, *Fundamentals of Social Psychology* (New York: Knopf, 1955).

39. *Children's Self-Help Project,* p. IV-b-6.

40. *Child Assault Prevention Training Center of Northern California Elementary Curriculum*.

41. *Talking About Touching II* (Seattle, WA: Seattle Institute for Child Advocacy, Committee for Children, 1986) (available from publisher, 172 20th Avenue, Seattle, WA 98122.

42. Ibid.

43. *Children's Self-Help Project*.

44. S. K. Kraizer, "Rethinking Prevention," *Child Abuse and Neglect*, 10 (1986): 259–261.

45. W. S. Rholes and D. N. Ruble, "Children's Understanding of Dispositional Characteristics of Others," *Child Development*, 55(2) (1984): 550–560.

46. N. M. Coppens, "Cognitive Characteristics as Predictors of Children's Understanding of Safety and Prevention," *Journal of Pediatric Psychology*, 11(2) (1986): 189–202.

47. T. Schultz and R. Mendelson, "The Use of Covariation as a Principle of Causal Analysis," *Child Development*, 46 (1975): 394–399.

48. *Children's Self-Help Project; Talking About Touching*, 1985, 1987; *Touch Program; Touch Safety Program*.

49. R. Ault, *Children's Cognitive Development* (New York: Oxford University Press, 1977); J. Piaget, *The Moral Judgment of the Child* (New York: Collier, 1962; original work published in 1932).

50. *Touch Safety Program*.

51. *Children's Self-Help Project*.

52. Bellum, *First Steps*, p. 20.

53. T. P. McGurn and C. N. Kelly, *The Woman's Bible for Survival in a Violent Society* (New York: Stein & Day, 1984).

54. M. Conroy and E. Ritvo, *Every Woman Can* (New York: Grosset & Dunlap, 1982).

55. S. E. Smith, *Fear or Freedom: A Woman's Options in Social Survival and Physical Self-Defense* (Racine, WI: Mother Courage Press, 1986).

56. D. Nibert, S. Cooper, L. K. Fitch, and J. Ford, *An Examination of Young Children's Ability to Learn about Prevention Strategies* (Columbus, OH: National Assault Prevention Center, 1988, unpublished manuscript).

57. D. Elkind, "Recent Research"; P. C. Kendall, "Social Cognition and Problem Solving: A Developmental and Child-Clinical Interface," in B. Gholson and T. C. Rosenthal, *Application of Cognitive-Developmental Theory* (New York: Academic Press, 1984); J. Piaget, *The Child's Conception of the World* (Totowa, NJ: Littlefield, Adams, 1960; original work published in 1926); J. Piaget, *The Child's*

*Conception of Physical Causality* (Totowa, NJ: Littlefield, Adams, 1960; original work published 1927); Piaget, *The Moral Judgment of the Child*. Also see, for example: J. S. Wallerstein and J. B. Kelly, *Surviving the Breakup: How Children and Parents Cope with Divorce* (New York: Basic Books, 1980).

58. S. C. Anderson, C. M. Bach, and S. Griffith, *Psychosocial Sequelae in Intrafamilial Victims of Sexual Assault and Abuse* (Paper presented at the Third International Conference on Child Abuse and Neglect, Amsterdam, The Netherlands, 1981); V. DeFrancis, *Protecting the Child Victim of Sex Crimes Committed by Adults* (Denver, CO: American Humane Association, 1969); W. N. Friedrich, A. J. Urquiza, and R. Beilke, "Behavioral Problems in Sexually Abused Young Children," *Journal of Pediatric Psychology*, 11 (1986): 47–57.

59. M. Tsai and N. N. Wagner, "Therapy Groups for Women Sexually Molested as Children," *Archives of Sexual Behavior*, 7 (1978): 417–427; D. Finkelhor, "What's Wrong with Sex Between Adults and Children?" *American Journal of Orthopsychiatry*, 49(4) (1979): 692–697.

60. "Preschool Child Abuse Efforts Seen as Ineffective," *Los Angeles Times*, 24 Feb. 1988, p. 3.

61. K. McFarlane and J. Waterman, *Sexual Abuse of Young Children* (New York, Guilford Press, 1986).

62. L. Berliner and J. R. Conte, *The Process of Victimization: The Victim's Perspective* (Chicago: University of Chicago, 1988, unpublished manuscript).

63. Kohlberg, "Children's Orientations," pp. 11–33; L. Kohlberg, "Stage and Sequence: The Cognitive-Developmental Approach to Socialization," in D. Goslin, ed., *Handbook of Socialization Theory and Research* (Chicago: Rand McNally, 1969).

64. J. M. Rich and J. L. DeVitis, *Theories of Moral Development* (Springfield, IL: Charles C. Thomas, 1985).

65. Piaget, *The Moral Judgment of the Child*.

66. H. Rosen, *Piagetian Dimensions of Clinical Relevance* (New York: Columbia University Press, 1985).

67. A. Bandura, "Social Learning of Moral Judgments," *Journal of Personality and Social Psychology*, 11 (1969): 275–279; A. Bandura and F. J. McDonald, "Influence of Social Reinforcement and the Behavior of Models in Shaping Children's Moral Judgments," *Journal of Abnormal and Social Psychology*, 67 (1963): 274–281; E. Turiel, "An Experimental Test of the Sequentiality of Developmental Stages in the Child's Moral Development," *Journal of Personality and Social Psychology*, 3 (1966): 261–274.

68. D. Morrison, M. Siegal, and R. Francis, "Control, Autonomy, and the Development of Moral Behavior: A Social-Cognitive Perspective," *Imagination, Cognition, and Personality*, 3 (1984): 337–351.

69. Piaget, *The Moral Judgment of the Child*, pp. 92, 111.

70. W. Damon, *The Moral Child* (New York: Free Press, 1988).

71. M. S. Tisak and E. Turiel, "Children's Conceptions of Moral and Prudential Rules," *Child Development*, 55 (1984): 1030–1039.

72. P. A. Cowan, J. Langer, J. Heavenrich, and J. Nathanson, "Social Learning and Piaget's Theory of Moral Development," *Journal of Personality and Social Psychology*, 11 (1969): 261–274.

73. W. Damon, "Early Conceptions of Positive Justice as Related to the Development of Logical Operations," *Child Development*, 46 (1975): 301–312; Kohlberg, "Children's Orientations"; Piaget, *The Moral Judgment of the Child*.

74. Bandura, "Social Learning"; Bandura and McDonald, "Social Reinforcement"; C. B. Keasey, "Experimentally Induced Changes in Moral Opinions and Reasoning," *Journal of Personality and Social Psychology*, 26(1) (1973): 30–38; D. Kuhn, "Imitation Theory and Research from a Cognitive Perspective," *Human Development*, 16 (1973); Turiel, "Experimental Test."

75. L. P. Nucci and M. S. Nucci, "Children's Social Interactions in the Context of Moral and Conventional Transgressions," *Child Development*, 53 (1982): 403–412; L. P. Nucci and M. S. Nucci, "Children's Responses to Moral and Social-Conventional Transgressions in Free-play Settings," *Child Development*, 53 (1982): 1337–1342; L. P. Nucci and E. Turiel, "Social Interactions and the Development of Social Concepts in Preschool Children," *Child Development*, 49 (1978): 400–407; J. G. Smetana, "Preschool Children's Conceptions of Moral and Social Rules," *Child Development*, 52 (1982): 1333–1336; J. G. Smetana, "Toddlers' Social Interactions Regarding Moral and Conventional Transgressions," *Child Development*, 55 (1984): 1767–1776; J. G. Smetana, "Preschool Children's Conceptions of Transgressions: The Effects of Varying Moral and Conventional Domain-related Attributes," *Developmental Psychology*, 21 (1985): 18–29; J. G. Smetana and J. L. Braeges, *The Development of Toddlers' Moral and Conventional Judgments* (Rochester, NY: University of Rochester, 1987, unpublished manuscript); J. G. Smetana, M. Kelly, and C. T. Twentyman, "Abused, Neglected, and Nonmaltreated Children's Conceptions of Moral and Conventional Transgressions," *Child Development*, 55 (1984): 277–287; M. S. Tisak and E. Turiel, "Children's Conceptions of Moral and Prudential Rules," *Child Development*, 55 (1984): 1030–1039; E. Turiel, *The Development of Social Knowledge: Morality and Convention* (Cambridge: Cambridge University Press, 1983); D. R. Weston and E. Turiel, "Act–Rule Relations: Children's Concepts of Social Rules," *Developmental Psychology*, 16(5) (1980): 417–424.

76. Damon, "Early Conceptions."

77. M. Laupa and E. Turiel, *Psychological Foundations of Moral Education* (Washington, DC: University Press of America, 1986); Turiel, *Social Knowledge*.

78. Nucci and Turiel, "Social Interactions"; Weston and Turiel, "Act–Rule Relations."

79. Nucci and Nucci, "Children's Social Interactions"; Nucci and Nucci, "Children's Responses."

80. Smetana and Braeges, *Toddlers*.

81. Smetana, "Preschool Children's Conceptions of Moral and Social Rules"; Smetana, "Toddlers' Social Interactions"; Smetana, "Preschool Children's Conceptions of Transgressions."

82. *Talking About Touching*, 1985.

83. *Children's Self-Help Project*.

84. *Child Assault Prevention Training*.

85. *Talking About Touching*, 1985.

86. For a discussion of the difficulty children may have in labeling a touch that feels good as a "bad" touch, see D. Finkelhor, *Child Sexual Abuse: New Theory and Research* (New York: Free Press, 1984); D. J. Tharinger, J. J. Krivacska, M. Laye-McDonough, L. Jamison, G. G. Vincent, and A. D. Hedlund, "Prevention of Child Sexual Abuse: An Analysis of Issues, Educational Programs, and Research Findings," *School Psychology Review*, 17(4) (1988): 614–634; B. Trudell and M. H. Whatley, "School Sexual Abuse Prevention: Unintended Consequences and Dilemmas," *Child Abuse and Neglect*, 12 (1988): 103–115.

87. M. deYoung, "Good Touch/Bad Touch," p. 64.

88. Cowan, *Piaget*.

89. E. Erickson, *Childhood and Society* (New York: Norton, 1950).

90. S. Lever, *CARE*, Unpublished material (available from Los Angeles Unified School District Elementary Curriculum, 1320 W. 3rd Street, Los Angeles, CA 90015).

91. *Child Assault Prevention Training*.

92. *Children's Self-Help Project*.

## Chapter 5. Age and Learning

1. The first-grade sample received a pretest and a posttest 6 months later. The third-grade children were given two posttests: one shortly after participation in the program and another also about 6 months later. For this group, an analysis of changes in scores between the initial posttest and the follow-up posttest showed no statistically significant differences. The findings in Table 5.2 refer to data from the pretests and 6-month posttests for both groups. The similarity between the third-grade initial posttest scores and the 6-month follow-up posttest scores suggest that there was little, if any, decay in knowledge over a 6-month period. In interpreting this result it should be borne in mind, however, that the third graders' pretest scores were rather high to begin with and showed only a marginal

increase after training. Correct responses in Table 5.1 are printed in bold. Because of rounding, percentages do not equal 100 in all cases.

2. Analyses were also run on children's gender and ethnicity. When responses to the total questionnaire were examined by gender, no differences were found on pretest; however, on posttest, girls had a somewhat higher score ($m = 11.64$) compared to boys' ($m = 10.90$). When responses to the questionnaire were analyzed by ethnicity, little variation was found among groups.

3. Table A.5 shows the mean score for each program, based on the number of concepts presented. To examine the extent to which differences in scores might be found statistically significant across programs, analysis of variance procedures were run. The analysis examined mean scores including only 10 questions (corresponding to 10 concepts) common to all of the programs studied. Third-grade posttest scores were similar across programs, and differences were not found to be statistically significant. Some differences were found, however, among first-grade programs. The CARE program demonstrated higher posttest scores than did the TAT or CAP programs. The CLASS program also revealed higher posttest scores than did the CAP program. Including 10 questions, results showed: $F = 7.37$, $df = 3$, $p = .000$. The mean posttest scores for first-grade programs, including only the 10 concepts, were as follows: TAT, 7.6; CLASS, 7.9; CARE, 9.0; CAP, 6.6.

4. Questions eliciting children's telling responses included numbers 2, 3, 8, 10, and 13.

5. Differences between the posttest and posttest-only group also did not show statistical significance.

6. Because Question 3 was not covered by either the third-grade CAP program or the TAT program, an analysis of variance procedure was also conducted to include only four of the five questions counted in this scale (only those questions pertaining to "telling responses"). This analysis resulted in the same findings as the results presented in the text. There were no statistically significant differences between posttest scores among the third-grade programs, and the first-grade programs evidenced the same differences on the Scheffe's multiple comparisons tests (a conservative test which identifies exactly where the significant differences lie among programs) as were seen in the analysis of all five questions.

7. N. Gilbert, J. Berrick, N. Le Prohn, and N. Nyman, *Protecting Young Children from Sexual Abuse: Does Preschool Training Work?* (Lexington, MA: Lexington Books, 1989).

8. Comparisons of posttest responses with answers from the posttest-only group showed few differences, indicating that the instrument itself had little, if any, influence on children.

9. The Children's Self-Help Project and the Talking About Touching programs (first and third grade) discuss tickling in the context of a mixed-up or confused feeling. The Touch Program discusses tight hugs to illustrate "confusing touch."

Data from these individual programs were examined in comparison to the total group's responses and no differences were found.

10. Gilbert et al., *Protecting Young Children*, p. 47.

11. Ibid., p. 56.

12. S. K. Wurtele and C. L. Miller, "Children's Conceptions of Sexual Abuse," *Journal of Clinical Child Psychology*, 16(3) (1987): 184–191 .

13. N. Ostblom, B. Richardson, and M. Galey, "Sexual Abuse Prevention Projects" (Des Moines, IA: National Committee for the Prevention of Child Abuse, 1987, Mimeographed); Y. Lutter and A. Weisman, "Sexual Victimization Prevention Project," (Final Report to the National Institute of Mental Health, 1985, Unpublished mimeograph); C. Plummer, "Preventing Sexual Abuse: What In-School Programs Teach Children" (Paper presented at the Second National Conference for Family Violence Researchers, Durham, NH, 1984).

14. Table A.10 includes the following studies:
R. L. Binder and D. E. McNiel, "Evaluation of a School-Based Sexual Abuse Prevention Program: Cognitive and Emotional Effects," *Child Abuse and Neglect*, 11 (1987): 497–506;

K. J. Kolko, J. T. Moser, J. Litz, and J. Hughes, "Promoting Awareness and Prevention of Child Sexual Victimization Using the Red Flag/Green Flag Program: An Evaluation with Follow-Up," *Journal of Family Violence*, 2(1) (1987): 11–35.

H. M. Leake, *A Study to Determine the Effectiveness of the Child Assault Prevention Program in Teaching First Grade Students to Recognize and Avoid Child Sexual Abuse and Assault* (Unpublished manuscript prepared for the Sexual Assault Center of San Joaquin County, 1986).

D. E. Nelson, *An Evaluation of the Student Outcomes and Instructional Characteristics of the "You're In Charge" Program* (Utah State Office of Education, 1985, unpublished manuscript).

S. C. Woods and K. S. Dean, *Evaluating Sexual Abuse Prevention Strategies* (Paper presented at the Seventh National Conference on Child Abuse and Neglect, Chicago: 1985).

D. A. Wolfe, T. MacPherson, R. Blount, and V. V. Wolfe, "Evaluation of a Brief Intervention for Educating School Children in Awareness of Physical and Sexual Abuse," *Child Abuse and Neglect*, 10 (1986): 85–92.

A. Downer, *Evaluation of Talking About Touching: Summary Report* (Committee for Children, Seattle, WA, 1984, unpublished manuscript).

G. E. Fryer, S. K. Kraizer, and T. Miyoshi, "Measuring Actual Reduction of Risk to Child Abuse: A New Approach," *Child Abuse and Neglect*, 11 (1987): 173–179.

P. Harvey, R. Forehand, C. Brown, and T. Homes, "The Prevention of Sexual Abuse: Examination of the Effectiveness of a Program with Kindergarten-Age Children," *Behavior Therapy*, 19 (1988): 429–435.

J. R. Conte, C. Rosen, L. Saperstein, and R. Shermack, R., "An Evaluation of a Program to Prevent the Sexual Victimization of Young Children," *Child Abuse and Neglect,* 9 (1985): 319–328.

S. K. Kraizer and G. E. Fryer, *Preventing Child Sexual Abuse: Measuring Actual Behavioral Change Attributable to a School-Based Curriculum* (Palisades, NY: Health Education Systems, n.d., unpublished manuscript).

S. Kraizer, S. S. Witte, and G. E. Fryer, "Child Sexual Abuse Prevention Programs: What Makes Them Effective in Protecting Children?" *Children Today,* Sept/Oct. 1989, pp. 23–27.

R. G. Miltenberger and E. Thiesse-Duffy, "Evaluation of Home-Based Programs for Teaching Personal Safety Skills to Children," *Journal of Applied Behavior Analysis,* 21 (Spring 1988): 81–87.

S. K. Wurtele, D. A. Saslawsky, C. L. Miller, S. R. Marrs, and J. C. Britcher, "Teaching Personal Safety Skills for Potential Prevention of Sexual Abuse: A Comparison of Treatments," *Journal of Consulting and Clinical Psychology,* 54 (1986): 688–692.

15. Fryer, Krailer, and Miyoshi, "Measuring Actual Reduction of Risk," pp. 173–179.

16. Conte, Rosen, Saperstein, and Shermack, "An Evaluation," pp. 319–328.

17. Kraizer and Fryer, *Preventing Child Sexual Abuse.*


## Chapter 6. Private Responsibility

1. Eighty-five percent of the California sample was married or living with a significant other. The mean age of mothers was 36; fathers' mean age was 38. Sixty-one percent of the sample was white, 20% Hispanic, 11% black, and the remaining 8% Asian or other. Most families either spoke English (78%) or both English and Spanish (10%) in the home. For the non-English-speaking participants, interview schedules and parent letters were translated into Spanish and Chinese and then back-translated. Spanish-speaking and Chinese-speaking staff conducted interviews with non-English-speaking parents. Participants included families with a range of incomes: 39% reporting annual incomes of over $40,000, 31% with incomes between $20,000 and $39,999, and 25% with incomes below $20,000 (5% declined to report their incomes).

2. N. Gilbert, J. Berrick, N. Le Prohn, and N. Nyman, *Protecting Young Children from Sexual Abuse: Does Preschool Training Work?* (Lexington, MA: Lexington Books, 1989); D. Nibert, S. Cooper, and J. Ford, "Parents' Observations of the Effects of a Sexual-Abuse Prevention Program on Preschool Children," *Child Welfare,* 68(5) (1989): 539–546.

3. D. Finkelhor, *Child Sexual Abuse: New Theory and Research* (New York: Free Press, 1984).

4. C. Adams and J. Fay, *No More Secrets: Protecting Your Child from Sexual*

*Assault* (San Luis Obispo, CA: Impact, 1981); S. K. Kraizer, *The Safe Child Book* (New York: Dell, 1985); L. Sanford, *The Silent Children: A Parent's Guide to the Prevention of Child Sexual Abuse* (New York: Doubleday, 1980); L. Sanford, *Come Tell Me Right Away* (Fayetteville, NY: Ed-U Press, 1982).

5. Nibert, Cooper, and Ford, "Parents' Observations."

6. Finkelhor, *Child Sexual Abuse*.

7. Gilbert et al., *Protecting Young Children*, p. 72.

8. Finkelhor, *Child Sexual Abuse*.

9. Nibert, Cooper, and Ford, "Parents' Observations."

10. Gilbert et al., *Protecting Young Children*, p. 76.

11. Ibid.

12. H. Swan, A. Press, and S. Briggs, "Child Sexual Abuse Prevention: Does It Work?" *Child Welfare* 64(4) (July/August, 1985): 395–405.

13. B. Stipak, "Citizens' Satisfaction with Urban Services: Potential Misuse as a Performance Indicator," *Public Administration Review*, 39 (January/February, 1979): 46–52; N. Gilbert and J. Eaton, "Who Speaks for the Poor?" *Journal of the American Institute of Planners*, 36 (November, 1970): 411–412; M. A. Scheirer, "Program Participants' Positive Perceptions: Psychological Conflict of Interest in Social Program Evaluation," in Lee Sechrest et al., eds., *Evaluation Studies Review Annual* (Beverly Hills, CA: Sage, 1979), pp. 767–783.

14. D. Finkelhor and Associates, *A Sourcebook on Child Sexual Abuse* (Beverly Hills, CA: Sage, 1986); J. Crewdson, *By Silence Betrayed: Sexual Abuse of Children in America* (Boston: Little, Brown, 1988).

15. S. K. Krazier, "Rethinking Prevention," *Child Abuse and Neglect*, 10 (1986): 259–261; D. Tharinger, J. Krivacska, M. Laye-McDonough, L. Jamison, G. Vincent, and A. Hedlund, "Prevention of Child Sexual Abuse: An Analysis of Issues, Educational Programs, and Research Findings," *School Psychology Review* 17(4) (1988): 614–634; N. Reppucci and J. Haugaard, "Prevention of Child Sexual Abuse: Myth or Reality," *American Psychologist* 44(10) (1989): 1266–1275; D. Finkelhor and N. Strapko, "Sexual Abuse Prevention Education: A Review of Evaluation Studies," in D. Willis, E. Holden, and M. Rosenberg, eds., *Child Abuse Prevention* (New York: Wiley, in press).

16. Reppucci and Haugaard, "Prevention."

17. Nibert, Cooper, and Ford, "Parents' Observations."

18. Swan, Press, and Briggs, "Child Sexual Abuse Prevention."

19. C. Kleemeier and C. Webb, *Evaluation of a School Based Prevention Program* (Paper presented at the American Psychological Association Convention, Washington, DC, 1986).

20. S. K. Wurtele and C. L. Miller-Perrin, "An Evaluation of Side Effects Associated with Participation in a Child Sexual Abuse Prevention Program," *Journal of School Health,* 57 (1987): 228–231.

21. R. Binder and D. McNiel, "Evaluation of a School-Based Sexual Abuse Prevention Program: Cognitive and Emotional Effects," *Child Abuse and Neglect,* 11 (1987): 497–506.

22. D. Finkelhor and Associates, *Sourcebook.*

23. A. Ray-Keil, *Intersect: Of Social Theory and Management Practice in Preventing Children's Exploitation* (Seattle, WA: Committee for Children, 1989).

24. Nibert, Cooper, and Ford, "Parents' Observations."

25. Reppucci and Haugaard, "Prevention."

26. Gilbert et al., *Protecting Young Children,* p. 90.

27. Finkelhor and Associates, *Sourcebook,* pp. 22–27.

28. N. Gilbert, "Teaching Children to Prevent Sexual Abuse," *The Public Interest,* 93 (1988): 3–15.

29. D. Tharinger et al., "Prevention of Child Sexual Abuse."

30. S. Kraizer, "Rethinking Prevention"; G. Melton, "The Improbability of Prevention of Sexual Abuse," in D. Willis, E. Holder, and M. Rosenberg, eds., *Child Abuse Prevention* (New York: John Wiley, in press); Tharinger et al., "Prevention of Child Sexual Abuse"; Reppucci and Haugaard, "Prevention."

31. D. Finkelhor and N. Strapko, "Sexual Abuse Prevention Education."

## Chapter 7. Public Responsibility

1. Carnegie Foundation for the Advancement of Teaching, *The Condition of Teaching: A State-by-State Analysis* (Princeton, NJ: Author, 1988).

2. N. Romano, K. Casey, and D. Daro, "Schools and Child Abuse: A National Survey of Principals' Attitudes, Beliefs, and Practices" (Chicago: National Committee for Prevention of Child Abuse, 1990).

3. R. S. Riggs, "Incest: The School's Role," *The Journal of School Health* 52(6) (August 1982): 365–370.

4. L. J. Henke, "The Health Educator's Role in the Problem of Child Abuse," *Health Education* 6(3) (May 1985): 15–18.

5. G. M. Stringer, "An Overview of Reporting." in M. Nelson and K. Clark, eds., *Preventing Child Sexual Abuse* (Santa Cruz, CA: Network Publications, 1986); Clearinghouse on Child Abuse and Neglect Information, *Who Must Re-*

*port: Laws* (Washington, DC: Author, 1982); and D. Besharov, "Gaining Control over Child Abuse Reports," *Public Welfare* 48(2) (Spring 1990): 34–40.

6. Commission on the Enforcement of Child Abuse Laws, California Attorney General John K. Van de Kamp's Final Report, 1985.

7. G. Ezell, "The Educator's Role in Child Abuse," *Health Education,* March 1977 pp. 16–17.

8. D. Finkelhor, B. Gomez-Schwartz, and J. Horowitz, "Professionals' Responses," in D. Finkelhor, ed., *Child Sexual Abuse: New Theory and Research* (New York: Free Press, 1984)

9. J. James, W. Womack, and F. Stauss, "Physician Reporting of Sexual Abuse of Children," *Journal of the American Medical Association,* 240 (1978): 1145–1146; S. C. Kalichman and M. E. Craig, "Victims of Incestuous Abuse: Mental Health Professionals' Attitudes and Tendency to Report," *Victimology: An International Journal* (in press); T. Muehleman and C. Kimmons, "Psychologists' Views on Child Abuse Reporting, Confidentiality, Life and the Law: An Exploratory Study," *Professional Psychology,* 12 (1981): 631–637; S. C. Kalichman, M. E. Craig, and D. R. Follingstad, "Mental Health Professionals and Suspected Cases of Child Abuse: An Investigation of Factors Influencing Reporting," *Community Mental Health Journal,* 24(1) (1988): 43–51.

10. A. Sedlak, *Study of National Incidence and Prevalence of Child Abuse and Neglect* (Bethesda, MD: Westat, 1987), pp. 3–19.

11. N. Abrahams and K. Casey, *Teachers Confront Child Abuse: A Survey of Teachers' Knowledge, Attitudes, and Beliefs* (Chicago: National Committee for Prevention of Child Abuse, 1989).

12. American Humane Association, *National Analysis of Official Child Abuse and Neglect* (Washington, DC: Author, 1981).

13. Eighty-six percent of the teachers were white. Three male teachers participated in the study. All teachers had a teaching credential, and 23% had one or more years of education beyond their initial degree. The average number of children teachers reported in their classrooms was 28.

14. K. MacFarlane and J. Waterman, *Sexual Abuse of Young Children* (New York: Guilford Press, 1986).

15. N. N. Nightingale and E. F. Walker, "Identification and Reporting of Child Maltreatment by Head Start Personnel: Attitudes and Experiences," *Child Abuse and Neglect,* 10 (1986): 191–199.

16. B. J. Meddin and A. L. Rosen, "Child Abuse and Neglect: Prevention and Reporting," *Young Children,* May 1986, pp. 26–30; E. Underhill, "The Strange Silence of Teachers, Doctors and Social Workers in the Face of Cruelty to Children," *International Child Welfare Review,* 21 (1974): 16–21.

17. B. Trudell and M. H. Whatley, "School Sexual Abuse Prevention: Un-

intended Consequences and Dilemmas," *Child Abuse and Neglect,* 12 (1988): 103–113.

18. S. Barvolek, *The Identification and Reporting of Child Abuse and Neglect among School Personnel in Wisconsin: An In-depth Study* (Eau Claire, WI: University of Wisconsin, 1981, unpublished manuscript).

19. A. Lynch, "Child Abuse in the School-age Population," *Journal of Public Health,* 45 (1975): 114–122.

20. Abrahams and Casey, *Teachers Confront.*

21. Barvolek, *Identification and Reporting.*

22. The Education Commission of the States, *Education Policies and Practices Regarding Child Abuse and Neglect and Recommendations for Policy Development* (Denver, CO: Author, 1977).

23. R. S. Riggs and D. W. Evans, "The Pre-professional Elementary Educators' Knowledge and Opinions Regarding Child Abuse," *College Student Journal,* 12 (1978): 290–293.

24. C. Gliszczinski, *The Student Teacher's Preparation for Identifying and Reporting Suspected Cases of Abuse and Neglect* (Madison, WI: University of Wisconsin, 1982, unpublished master's thesis).

25. N. Romano, K. Casey, D. Daro, "Schools and Child Abuse: A National Survey of Principals' Attitudes, Beliefs, and Practices" (Chicago: National Committee for Prevention of Child Abuse, 1990).

26. P. G. Levin, "Teachers' Perceptions, Attitudes, and Reporting of Child Abuse/Neglect," *Child Welfare,* 62(1) (1983): 14–20.

27. See, for example, Abrahams and Casey, *Teachers Confront;* and H. Swan, A. Press, and S. Briggs, "Child Abuse Prevention: Does It Work?" *Child Welfare,* July/August 1985, pp. 395–405.

28. B. Olmstead, "Teachers' Hugging Ban Hit," *Chicago Sun-Times,* April 3, 1986, p. 22.

29. J. D. Berrick, "Parental Involvement in Child Abuse Prevention Training: What Do They Learn?" *International Journal of Child Abuse and Neglect,* 12(4) (1988): 542–554.

30. A. Molnar and C. Gliszczinski, "Child Abuse: A Curriculum Issue in Teacher Education," *Journal of Teacher Education,* 34(5) (1983): 39–41.

31. R. W. ten Bensel and J. Berdie, "The Neglect and Abuse of Children and Youth: The Scope of the Problem and the Schools' Role," *Journal of School Health,* 46 (October 1976): 458–459.

32. M. McCaffrey and S. Tewey, "Preparing Educators to Participate in the Community Response to Child Abuse and Neglect," *Exceptional Children,* 45 (October 1978): 144–122.

33. W. L. McNab, "Staying Alive: A Mini-Unit on Child Molestation Prevention for Elementary School Children," *Journal of School Health*, 55(6) (1985): 226–229; S. Koblinsky and N. Behana, "Child Sexual Abuse: The Educator's Role in Prevention, Detection, and Intervention," *Young Children* (September 1984), pp. 3–15; M. Nelson and K. Clark, *The Educator's Guide to Preventing Child Sexual Abuse* (Santa Cruz, CA: Network Publications, 1986); J. T. Francisco, *Child Abuse: An Inservice Intervention Program for Elementary School Teachers* (New Brunswick, NJ: Rutgers University, 1979, unpublished dissertation).

34. This program was developed by Shayla Lever, director, District Child Abuse Prevention Office, Los Angeles Unified School District.

35. A. Hazzard, "Training Teachers to Identify and Intervene with Abused Children, *Journal of Clinical Child Psychology*, 13(3) (1984): 288–293; C. Kleemeier, C. Webb, A. Hazzard, and J. Pohl, "Child Sexual Abuse Prevention: Evaluation of a Teacher Training Model," *Child Abuse and Neglect*, 12(4) (1988): 555–561.

36. R. D. Felner, and T. Y. Felner, "Primary Prevention Programs in the Educational Context: A Transactional-Ecological Framework and Analysis," in L. A. Bond and B. E. Compas, eds., *Primary Prevention and Promotion in the Schools* (Beverly Hills, CA: Sage, 1989).

37. R. Barth and D. Derezotes, *Preventing Adolescent Abuse* (Lexington, MA: Lexington Books, 1990); J. J. Krivacska, "Your First Step in Preventing Abuse: Look Critically at Prepackaged Programs," *American School Board Journal*, (April 1989), pp. 35–37; N. D. Reppucci and J. J. Haugaard, "Prevention of Child Sexual Abuse: Myth or Reality," *American Psychologist*, 44(10) (1989): 1266–1275; D. J. Tharinger, J. J. Krivacska, M. Laye-McDonough, L. Jamison, G. G. Vincent, and A. D. Hudland, "Prevention of Child Sexual Abuse: An Analysis of Issues, Educational Programs and Research Findings," *School Psychology Review*, 17 (1988): 614–634.

38. T. McIntyre, "The Teacher's Role in Cases of Suspected Child Abuse," *Education and Urban Society*, 22(3) (1990): 300–306.

39. N. Romano, K. Casey, and D. Daro, "Schools and Child Abuse: A National Survey of Principals' Attitudes, Beliefs, and Practices" (Chicago: National Committee for Prevention of Child Abuse, 1990).

*Chapter 8. Prevention Policy*

1. M. Kessler and G. Albee, "Primary Prevention," *Annual Review of Psychology*, 26 (1975): 557–591. Also see H. R. Lamb and J. Zusman, "Primary Prevention in Perspective," *American Journal of Psychiatry*, 136(1) (1979): 12–17; and A. S. Mariner, "Benevolent Gambling: A Critique of Primary Prevention Programs in Mental Health," *Psychiatry*, 43 (1980): 95–105. This represents the perspective in the psychology/mental health literature. As indicated in Chapter 1, there is a slightly different definition of these levels in the child abuse literature. Here, for

instance, primary prevention is defined as efforts aimed at preventing child abuse in the general population, secondary prevention involves measures to stop abuse from happening (directed more narrowly toward high-risk groups), and tertiary prevention aims to reduce the severity and effects of abuse after it has occurred. See, for example, R. D. Helfer, "A Review of the Literature on Prevention of Child Abuse and Neglect," *Child Abuse and Neglect*, 6 (1982): 251–256.

2. L. Rapoport, "The Concept of Prevention in Social Work," *Social Work*, 6 (January 1961): 3–12.

3. M. Wittman, "Preventive Social Work: What? How? Where?" (Paper presented at the Eleventh Annual Symposium on Issues in Social Work Education, University of Utah, Graduate School of Social Work, April 17, 1980).

4. Reported in the Bay Area Child Health Network newsletter, Dec. 20, 1989.

5. See, for example, R. Merton, *Social Theory and Social Structure* (New York: Free Press, 1957), pp. 421–436; and P. Rains, "Imputations of Deviance: A Retrospective Essay on the Labeling Perspective," *Social Problems*, 23(1) (1975): 1–11.

6. For a detailed review of the risk factors associated with abuse, see D. Finkelhor and Associates, *A Sourcebook on Child Sexual Abuse* (Beverly Hills, CA: Sage, 1986).

7. F. Rivara, A. Bergman, and C. Drake, "Parental Attitudes and Practices toward Children as Pedestrians," *Pediatrics*, 84(6) (1989): 1017–1021.

8. K. Beland, *Talking About Touching II* (Seattle, WA: Committee for Children, 1986).

9. L. Robertson and P. Zader, "Driver Education and Fatal Crash Involvements of Teenaged Drivers," *American Journal of Public Health*, 70 (June 1980): 599–603.

10. D. Finkelhor and N. Strapko, "Sexual Abuse Prevention Education: A Review of Evaluation Studies," in D. Willis, E. Holder, and M. Rosenberg eds., *Child Abuse Prevention* (New York: Wiley, in press).

11. Finkelhor and Associates, *Sourcebook*, pp. 18–44.

12. N. Gilbert, "Teaching Children to Prevent Sexual Abuse," *The Public Interest*, 93 (Fall 1988): 3–15.

13. H. Ahn, *Intimacy and Discipline in Family Life: A Cross-Cultural Analysis with Implications for Theory and Practice in Child Abuse Prevention* (Berkeley, CA: University of California, Family Welfare Research Group, 1990).

14. J. J. Krivacska, "Your First Step in Preventing Abuse: Look Critically at Prepackaged Programs," *American School Board Journal*, April 1989, pp. 35–37.

15. D. Finkelhor, *Child Sexual Abuse: New Theory and Research* (New York: Free Press, 1984).

16. D. Finkelhor, "Abusers: Special Topics," in D. Finkelhor and Associates, eds., *A Sourcebook on Child Sexual Abuse* (Beverly Hills, CA: Sage, 1986); P. Gebhard, J. Gagnon, W. Pomeroy, and C. Christenson, *Sex Offenders: An Analysis of Types* (New York: Harper & Row, 1965); R. Langevin, ed., *Erotic Preference, Gender Identity and Aggression* (New York: Erlbaum, 1985).

17. K. Freund, "Erotic Preference in Pedophilia," *Behavioral Research and Therapy,* 5 (1967): 339–348; K. Freund, C. K. McKnight, R. Langevin, and S. Cibiri, "The Female Child as Surrogate Object," *Archives of Sexual Behavior,* 2 (1972): 119–133; N. Groth, *Men Who Rape* (New York: Plenum, 1979); S. Sgroi, *Handbook of Clinical Intervention in Child Sexual Abuse* (Lexington, MA: Lexington Books, 1982); D. Finkelhor, *Child Sexual Abuse*.

18. J. R. Conte, S. Wolf, and T. Smith, "What Sexual Offenders Tell Us about Prevention Strategies," *Child Abuse and Neglect,* 13 (1989): 293–301.

19. Ibid., p. 298.

20. L. E. Budin and C. F. Johnson, "Sex Abuse Prevention Programs: Offenders' Attitudes about Their Efficacy," *Child Abuse and Neglect,* 13 (1989): 77–87.

21. Conte, Wolf, and Smith, "What Sexual Offenders Tell Us," pp. 293–301.

22. L. Berliner and J. R. Conte, *The Process of Victimization: The Victim's Perspective* (University of Chicago, 1988, unpublished manuscript), p. 21.

23. J. R. Conte, S. Wolf, and T. Smith (1989), "What Sexual Offenders Tell Us."

24. D. Finkelhor, "Perils Seen in Warnings about Abuse," *The New York Times,* November 21, 1989, p. B9.

25. For some discussion regarding the concerns in the professional community regarding the effects of prevention programs on sexual development, see D. Finkelhor and N. Strapko, "Sexual Abuse Prevention Education"; J. J. Krivacska, "Your First Step in Preventing Abuse, pp. 35–37; J. J. Krivacska, *Child Abuse Prevention Programs and False Allegations of Abuse* (Educational Program Consultants, Milltown, NJ, unpublished manuscript, n.d.); G. Melton, "The Improbability of Prevention of Sexual Abuse," in D. J. Willis, E. W. Holder, and M. Rosenberg, eds., *Child Abuse Prevention* (New York: Wiley, in press); D. J. Tharinger, J. J. Krivacska, M. Laye-McDonough, L. Jamison, G. G. Vincent, and A. D. Hedlund, "Prevention of Child Sexual Abuse: An Analysis of Issues, Educational Programs, and Research Findings," *School Psychology Review,* 17(4) (1988): 614–634.

26. J. Garbarino and K. Kostelny, "Children in Dangerous Environments," in D. Cicchetti and S. Toth, eds., *Child Abuse, Child Development, and Social Policy* (New York: Ablex, in press).

27. In some cultures it may also be inappropriate to encourage children to assert themselves with adults. The Hispanic and Asian cultures place a high value on children's respect for their elders and their humble assent to adults' wishes. Providing education that is sensitive to the cultural diversity in California and across the country should account for this value. For these cultural groups in

particular, it is especially important that we teach young children to rely on other adult figures as helpers so that they can elicit support when necessary.

28. K. Beland, *Talking about Touching, II*.

29. H. N. Ahn, *Intra-ethnic Study of Family Intimacy and Discipline in Korean Families: Implications for Defining Child Abuse* (University of California, Berkeley, 1989, unpublished manuscript).

30. D. Besharov, *Recognizing Child Abuse* (New York: Free Press, 1990); A. W. Burgess, A. N. Groth, and M. P. McCausland, "Child Sex Initiation Rings," *American Journal of Orthopsychiatry*, 51 (1981): 110–119; J. Goodwin, ed., *Sexual Abuse: Incest Victims and Their Families* (Boston: John Wright, 1982); J. J. Haugaard and N. D. Reppucci, *The Sexual Abuse of Children* (San Francisco: Jossey-Bass, 1988); K. MacFarlane and J. Waterman, *Sexual Abuse of Children* (New York: Guilford, 1986); D. D. Mayhall and K. E. Norgard, *Child Abuse and Neglect: Sharing Responsibility* (New York: Wiley, 1983); J. Sebold, "Indicators of Child Sexual Abuse in Males," *Social Casework*, 68 (1987): 75–80; S. M. Segroi, ed., *Handbook of Clinical Intervention in Child Sexual Abuse* (Lexington, MA: Lexington Books, 1982); K. Simrel, R. Berg, and J. Thomas, "Crisis Management of Sexually Abused Children," *Pediatric Annals* 8 (1979): 59–72.

31. D. Finkelhor, *Child Sexual Abuse*.

32. Ibid.

33. A. Cohn, "Preventing Adults from Becoming Sexual Molesters," *Child Abuse and Neglect*, 10 (1986): 559–562.

34. D. Finkelhor, *Child Sexual Abuse*.

35. C. Newberger and E. Newberger, *Sex with Children: A Moral Analysis* (1986, unpublished manuscript); F. Rush, *The Best Kept Secret: Sexual Abuse of Children* (Englewood Cliffs, NJ: Prentice-Hall, 1980).

36. S. E. Smith, *Fear or Freedom: A Woman's Options in Social Survival and Physical Self-Defense* (Racine, WI: Mother Courage Press, 1986), p . 12.

37. Bribes also have two dimensions for most children. Many american children are regularly offered bribes (e.g., "If you finish your beans, you can have dessert"). So how does a child distinguish between the benign bribe about dessert and the bribe of a dollar if they don't tell about the touching game? Krivacska has also suggested that many families have secrets that they keep from the public— some of which serve useful purposes and some that further the family's dysfunction—and that it becomes very difficult for children to sort out only the family secrets from the threats or bribes that are related to touching. For Krivacska's comments, see J. J. Krivacska, *Designing Child Sexual Abuse Prevention Programs: Current Approaches and A Proposal for The Prevention, Reduction and Identification of Sexual Misuse* (Springfield, IL: Charles C. Thomas, 1990).

38. M. Zald and J. McCarthy, *Social Movements in an Organizational Society* (New Brunswick, NJ: Transaction, 1987), pp. 121–133.

A·P·P·E·N·D·I·X  A

# Supplemental Tables

TABLE A.1. Concepts Chart—Preschool

| Concepts | Oakland CAP | San Francisco CSHP | Marin TSP | San Mateo TAT | Los Angeles YSAP | San Bernardino CAPIE | El Cajon SAFE |
|---|---|---|---|---|---|---|---|
| Good touches | N/C[a] | A heart touch. That's a touch that feels good and safe. It's a touch that both people like and both people want. | We say "mmm" when we get a green touch. A green light touch makes us feel happy. We say go. We want it to go on and on. | Safe touches are caring touches. Safe touches don't hurt our bodies or our feelings. | OK touch. A touch that feels good to you. | Touches that don't hurt. | Most of the touches you get are good kinds of touches, like when you get hugs or kisses or when you get a pat on the back. |
| Bad touches | N/C | You do not like this kind of touch. You want a 'no' touch to stop. | We say "ouch" when we get a red light touch. A red light touch makes us feel sad or mad. | Unsafe touches. Touches which hurt our bodies or our feelings. | A touch that feels bad inside. Or a touch that makes you feel yucky inside. Or a touch that does not feel okay. | Something that hurts us. | Some touches do not feel good and are not okay. |

(continued)

157

TABLE A.1. (continued)

| Concepts | Oakland CAP | San Francisco CSHP | Marin TSP | San Mateo TAT | Los Angeles YSAP | San Bernardino CAPIE | El Cajon SAFE |
|---|---|---|---|---|---|---|---|
| Mixed-up touches | N/C | A '?' touch is a mixed-up touch. It's kind of confusing. You may want it at first but then change your mind. | The yellow light touch makes us feel mixed up. It starts out feeling good and then it doesn't feel good. | Confusing touches start out being safe and then don't seem safe after awhile. | A touch that starts feeling comfortable and fun then goes too far and you might want it to stop. | "Uh-oh" touch. When you're not sure if it's good or bad. | N/C |
| Good secrets | A good secret is one you can tell sooner or later. | Like a surprise that you keep for a little while, and after you tell, everyone has a good time. | A good secret will make you feel good when you tell it. | Surprises about presents and costumes. When secrets don't hurt anyone. | (Example given in role play.) | (Example given in role play.) | N/C |

| | | | | | | | |
|---|---|---|---|---|---|---|---|
| Bad secrets | A bad secret is one you can't tell. A bad secret doesn't make you feel good. | When someone says, "Don't tell anyone ever." When they touch you in your private parts or want you to touch them, you can tell someone. | Secret touching is when somebody bigger or older than you asks to touch your private parts or asks you to touch theirs, and tells you to keep it a secret. | Secrets about touching, secrets hiding something you are not supposed to do. | (Example given in role play.) | (Example given in role play.) | N/C |
| What to do if told a secret | You can tell someone. | You can tell someone. | Tell someone. | Tell. | Tell. | Tell. | N/C |
| Body rights | Rights are something that all children have. You have the right to sleep. You have the right to eat. You have the right to be SAFE, STRONG, and FREE. | Your body is your own special property. | Everyone of you has your very own body. Nobody bigger or older than you has the right to touch you in your private parts except to keep you clean and healthy. | Your body is your own. | Your body is special because it belongs to you and nobody else. | N/C | You have the right to keep your whole body safe. |

(continued)

TABLE A.1. (*continued*)

| Concepts | Oakland CAP | San Francisco CSHP | Marin TSP | San Mateo TAT | Los Angeles YSAP | San Bernardino CAPIE | El Cajon SAFE |
|---|---|---|---|---|---|---|---|
| People you know can abuse you | (Role-play with uncle.) | We know there are two kinds of people who touch children in private parts of their bodies when they don't like it or it feels funny: strangers (or people you don't know) and people you know. | It might be a stranger or it might be someone you know, someone in your family, someone your parents know well, or your teacher, your friend, or babysitter. | (Examples in stories with stranger, babysitter, friend of a parent.) | A friend of yours. A grown-up person that you know or your family knows. | N/C | |
| Strangers | Someone you don't know. People you don't know. | A stranger is someone who does not live with you and your parents do not know well. | Never go with strangers. | Strangers can touch you. | N/C | N/C | |

| | | | | | | | |
|---|---|---|---|---|---|---|---|
| Say no | Say no. | Say no. | Say no. | You can say no, push the person's hand away, run away, and tell. | Say no. Just think of words that mean "stop" to you. | Stand up, chin up, shoulder raised, fist clenched, look mean. Say no. | Stop it! Get away! Tell, tell, tell! |
| Run away | You want to run away. | Walk away. | Go. | N/C | Walk or run away. | Run. | Get away. |
| Tell someone | Get help and tell your teacher. | You can tell your mom and say, "Stop it." | Even when you have to, you should tell. Sometimes it is not easy to tell. Even if you are afraid to tell, it is always a very good idea to tell. | You should tell someone. | Tell someone. | Tell someone. | Tell, tell, tell. |
| Whom to tell | You can tell someone like your mom, dad, teacher or grandma or grandpa. | Daddy or mommy, uncle, grandparents, teacher. | (Encourages children to list names.) | Your mother, a grown-up friend, a babysitter, or teacher. | (Encourages children to give names.) | (Encourages children to give names.) | Mom, dad, teacher, etc. |

(continued)

TABLE A.1. (continued)

| Concepts | Oakland CAP | San Francisco CSHP | Marin TSP | San Mateo TAT | Los Angeles YSAP | San Bernardino CAPIE | El Cajon SAFE |
|---|---|---|---|---|---|---|---|
| Keep telling if they don't believe you | N/C | Sometimes the first person a child tells doesn't believe it. That's why it's important to tell until someone does believe you. | If mom or dad don't understand, you could tell someone else in your family or at school. | N/C | N/C | N/C | N/C |
| Stand an arm's distance away | There is a special way that you should stand if you meet someone you don't know. Stick out you arm. You should stand more than this far away from someone you don't know. | He kept an arm's distance. He's moving away from a touch that doesn't feel safe. | A safety space is as big as a broomstick. | N/C | Stand an arm's distance away from a stranger. | N/C | N/C |

| | | | | | | | |
|---|---|---|---|---|---|---|---|
| Yell | My mom also taught me a very special yell. It is very ferocious and it means two things. It means I am strong so don't mess with me and it means I need help. | The safety yell. It's a yell that will help you to keep you safe. | A safety yell is a yell that scares the stranger away. You can yell from deep in your belly. | N/C | N/C | N/C | N/C |
| Self-defense | You can stomp on their foot. And you can bite, scratch, punch—you can do any-thing you can do to get away. | N/C | N/C | N/C | N/C | N/C | N/C |

*(continued)*

163

| Concepts | Oakland CAP | San Francisco CSHP | Marin TSP | San Mateo TAT | Los Angeles YSAP | San Bernardino CAPIE | El Cajon SAFE |
|---|---|---|---|---|---|---|---|
| Private parts | Breasts, penis, vagina. | The mouth, the chest, between the legs, and the bottom. | The parts you cover with your underwear. The names for the private parts are penis, vagina, and anus. | Private body parts. Parts covered by a bathing suit. | Parts of the body your bathing suit covers. Special parts of your body you need to keep safe. | Parts covered by a bathing suit. You don't have to share with anybody. | Private parts are the parts between your legs covered by your underwear. Private parts have openings that you use to go to the bathroom. |
| Rules about touching | Your body is your own and if someone touches you anywhere it is okay to tell an adult about it. | N/C | Nobody bigger or older than you has the right to touch you in your private parts. | Now we are going to talk about personal safety rules for touching. An unsafe touch to which you should always say no. It is not okay for people to touch kids' private parts unless it is for health reasons. | You should tell if anyone touches your private parts. | N/C | When an older or bigger person wants to touch you in your private parts when you don't need any help, that's not okay. |

| | | | | | | |
|---|---|---|---|---|---|---|
| When can people touch private parts | N/C | N/C | To keep you clean or healthy. | Health reasons: like getting clean in the bathtub or after using the toilet, changing a diaper, or being looked over by a doctor. | When they are cleaning you. | When kids need help with their private parts. |
| When can't people touch private parts | N/C | N/C | N/C | Unless it is for health reasons. | N/C | N/C |
| Bribes | N/C | (Example in role play.) | N/C | (Example in storytelling.) | N/C | N/C |
| Abduction | N/C | N/C | Yell "Help! Kidnap!" | N/C | N/C | N/C |
| Intuition | N/C | A funny feeling is a little voice inside you that tells you that something is about to happen. | Red light feelings. | When we think something is unsafe or we are doing something we are not supposed to, we sometimes get an "Uh-Oh" feeling. | N/C | N/C |

*(continued)*

TABLE A.1. (*continued*)

| Concepts | Oakland CAP | San Francisco CSHP | Marin TSP | San Mateo TAT | Los Angeles YSAP | San Bernardino CAPIE | El Cajon SAFE |
|---|---|---|---|---|---|---|---|
| Guilt/blame | N/C | If a child is touched in private parts and doesn't want to be, it's never the child's fault. It's always the fault of the person that's touching the child or asking the child to touch him or her. | It's not your fault (told in a puppet play). | If a grown-up touches your private body parts, you are not bad. It is not your fault. | It's not your fault. | N/C | If it happens, it's not the kid's fault. |
| Bullies | (Example given in role play.) | (Example given in role play.) | (Example given in role play.) | (Example given in role play.) | (Example given in role play.) | (Example given in role play.) | N/C |
| Physical abuse | N/C | N/C | (Example given in role play.) | N/C | N/C | N/C | (Example of a child with bruises on legs and her bottom.) |
| Emotional abuse | N/C | N/C | (Example given in a puppet play.) | N/C | N/C | N/C | N/C |
| Neglect | N/C | N/C | (Example given in a puppet play.) | N/C | N/C | N/C | N/C |

[a]N/C: Not covered in curriculum.

166

TABLE A.2. Concepts Chart—First Grade

| Concepts | San Mateo TAT | Marin CLASS | Los Angeles CARE | Auburn CAPP |
|---|---|---|---|---|
| Good touches | Let's talk about touch that is safe or appropriate. Everybody needs safe, positive touch. | A green light touch is a safe touch. | N/C[a] | Good touches are not secrets. |
| Bad touches | Another kind of touch is unsafe or inappropriate. This includes any touch that injures others, as well as forced or tricked touch. | A red light touch is *not* a safe touch. | N/C | When a touch gives you the "Uh-Oh" feeling. |
| Mixed-up touches | There is another kind of touch I'm thinking about. That is confusing touch. It makes you feel "mixed up." The kind of touch that can be fun at the beginning but can end up hurting or you can like the person giving it but not the kind of touch. | N/C | Funny feeling—if something doesn't seem, feel right. | N/C |

167

| Concepts | San Mateo TAT | Marin CLASS | Los Angeles CARE | Auburn CAPP |
|---|---|---|---|---|
| Good secrets | N/C | A good secret is a secret that makes you feel good when you tell it—like a surprise (e.g., birthday party). | Some secrets are good, like surprise birthday parties. Good secrets make both people feel good and can eventually be told. | Good secrets are like surprise parties, Christmas, and it is okay to keep these. |
| Bad secrets | Never keep secrets about touching with an older person. This is not an okay secret. | A bad secret is a secret that makes you or someone else feel bad. | Some secrets are not good, like touching or looking at your private parts. Bad secrets have no time limit. They are usually scary. Bad secrets: stealing, touching private parts for no good reason. | When someone is doing something we don't like to us or someone we love. These must not be kept. |
| What to do if told a secret | Tell someone. | Tell. "Why?" Always tell if a secret hurts you or somebody else. | Tell. This isn't tattling—tattling is just to get someone in trouble. Telling is to protect yourself. | Must tell a trusted adult. To get help for a friend, you sometimes must tell a secret. |
| Body rights | N/C | N/C | Child's right not to be hurt and to get help. | Your body is yours alone. |

| | | | | |
|---|---|---|---|---|
| People you know can abuse you | Safety rules apply to everyone. | You can tell—no matter who the person is—even if it is someone you know. | People could do things to you that make you feel uncomfortable or could even hurt you. These people can be anyone, even people you know very well or people you love. Most people would never hurt you, but sometimes even grown-ups do the wrong things. | People we love may hurt us. Must tell to get help. |
| Strangers | (Don't define) Make decisions based on family rules. Don't get into strangers' cars, houses. | N/C | Any person the child does not know. | Anyone they don't know is a stranger. Not all are bad. Not all are good. You can't tell, so stay a safe distance. |
| Say no | Say no to a touch that makes you uncomfortable or confused. Or anytime someone touches you on your private parts (except for health reasons). | You can say "stop" to a red light touch—even to a grown-up (practice saying no to an adult). | If anyone, even an adult, bothers you, makes you feel yucky, or bad, or uncomfortable, you should tell him or her "NO," that you don't like what he's/she's doing and to stop. | Say no, but you must tell to get help. |
| Run away | N/C | N/C | The first step in protecting yourself is to tell someone. The next step is to get away from that person as soon as you can. | Stay far enough away so if someone tries to grab you, you can run. Running and yelling what is wrong is good. |

*(continued)*

169

| Concepts | San Mateo TAT | Marin CLASS | Los Angeles CARE | Auburn CAPP |
|---|---|---|---|---|
| Tell someone | Talk to a trusted adult anytime you feel uncomfortable or mixed up about an affectionate touch. It's never too late to tell. | You can tell, no matter what the problem is, even if you're told not to tell. Your teacher and parents care about you and want to help you. Tattling is when you tell just to be mean and get someone in trouble. Telling is getting help for yourself. | Telling someone how you feel is one of the most important ways of protecting yourself. Then tell someone you trust how you're feeling. Tell someone you trust about anything that is bothering you. | Must always tell if someone tries to or does hurt or frighten them. Hard to do, but must; this time, tell an adult you trust. |
| Whom to tell | Talk to a trusted adult about it. | Family members, teachers, teachers' aides, school principal, neighbor. | Tell someone you trust, like mom or dad, or your teacher, how you are feeling and what happened. | Tell teacher, mom, dad, grandparents, aunts, uncles, us, or someone you trust to help you. |
| Keep telling if they don't believe you | Keep telling until someone believes you. | What if you told your mom but she didn't help you? Who else could you tell? | If the first person you tell doesn't believe you or can't help you, keep telling until someone does believe and help you. | Tell till someone tries to help you. May have to tell a lot of people. |
| Stand arm's distance away | N/C | N/C | N/C | A safe distance is a feeling we just have inside. |

|  |  |  |  |  |
| --- | --- | --- | --- | --- |
| Yell | N/C | N/C | N/C | Yell and say what is wrong. No one can understand us when we cry. Make a lot of noise. |
| Self-defense | N/C | N/C | N/C | Yell and run away. |
| Private parts | Either: anatomical words such as breast, penis, anus, clitoris, vagina. Or parts of the body that bathing suits cover up. | Your private parts are the parts of your body that you cover with your bathing suit or underwear. | The parts that are covered by your bathing suit. They stay covered unless you take a bath or change into pajamas, or go to the doctor. | N/C |
| Rules about touching | It is never okay for another, more powerful person to touch your private body parts except for health reasons. It's against the law. | No one bigger or older than you is allowed to touch you in your private parts. | N/C | When a touch makes you feel uncomfortable inside, you should always tell someone you trust. |
| When *can* people touch private parts | Changing diapers, health reasons, taking a bath. | Except to keep you clean and healthy (bathing, doctor). | Anytime you uncover your private parts, let someone see your private parts, or touch your private parts, there has to be a *very* good reason (during doctor's examination, if child is hurt). | Medical needs or for parents to help us clean ourselves. |

*(continued)*

## TABLE A.2. (continued)

| Concepts | San Mateo TAT | Marin CLASS | Los Angeles CARE | Auburn CAPP |
|---|---|---|---|---|
| When people *can't* touch private parts | Rule #1: It is never okay for an older, more powerful person to touch your private parts, except for health reasons. | A person can't touch you for no reason at all. | If anyone wants to see or touch your private parts or any part of you for no good reason, you tell them no. When there's no good reason or when child doesn't want to be touched. | When they say it is a secret or say they will hurt if we tell. |
| Bribes | A bribe is something desirable offered in exchange for something else. | N/C | (Situations of people enticing a child.) | It's okay to want new things, but you should not have to let anyone touch you in ways you feel uncomfrotable with to get new things. |
| Abduction | N/C | N/C | N/C | There are people who want to take you; we call these strangers. |
| Intuition | N/C | N/C | Funny/uncomfortable feeling. | You can judge a safe distance from a stranger by your feelings. |

172

| | | | | |
|---|---|---|---|---|
| Guilt/blame | It is the other person's fault (if a child is touched on the private parts). It is never the child's fault. | Do you think it was ___ fault? "No." Why not? It was his uncle's. Uncle has the touching problem. ___ didn't do anything wrong. He was brave to tell. | If (this has) ever happened to you, remember: it was not your fault; it is never your fault when a bigger person/adult does something wrong. It is never too late to tell someone. | N/C |
| Bullies | Someone who bothers other people who are usually younger or smaller than him/herself. | N/C | N/C | Bullies are really not as brave as you think. If bullies were, they wouldn't pick on kids younger or smaller. |
| Physical abuse | Children are abused when they are punished in a way that causes a lot of pain or injury that lasts for a long time. Any punishment that lasts for a long time. Any punishment that causes welts, cuts, bruises, or broken bones. | Puppet show: My mom spanks me so hard I get black and blue marks that last a long time, and I'm afraid. Gee, I get spankings, but they don't leave any marks and I'm not afraid. | N/C | No one has the right to hurt you. |
| Emotional abuse | N/C | N/C | N/C | This hurts your feelings, not your bodies, but you still need to tell someone. |

*(continued)*

173

TABLE A.2. (*continued*)

| Concepts | San Mateo<br>TAT | Marin<br>CLASS | Los Angeles<br>CARE | Auburn<br>CAPP |
|---|---|---|---|---|
| Neglect | Children are neglected when their basic needs aren't met (love, food, clothing, shelter, medical care). | Low income: My parents love me a lot but sometimes we don't have any money so sometimes I don't have enough to eat or enough clothes to wear.<br><br>High income: My mom and dad both work all the time and I hardly see them. Sometimes I go home, and there's nothing to eat. I get scared, and I don't know my mommy's phone number. They leave me alone a lot. | N/C | You have the right to sleep, eat, dress according to the weather, have shelter. |

[a]N/C: Not covered in curriculum.

174

TABLE A.3. Concepts Chart—Third Grade

| Concepts | Oakland CAP | San Francisco CSHP | San Mateo TAT | San Luis Obispo TP |
|---|---|---|---|---|
| Good touches | N/C[a] | A "heart" touch feels good and both people like and want it. An "ok" touch. | Mutual. Both people like it. Good touch is good to both people. | Both people like the touch and it makes them feel good. Hugs, kisses, tucks into bed. |
| Bad touches | Sometimes someone that you know—a friend of your family, a neighbor, cousin or uncle—might try to hurt or scare you by touching you in a way that is confusing or a way you do not like. | A "no" touch feels bad. You don't like it and want this kind of touch to stop. A "not okay" touch. | Bad touch is not mutual; one that hurts. It makes you feel bad. | It hurts and makes you angry. Punches, kicks, touches that hurt and make both people *mad* and angry. |
| Mixed-up touches | N/C | A "?" touch is a mixed-up, confusing kind of touch. You're not sure how you feel about this touch. Maybe you liked the touch at first, but then you changed your mind and don't like it anymore. Or maybe you like the person who's touching you, but don't like the touch. | Confusing touch. It makes you feel "mixed up." The kind of touch that can be fun at the beginning, but can end up hurting. | One person may like the touch but the other person doesn't like the touch. Mixed up—you don't understand something. When you don't want or need the touch, but the other person touches you anyway. Unwanted hugs, kisses on private parts. |

*(continued)*

| Concepts | Oakland CAP | San Francisco CSHP | San Mateo TAT | San Luis Obispo TP |
|---|---|---|---|---|
| Good secrets | Kisses that feel good don't have to be a secret. Is this a good secret? | An okay secret. One you keep for a little while, like for a surprise birthday party. | A surprise that will eventually be known by others. | A good secret might be a surprise for someone. |
| Bad secrets | | When someone forces or tricks you into touching private parts of your body or the other person's body and tells you not to tell, ever, that's not the kind of secret you need to keep. A secret that's not OK. | A bad secret engenders bad feelings inside. | You have to keep this touch a secret. |
| What to do if told a secret | N/C | If not an okay secret, that's their secret, not yours. You can tell someone you trust. | N/C | If a person tells you to keep a secret, you need to tell to get some help. Tell someone if it is a bad secret. |
| Body rights | You have the right to be safe, strong, and free. | The right to feel safe from forced or tricked touch; the right to ask questions about forced or tricked touch to private parts of your body or the other person's body; and the right to say no to forced or tricked touch. | N/C | You have the right to keep your body safe. |

| | | | |
|---|---|---|---|
| People you know can abuse you | Sometimes, someone you know, a friend of your family, neighbor, cousin, may try to hurt or scare you by touching you in a way that is confusing or in a way you do not like. | There are two kinds of people who sexually abuse children: strangers and people you know. Most of the time it is someone the child knows. When someone in a kid's family sexually abuses a child, it is called incest. | There are people called "child molesters" who try to touch children's private body parts. It might be a stranger, but it could be someone you know, too. | Sometimes even people you love, or someone in your family might try to give you a confusing touch. |
| Strangers | Someone that you don't know (role play). | (Used in role play.) People who sexually abuse kids can be strangers or people you know. | (Discussed in stories.) | You can never tell whether a person is good or bad by looking at them. If you don't know them, don't go with them. |
| Say no | "No" is a safe, strong, and free word. | You can say no or "stop." | Say no. | He should say, "Stop that, I don't like that." He should use a big, strong voice. Say no in a strong voice. |
| Run away | N/C | You can run away. | Run away. | He should walk away. Get away—run to a safe place. |
| Tell someone | Whom could I tell? (Ask for requests.) | And if you can't stop the forced or tricked touch, you can tell someone afterwards, so that you can get the touching to stop. | Tell someone. | Tell someone to make sure that it doesn't happen again to him or to anyone else. If someone bothers you or touches you, tell someone you know and trust. |

*(continued)*

177

| Concepts | Oakland CAP | San Francisco CSHP | San Mateo TAT | San Luis Obispo TP |
|---|---|---|---|---|
| Whom to tell | Mom or aunt or someone you trust. | Tell someone you trust. | Family (mom, dad, stepparents, uncles, etc.), teacher, school counselor, Brownie leader, minister, police. | Mom, dad, siblings, cousins, teachers, babysitters, etc. Grandparents, family. 549-KIDS. |
| Keep telling if they don't believe you | The most important thing is that I keep telling people that I trust until I find someone who will listen to me, believe me, and help me. | It's important to tell, and tell, and tell till someone believes you. | Keep telling until someone believes you. | Tell someone else. And if he runs out of people to tell, then Gene can call 549-KIDS. If the first person you tell doesn't believe you, tell someone else. |
| Stand arm's distance away | It's a good idea to keep a couple of arms' distance between you and the stranger. | Because she's keeping an arms' distance away, that will give you extra time to turn and run for help. | N/C | If a stranger asks you a question, stand at a distance. |
| Yell | This is a safety yell so you should only use it when you're in trouble. The yell doesn't come from the top of the throat; it comes from the small place between your ribs. | You can yell. We're going to show you a special self-defense yell. A yell that people will know is serious and will come to help when they hear it. | N/C | Say no in a big, strong voice. Yell if you need to get attention. |

178

| | | | | |
|---|---|---|---|---|
| Self-defense | Kicking is a good idea. You can kick him in the shin. Scraping down the shin and stomping on the strangers' foot are also good ideas. Your elbow is a good weapon because it's sharp. Push your elbow really hard into the stranger's stomach. If you're tall enough you can aim for the throat. You can bite or grab hold of his little finger. | (Role play—man grabs boy. Boy brings arms down quickly to break man's hold.) | N/C | As a last resort, bite or kick or yell. |
| Private parts | N/C | The mouth, the chest, between the legs, and the bottom. | Private parts of your body covered by a bathing suit. | Private parts are those areas covered by a bathing suit. Girls—two-piece. Boys—swimming trunks. |
| Rules about touching | N/C | N/C | Anytime someone touches you on your private parts (except for health reasons) or you feel uncomfortable or mixed up about a touch, say no and tell someone. It's against the law. | Parents or grown-ups can touch your private area when they are helping you. |

(continued)

TABLE A.3. *(continued)*

| Concepts | Oakland CAP | San Francisco CSHP | San Mateo TAT | San Luis Obispo TP |
|---|---|---|---|---|
| When *can* people touch private parts | N/C | N/C | These touches are okay in love relationships between two adults, but not when one person forces the other or is in a position of power over the other person. | To help you or to make sure you are alright. |
| When people *can't* touch private parts | N/C | N/C | It is never okay for an older, more powerful person to touch your private parts except for health reasons. | Just because the grown-up wants to. |
| Bribes | N/C | When someone offers to give you something to do something for them. | (Story demonstrates bribe to keep secret about breaking family rules.) Discussion follows. | Might offer you candy, money, or toys in exchange for a touch. |
| Abduction | N/C | (Used in role play with stranger.) | N/C | Stranger or parents who are divorced might try to take you away. |

| | | | | |
|---|---|---|---|---|
| Intuition | N/C | Funny feelings are kind of hard to describe because everyone's funny feelings are different. A funny feeling is something inside you. It's maybe like a little voice that tells you something's not okay. The little voice is like a warning saying, "Uh-oh, better say no." | N/C | A feeling like an alarm going off inside your body and tells you when something is wrong—the Uh-Oh feeling, or intuition. Your Uh-Oh feeling, goosebumps, thoughts in your head. |
| Guilt/blame | N/C | It is never the child's fault. It is always the fault of the bigger or older person who is forcing or tricking the child into touching. | It is the molester's fault. It is never the child's fault. | Would any of this be the child's fault? No, this would never be the child's fault. It is *never* the child's fault. |
| Bullies | They're not looking for a fair fight. They're looking for kids who are scared, quiet and confused. (Role play.) | Nobody likes to be bullied or pushed around, and its important to get help if someone gives you a "no" touch or scares you. | Problem-solve and come up with a solution so a bully doesn't ruin the day for the children. | If someone bothers you, act assertive. Say no, go, tell. |

*(continued)*

181

TABLE A.3. *(continued)*

| Concepts | Oakland CAP | San Francisco CSHP | San Mateo TAT | San Luis Obispo TP |
|---|---|---|---|---|
| Physical abuse | N/C | If a grown-up hurts a child so that it leaves marks or bruises, that is a kind of abuse. | (Discuss welts or bruises in story.) | When a parent hurts a child's outside body in a way that really hurts or harms a child. If a parent hits a child on purpose, hard enough to leave cuts, bruises, broken bones, bleeding, that's too hard. Get help. |
| Emotional abuse | N/C | If a grown-up always is telling a child that they never do anything good or right until the child starts to believe it. | N/C | Emotional abuse is harming the inside, or the person you are inside, harming feelings in such a way that the child feels like he/she is worthless. When an adult *constantly* yells at a child. |
| Neglect | N/C | If a child doesn't get enough food or clothing or even love, that is a kind of abuse. | N/C | Neglect means to ignore something or someone, to pretend they aren't even there. When an adult doesn't provide a child with enough food, proper clothes, place to live, doesn't pay attention. |

[a]N/C: Not covered in curriculum.

TABLE A.4. Item Analysis of Pre- and Posttest Questionnaire Results

| Questions | Pretest | | | Posttest | | |
|---|---|---|---|---|---|---|
| | Total Sample n (%) | Third Grade n (%) | First Grade n (%) | Total Sample n (%) | Third Grade n (%) | First Grade n (%) |
| 1. Who could help you if you had a problem? | | | | [b] | | |
| a. **Could grown-ups you like help you?**[a] | 110 (48%) | 38 (43%) | 72 (51%) | 133 (58%) | 55 (63%) | 78 (55%) |
| b. Could only people in your family help you? | 113 (50%) | 50 (57%) | 63 (44%) | 95 (41%) | 31 (35%) | 64 (45%) |
| c. Could no one help you? | 7 (3%) | 0 (0%) | 7 (5%) | 3 (1%) | 2 (2%) | 1 (1%) |
| 2. What would you do if a big person tried to do something to you that you did not like? | | | | | | |
| a. Would you hit or kick the big person? | 37 (16%) | 24 (27%) | 13 (9%) | 42 (18%) | 24 (28%) | 18 (13%) |
| b. **Would you tell a grown-up you know?** | 165 (71%) | 62 (71%) | 103 (72%) | 176 (77%) | 63 (72%) | 113 (79%) |
| c. Would you let the bigger person do it? | 29 (13%) | 2 (2%) | 27 (19%) | 12 (5%) | 0 (0%) | 12 (8%) |
| 3. What would you do if a big person told you to keep a secret about touching? | | | | | | |
| a. Would you tell your friend? | 12 (5%) | 4 (5%) | 8 (6%) | 14 (6%) | 5 (6%) | 9 (6%) |
| b. Would you keep the secret? | 28 (12%) | 2 (2%) | 26 (18%) | 11 (5%) | 1 (1%) | 10 (7%) |
| c. **Would you tell a grown-up you know?** | 191 (83%) | 82 (93%) | 109 (76%) | 205 (89%) | 82 (93%) | 123 (87%) |
| 4. When would it be okay for a grown up you know to spank you? | | | | | | [c] |
| a. **Would it be okay if it were just a little spank?** | 145 (63%) | 47 (54%) | 98 (69%) | 126 (55%) | 43 (49%) | 83 (58%) |

| | | | | | | |
|---|---|---|---|---|---|---|
| **b. Would it never be okay?** | 62 (27%) | 36 (41%) | 26 (18%) | 92 (40%) | 43 (49%) | 49 (34%) |
| c. Would it be okay if it left a bruise? | 22 (10%) | 4 (5%) | 18 (13%) | 13 (6%) | 2 (2%) | 11 (8%) |

5. What would you do if you got a funny feeling inside you when a big person touched you? *d* *e*

| | | | | | | |
|---|---|---|---|---|---|---|
| **a. Would you tell the big person to stop?** | 121 (75%) | 79 (91%) | 92 (65%) | 209 (91%) | 80 (92%) | 129 (90%) |
| b. Would you keep your feelings a secret? | 12 (5%) | 2 (2%) | 10 (7%) | 2 (1%) | 1 (1%) | 1 (1%) |
| c. Would you tell the big person it feels funny? | 46 (20%) | 6 (7%) | 40 (28%) | 19 (8%) | 6 (7%) | 13 (9%) |

6. What if a big person touched you in a way that you did not like, whose fault would it be?

| | | | | | | |
|---|---|---|---|---|---|---|
| **a. Would it be the big person's fault?** | 204 (89%) | 76 (87%) | 128 (90%) | 210 (91%) | 83 (94%) | 127 (89%) |
| b. Would it not be anyone's fault? | 13 (6%) | 3 (3%) | 10 (7%) | 9 (4%) | 3 (3%) | 6 (4%) |
| c. Would it be your fault? | 13 (6%) | 8 (9%) | 5 (4%) | 12 (5%) | 2 (2%) | 10 (7%) |

7. Who might try to touch you in a way that you did not like? *f*

| | | | | | | |
|---|---|---|---|---|---|---|
| a. Would only strangers? | 104 (45%) | 30 (34%) | 74 (52%) | 88 (38%) | 5 (6%) | 83 (59%) |
| b. Would only people you know? | 32 (14%) | 8 (9%) | 24 (17%) | 19 (8%) | 6 (7%) | 13 (9%) |
| **c. Would anybody?** | 95 (41%) | 50 (57%) | 45 (32%) | 122 (53%) | 76 (87%) | 46 (32%) |

8. What would you do if your friend told you that a bigger person touched hir or her private parts? *g* *h*

| | | | | | | |
|---|---|---|---|---|---|---|
| **a. Would you help your friend to find a grown-up to tell?** | 186 (81%) | 79 (90%) | 107 (75%) | 220 (95%) | 86 (98%) | 134 (94%) |

*(continued)*

TABLE A.4. *(continued)*

| Questions | Pretest | | | Posttest | | |
|---|---|---|---|---|---|---|
| | Total Sample n (%) | Third Grade n (%) | First Grade n (%) | Total Sample n (%) | Third Grade n (%) | First Grade n (%) |
| b. Would you tell your friend to keep it a secret? | 16 (7%) | 1 (1%) | 15 (11%) | 5 (2%) | 0 (0%) | 5 (4%) |
| c. Would you tell your friend you feel sorry for him or her? | 29 (13%) | 8 (9%) | 21 (15%) | 6 (3%) | 2 (2%) | 4 (3%) |
| 9. What would you do if a grown-up wanted you to do something that you did not think was okay? | | | | *i* | | *j* |
| a. Would you do what the grown-up told you to do? | 27 (12%) | 8 (9%) | 19 (13%) | 8 (4%) | 1 (1%) | 7 (5%) |
| **b. Would you not do what the grown-up told you to do because your feelings are right?** | **174 (75%)** | **78 (89%)** | **96 (67%)** | **213 (92%)** | **84 (96%)** | **129 (90%)** |
| c. Would you wonder what to do? | 30 (13%) | 2 (2%) | 28 (20%) | 10 (4%) | 3 (3%) | 7 (5%) |
| 10. What would you do if you told a grown-up something that bothered you and the grown-up did not believe you? | | | | *k* | | *l* |
| a. Would you forget about it? | 42 (18%) | 3 (3%) | 39 (27%) | 28 (12%) | 3 (3%) | 25 (18%) |
| **b. Would you find someone else to tell?** | **161 (70%)** | **79 (90%)** | **82 (57%)** | **188 (82%)** | **84 (94%)** | **106 (74%)** |
| c. Would you not know what to do? | 28 (12%) | 6 (7%) | 22 (15%) | 14 (6%) | 2 (2%) | 12 (8%) |

11. When would it be all right for someone you know to touch you?

| | | | | | | |
|---|---|---|---|---|---|---|
| a. Would it be all right if the other person liked it? | 24 (10%) | 3 (3%) | 21 (15%) | 16 (7%) | 1 (1%) | 15 (11%) |
| b. Would it never be all right? | 82 (36%) | 38 (43%) | 44 (31%) | 99 (43%) | 40 (46%) | 59 (41%) |
| **c. Would it be all right if you liked it?** | 125 (54%) | 47 (53%) | 78 (55%) | 116 (50%) | 47 (53%) | 69 (48%) |

12. What would you do if a big person did something to you that you did not like?

| | | | | *m* | *n* | *o* |
|---|---|---|---|---|---|---|
| **a. Would you say no?** | 110 (49%) | 67 (76%) | 43 (31%) | 143 (63%) | 80 (92%) | 63 (45%) |
| b. Would you say no only if it were a stranger? | 110 (44%) | 18 (21%) | 82 (60%) | 84 (36%) | 7 (8%) | 77 (55%) |
| c. Would you let the big person do it? | 15 (7%) | 3 (3%) | 12 (9%) | 1 (1%) | 0 (0%) | 1 (1%) |

13. What would you do if a big person tried to touch you in a way you did not like?

| | | | | | | |
|---|---|---|---|---|---|---|
| a. Would you not tell anyone about it? | 10 (4%) | 0 (0%) | 10 (7%) | 3 (1%) | 0 (0%) | 3 (2%) |
| **b. Would you tell a grown-up about it?** | 214 (93%) | 87 (99%) | 127 (89%) | 219 (96%) | 82 (97%) | 137 (96%) |
| c. Would you tell your friend? | 7 (3%) | 1 (1%) | 6 (4%) | 6 (3%) | 3 (3%) | 3 (2%) |

14. What would you do if someone you did not know wanted to give you something?

| | | | | | | |
|---|---|---|---|---|---|---|
| **a. Would you say no?** | 124 (54%) | 65 (74%) | 59 (42%) | 110 (48%) | 57 (65%) | 53 (37%) |

(continued)

TABLE A.4. *(continued)*

| Questions | Pretest | | | Posttest | | |
|---|---|---|---|---|---|---|
| | Total Sample n (%) | Third Grade n (%) | First Grade n (%) | Total Sample n (%) | Third Grade n (%) | First Grade n (%) |
| b. Would you take it? | 4 (2%) | 0 (0%) | 4 (3%) | 5 (2%) | 1 (1%) | 4 (3%) |
| c. **Would you ask your mom if you could have it?** | 101 (44%) | 23 (26%) | 78 (55%) | 115 (50%) | 30 (34%) | 85 (60%) |

[a]Correct responses are shown in bold.
[b]Indicates a significant difference between pre- and posttest scores for third-grade children to Question 1 ($\chi^2 = 9.56$, $df = 2$, $p < .005$).
[c]Indicates a significant difference between pre- and posttest scores for first-grade children at ($\chi^2 = 9.98$, $df = 2$, $p < .01$).
[d]$\chi^2 = 22.16$, $df = 2$, $p < .000$.
[e]$\chi^2 = 27.31$, $df = 2$, $p < .000$.
[f]$\chi^2 = 23.50$, $df = 2$, $p < .000$.
[g]$\chi^2 = 23.72$, $df = 2$, $p < .000$.
[h]$\chi^2 = 19.58$, $df = 2$, $p < .000$.
[i]$\chi^2 = 24.24$, $df = 2$, $p < .000$.
[j]$\chi^2 = 22.98$, $df = 2$, $p < .000$.
[k]$\chi^2 = 9.55$, $df = 2$, $p < .01$.
[l]$\chi^2 = 9.07$, $df = 2$, $p < .01$.
[m]$\chi^2 = 17.93$, $df = 2$, $p < .000$.
[n]$\chi^2 = 8.98$, $df = 2$, $p < .01$.
[o]$\chi^2 = 13.18$, $df = 2$, $p < .001$.

TABLE A.5. Questionnaire Scores by Program

| Scores | Third-Grade Programs | | | | First-Grade Programs | | | |
|---|---|---|---|---|---|---|---|---|
| | CAP | CSHP | TAT | TP | TAT | CLASS | CARE | CAPP |
| Total score possible | 11 | 13 | 12 | 14 | 14 | 12 | 13 | 14 |
| Mean pretest | 8.92 | 10.50 | 9.90 | 11.08 | 8.90 | 7.98 | 9.05 | 9.00 |
| | $(n = 24)$ | $(n = 20)$ | $(n = 20)$ | $(n = 24)$ | $(n = 39)$ | $(n = 41)$ | $(n = 19)$ | $(n = 19)$ |
| SD | 1.47 | 1.85 | 1.17 | 1.67 | 2.46 | 1.53 | 1.84 | 2.56 |
| % correct | 81% | 81% | 83% | 79% | 64% | 67% | 70% | 64% |
| Mean posttest | 9.92 | 11.40 | 9.80 | 12.42 | 10.28 | 8.90 | 10.59 | 9.26 |
| SD | 1.21 | 2.16 | 1.20 | 1.18 | 1.81 | 1.61 | 1.40 | 1.79 |
| % correct | 90% | 88% | 82% | 89% | 73% | 74% | 81% | 66% |
| % change | +9% | +7% | −1% | +10%[a] | +9%[b] | +7%[c] | +11%[d] | +2% |

[a]Indicates a significant difference between pre- and posttest scores in the Touch Program at $t = 3.20$, $p = .003$.
[b]$t = 2.84$, $p = .006$.
[c]$t = 2.68$, $p = .009$.
[d]$t = 4.43$, $p = .000$.

TABLE A.6. Responses to Telling Questions—Written
Questionnaire

| Scores | Total | Third Grade | First Grade |
|---|---|---|---|
| Mean pretest | 3.97 | 4.42 | 3.69 |
| | $(n = 231)$ | $(n = 88)$ | $(n = 143)$ |
| SD | 1.16 | .71 | 1.29 |
| % correct | 79% | 88% | 74% |
| Mean posttest | 4.36* | 4.49 | 4.29** |
| SD | .92 | .76 | 1.00 |
| % correct | 87% | 90% | 86% |
| % change | +8% | +2% | +12% |
| Posttest-only | 4.27 | 4.44 | 4.12 |
| | $(n = 74)$ | $(n = 36)$ | $(n = 38)$ |
| SD | 1.02 | 1.05 | 1.01 |
| % correct | 85% | 89% | 82% |

*$t = 4.04$. $p = .000$.
**$t = 4.35$. $p = .000$.

TABLE A.7. Questionnaire Scores on Telling Lessons by Program

| Scores | Third-Grade Programs | | | | First-Grade Programs | | | |
|---|---|---|---|---|---|---|---|---|
| | CAP | CSHP | TAT | TP | TAT | CLASS | CARE | CAPP |
| Total score possible | 4 | 5 | 4 | 5 | 5 | 5 | 5 | 5 |
| Mean pretest | 3.50 | 4.35 | 3.60 | 4.38 | 3.23 | 3.81 | 3.98 | 3.74 |
| | (n = 24) | (n = 20) | (n = 20) | (n = 24) | (n = 39) | (n = 41) | (n = 44) | (n = 19) |
| SD | .66 | .81 | .60 | .77 | 1.50 | 1.29 | .90 | 1.45 |
| % correct | 88% | 87% | 90% | 88% | 65% | 76% | 80% | 75% |
| Mean posttest | 3.71 | 4.40 | 3.35 | 4.46 | 3.92 | 4.61 | 4.57 | 3.68 |
| SD | .55 | 1.00 | .67 | .78 | 1.27 | .70 | .66 | 1.16 |
| % correct | 93% | 88% | 84% | 89% | 78% | 92% | 91% | 74% |
| % change | +5% | +1% | −6% | +1% | +13% | +17%[a] | +11%[b] | −1% |

[a] Indicates a significant difference between pre- and posttest scores in CLASS program at $t$ = 3.51, $p$ = 001.
[b] $t$ = 3.51, $p$ = .001.

190

TABLE A.8. Appropriate Connections between
Emotional State and Touching at Different
Grades

| | Appropriate response to mixed-up face | | |
|---|---|---|---|
| Sample group | Pretest | Posttest | Post-only |
| Total sample | 76% | 84%* | 80% |
| Third grade | 95% | 98% | 100% |
| First grade | 57% | 73% | 62% |
| Preschool | 16% | 37% | 28% |

*Indicates a significant difference between pre- and
posttest responses among the total elementary sample:
$\chi^2 = 17.28$, $p < .01$.

TABLE A.9. Children's Responses to "Who Touched Him?"

| | Mixed-up face | | Sad face | | Happy face | |
|---|---|---|---|---|---|---|
| Response | Pre | Post | Pre | Post | Pre | Post |
| Known person | | | | | | |
| Total sample | 25.7% | 18.1% | 24.0% | 20.5% | 80.8% | 89.2% |
| Third grade | 11.3% | 13.4% | 12.5% | 22.5% | 77.7% | 92.6% |
| First grade | 38.1% | 22.1% | 31.7% | 19.2% | 83.2% | 86.6% |
| Unknown person | | | | | | |
| Total sample | 59.5% | 68.1% | 56.5% | 60.0% | 10.8% | 6.1% |
| Third grade | 72.2% | 71.1% | 56.5% | 56.3% | 12.8% | 5.3% |
| First grade | 48.7% | 65.5% | 55.8% | 62.5% | 9.2% | 6.7% |
| Unspecified | | | | | | |
| Total sample | 14.8% | 13.8% | 19.5% | 19.5% | 8.5% | 4.7% |
| Third grade | 16.5% | 15.5% | 30.0% | 21.3% | 9.6% | 2.1% |
| First grade | 13.3% | 12.4% | 12.5% | 18.3% | 7.6% | 6.7% |

TABLE A.10. Evaluation of Prevention Programs in Elementary Schools

| Study[a] | Curriculum title | Design | Auspices | Sample-size | Sample size | Scoring | Experimental results | Control results |
|---|---|---|---|---|---|---|---|---|
| | | | | Studies Demonstrating 10% Knowledge Gain or Less | | | | |
| Binder & McNiel | Child Assault Prevention | Pre/post 2–4 wk/post No control | External[b] | 88 | 5–8 & 9–12 | 0–5 | Younger: $m_{pre}$ = 4.63 (.39)[c]; $m_{post}$ = 4.75 (.24); Older: $m_{pre}$ = 4.58 (.33); $m_{post}$ = 4.75 (.32) | — |
| Kolko et al. | Red Flag/Green Flag | Pre/post/post II 2 mo/post 6 mo/post II | Unclear | 337 | 3rd grade | 1–11 | $m_{pre}$ = 8.0 (1.6); $m_{post}$ = 8.9 (.9); $m_{postII}$ = 8.7 (1.0) | $m_{pre}$ = 8.5 (1.4); $m_{post}$ = 8.1 (1.5); $m_{postII}$ = 8.1 (1.4) |
| Leake | Child Assault Prevention | Post-only 1 wk/post Control | Internal[b] | 30 | 1st grade | 0–50 | $m_{post}$ = 37.07 (6.02) | $m_{post}$ = 33.13 (6.11) |
| Nelson | You're In Charge & Video | Post-only Control | Internal | 1,931 | 5th and 6th grades | 0–20 | $1m_{post}$ = 15.5 (2.8); $2m_{post}$ = 16.0 (2.8) | $cm_{post}$ = 13.3 (2.9) |

192

| Study | Program | Design | | N | Grade | Range | | |
|---|---|---|---|---|---|---|---|---|
| Woods & Dean | Talking About Touching & Spiderman | Pre/post Control | External | 1,579 | 3rd–5th grade | 0–15 | $1m_{pre} = 10.56$<br>$1m_{post} = 12.57$<br>$2m_{pre} = 10.40$<br>$2m_{post} = 11.06$ | $cm_{pre} = 10.34$<br>$cm_{post} = 10.89$ |
| Wolfe et al. | Untitled Two 5 min. skits | Post-only 3–5 day/post Control | Internal | 290 | 4th & 5th grades | 0–7 | $m_{post} = 5.30$ (1.32) | $m_{post} = 4.71$ (1.55) |

Studies Demonstrating Greater than 10% Knowledge Gain

| Study | Program | Design | | N | Grade | Range | | |
|---|---|---|---|---|---|---|---|---|
| Conte et al. | Untitled: Cook County Sheriff's Office | Pre/post 1 wk/post Control | External | 40 | 4–5 & 6–10 | Unclear | Older:<br>Abstract concepts:<br>$m_{pre} = 2.7$ (.82)<br>$m_{post} = 6.1$ (1.7)<br>Explicit concepts:<br>$m_{pre} = 11.4$ (4.2)<br>$m_{post} = 21.4$ (3.95) | $m_{pre} = 3.3$ (1.6)<br>$m_{post} = 3.7$ (2.1)<br>$m_{pre} = 13.0$ (5.4)<br>$m_{post} = 14.4$ (5.2) |
| Downer | Talking About Touching | Pre/post Control | Internal | 85 | 9–10 | — | $m_{pre} = 67.14$ (15.7)<br>$m_{post} = 71.0$ (10.4) | $m_{pre} = 65.13$ (16.1)<br>$m_{post} = 87.43$ (14.5) |

(continued)

TABLE A.10. (*continued*)

| Study[a] | Curriculum title | Design | Auspices | Sample size | Sample size | Scoring | Experimental results | Control results |
|---|---|---|---|---|---|---|---|---|
| Fryer et al. | Children Need to Know Personal Safety Training Program | Pre/post Control Stranger Simulation | Internal | 44 | K–2nd grade | — | Pretest 43.5% passed Posttest 78.3% passed | Pretest 52.4% passed Posttest 52.4% passed |
| Harvey et al. | Good Touch Bad Touch | Pre/post/postII 3 wk/post 7 wk/postII Control | External | 71 | Kindergarten | 1–5 | $m_{post}$ = 3.50 $m_{post\overline{II}}$ 3.57 | $m_{post}$ = 2.05 $m_{post\overline{II}}$ 2.08 |
| Kraizer & | Children Need to | Pre/post | Internal | 91 | 3–8 | 0–14 Behavior Scale | $m_{p43}$ = 3.84 | $m_{p43}$ = 3.49 |
| Fryer | Know Personal Safety Program | 1 day/post Control | | | | | $m_{post}$ = 9.40 | $m_{post}$ = 3.68 |
| Kraizer et al. | Safe Child Personal Safety Training Program | Pre/post 1 wk/post Control | Internal | 670 | 3–10 | 1–14 | $m_{pre}$ = 4.4 (2.25) $m_{post}$ = 8.3 (2.06) | $m_{pre}$ = 4.5 (2.76) $m_{post}$ = 5.0 (2.24) |
| Miltenberger et al. | Red Flag, Green Flag | Pre/post/postII 1 wk/post 2 mo/postII | External | 24 | 4–5 6–7 | 0–3 | Older: $m_{pre}$ = 1 $m_{post}$ = 3 $m_{postII}$ = 3  Younger: $m_{pre}$ = 1 $m_{post}$ = 3 $m_{postII}$ = 1 or 2 | |

| | | | | | |
|---|---|---|---|---|---|
| Wurtele et al. | Illusion Theatre "Touch" video vs. Behavioral Skills Training Program vs. combined | Post/postII<br>3 exp. groups<br>Just after/post<br>3 mo/post<br>Control | Internal | 71 | K–6th grade | 0–13 | $1m_{post}$ = 12.40 (.74)<br>$1m_{postII}$ = 12.28 (.91)<br>$2m_{post}$ = 10.95 (2.20)<br>$2m_{postII}$ = 11.41 (2.03)<br>$3m_{post}$ = 11.42 (2.09)<br>$2m_{postII}$ = 12.21 (1.72)<br>$cm_{post}$ = 9.72 (2.76) |

[a] See note 14 for Chapter 5 for the full citations for these studies.

[b] "External" refers to evaluations conducted by individuals who were not associated with the curriculum design or dissemination. "Internal" indicates that the evaluation author was involved in the design and/or the implementation of the program.

[c] Standard deviations in parentheses.

TABLE A.11. Parental Assessment of Children's Coping Abilities

| Children would | % Before the program | % After the program |
|---|---|---|
| 1. Know the difference between abusive and nonabusive touches | 82% | 90% |
| 2. Tell if an adult tried to touch them in ways that felt uncomfortable | 88% | 95% |
| 3. Think it was their fault if abused | 69% | 71% |
| 4. Yell or otherwise make a fuss if grabbed by an adult | 86% | 91% |

TABLE A.12. Hypothetical Disclosure of Sexual Abuse: What Would Teachers Do?

| Type of abuse | Call child's parents | Call CPS | Call police | Comfort child | Check story | Talk to principal | Call prevention agency |
|---|---|---|---|---|---|---|---|
| Stranger abuse % Yes[a] (n = 22) | 18% | 27% | 14% | 5% | 14% | 73% | 0 |
| Parent abuse % Yes[a] (n = 22) | 5% | 36% | 5% | 5% | 14% | 82% | 5% |

[a]Percentages do not sum to 100; teachers could give multiple responses.

# Research Methods

The study of the eight California programs involved a quasi-experimental pretest–posttest design with a 6-month follow-up. Approximately 30% of the total sample was held out for post-test only to control for the possible effects of testing. The pretest was administered 1 week before children received their training in child abuse prevention. The initial posttest occurred 1 month following the training and measured the children's knowledge gain. The six month follow-up was employed to indicate how well any gains in knowledge were sustained.

In the first year of the study, data were collected for third-grade children. In the second year, first graders were examined. In the second year of the study we focused on the knowledge gain at 6 months and did away with the initial posttest (which revealed no significant differences from the 6-month follow-up for third graders). Thus, first graders received the 6-month posttest as the strongest indicator of their sustained gain in knowledge.

Because of the nature of the intervention, the child abuse prevention training was not withheld from any child, precluding the inclusion of a conventional control group. Thus, the extent to which findings are influenced by history and maturation could not adequately be controlled through the study design. However, the posttest-only group was useful in controlling for the effects of testing.

## SAMPLING

In California, 84 prevention agencies are responsible for conducting child abuse prevention programs in the schools. Of the 84 providers, 8 were selected for participation in this study. Five of the agencies chosen for study were community-based, with providers who were outside the school system. Three providers were school-based: teachers or other school personnel were trained to use the curriculum with classroom children. Further criteria for selection were based on recommendations from the California Office of Child Abuse Prevention. The recommendations were made based on an agency's duration of service and its established record as a stable program. California's program delivery is monitored by a northern California and a southern California Training Center; six of the agencies were chosen from the northern California catchment area, and two were chosen from the south. Three agencies were located in urban districts, three were located in suburban areas, and two were situated in rural areas.

Each of the eight providers were responsible for making contact with school district personnel to apprise them of the study and to obtain their approval for school participation. Where school districts were used rather than community-based agencies, appropriate school district officials were contacted to gain access to the schools. Each school district or community agency was responsible for selecting at least two elementary schools. Any correspondence or meetings that were required to grant entrance to the school district or to individual schools were done jointly between the prevention provider and research staff. Study sites were selected with an eye to providing a cross-section of various socioeconomic and ethnic groups within the community. Additionally, prevention agencies chose schools with whom they had a strong working relationship and where parent or school personnel might facilitate the advancement of the study.

All children in the first and third grades of participating schools were invited to participate in the study. Parents of all children received letters fully explaining the study and asking for their child's participation. Following this procedure, parents self-selected their child's participation.

Sampling by this technique has certain advantages and limitations. The primary disadvantage of this sampling method is that one cannot generalize to the greater population from a self-selected sample. However, to assess the similarity of the sample with the total school population, demographic characteristics on all children participating in the study were compared to those of all first- or third-grade children in the schools. Three hundred thirty-four children completed pre- and posttest interviews; 305 completed the written survey. Although 45% of the targeted population participated in the study, the characteristics of the study sample, with respect to both gender and ethnicity, closely resembled the school population.

Almost equal numbers of boys and girls participated in the study (52% boys and 48% girls). Sixty-two percent of the sample was white, 8% black, 14% Hispanic, 4% Asian, and 8% other (or multiracial). This mirrored the complexion of the schools from which the children were drawn. The mean age of study participants was 7.58 years, ranging from 5.6 to 9.89 years.

Certain biases are inescapable when sampling among parents who volunteer their child's participation.[1] Some parents may be more friendly to the notion of prevention; others may already be confident of their child's abilities. Regardless, given the population being interviewed, human subjects considerations required the use of voluntary participation under informed consent.

In each school, all children who were given consent to participate took part in the study. The number of families granting consent varied, depending on the size of the classrooms in each school, administrative support for the study, or prior experience with prevention programs. Table B.1 describes the sample frame used in the study.

## INSTRUMENTATION

Two instruments were used in the elementary study.[2] One instrument involved a paper-and-pencil written questionnaire. The other was an in-person interview. Before developing each of the instruments, a review of the developmental literature was conducted. Other prevention studies involving children in the early elementary school grades were reviewed, as were standardized instruments designed for elementary-school-age children.[3] One prevention study made use of a paper-and-pencil survey with pictures of human stick figures.[4] Another study included a 25-item multiple-choice questionnaire designed for older elementary school children.[5] These instruments inspired much of the development of the written questionnaire. Before pilot-testing the instruments, a 1-day consulting session was held with a child development specialist, child abuse prevention researchers, and the chief of the State Office of Child Abuse Prevention; a speech and language specialist at the University of California, San Francisco, Langley Porter Psychiatric Institute was also consulted before the instruments were completed.[6] Finally, the instruments were reviewed by each of the prevention agency administrators involved in the study. Their observations and suggestions were incorporated in the final revision of the instruments.

Pilot testing was conducted at five sites in Alameda County; the sites represented schools, a day care center, and a children's summer camp. These settings gave us access to children from diverse socioeconomic backgrounds. Thirty-six first grade and 35 third grade children were pilot-tested. One researcher conducted the interviewing session while another observed the child to assess the child's comfort with the questions, conceptual difficulties, and focus on the task.

TABLE B.1. Description of Sample

| Geographic location | Auspices | Descriptive location | Grade | Written survey sample N | Written survey posttest only | Oral interview sample N | Oral interview posttest only |
|---|---|---|---|---|---|---|---|
| Northern California | Community-based agency | Urban | Third | 10 | 4 | 17 | 4 |
| Northern California | Community-based agency | Urban | Third | 10 | 5 | 12 | 5 |
| Northern California | Community-based agency | Urban | Third | 7 | 0 | 7 | 2 |
| Northern California | Community-based agency | Urban | Third | 17 | 3 | 17 | 4 |
| Northern California | School-based program | Suburban | Third | 13 | 8 | 19 | 3 |
| Northern California | School-based program | Suburban | Third | 7 | 5 | 10 | 4 |
| Southern California | Community-based agency | Rural | Third | 13 | 7 | 23 | 7 |
| Southern California | Community-based agency | Rural | Third | 11 | 4 | 15 | 5 |
| | | Third-grade totals | | 88 | 36 | 120 | 34 |
| Northern California | Community-based agency | Rural | First | 14 | 5 | 13 | 6 |
| Northern California | Community-based agency | Rural | First | 5 | 1 | 5 | 1 |
| Northern California | Community-based agency | Suburban | First | 13 | 4 | 13 | 4 |
| Northern California | Community-based agency | Suburban | First | 28 | 5 | 28 | 5 |
| Northern California | School-based program | Suburban | First | 25 | 7 | 25 | 7 |
| Northern California | School-based program | Suburban | First | 14 | 3 | 13 | 4 |
| Southern California | School-based program | Urban | First | 25 | 8 | 23 | 9 |
| Southern California | School-based program | Urban | First | 19 | 5 | 19 | 5 |
| | | First-grade totals | | 143 | 38 | 139 | 41 |

Before implementing the evaluation, master's degree level research assistants were given 4 hours of training in interviewing techniques. Interviewers were taught how to follow the interview schedule format in a uniform manner, and they practiced asking questions in a nonleading fashion. Because interviewers were mandated reporters, they were also taught how to handle possible disclosures of child abuse.

## QUESTIONNAIRE

The questionnaire utilized a three-item multiple-choice format accompanied by a small drawing that represented each of the response categories. The questionnaire included 14 items. Questions were representative of the range of prevention concepts presented to children across programs. Children were given three possible response categories for each question. For most questions, there was only one correct answer. For two of the questions, however, two response categories were considered correct. For example, Question 4 asked: "When would it be okay for a grown-up you know to spank you?" Response categories were as follows: (1) "Would it be okay if it were just a little spank?" (2) "Would it never be okay?" (3) "Would it be okay if it left a bruise?" Some programs teach children that spanking is acceptable if parents do it to discipline a child and if the spanking is not excessive. Therefore, Category 1 was the correct response. Yet many adults think that spanking is abusive and should not be allowed and may convey this view to children. Out of regard for this view, the second response category was also considered correct in the scoring system. The final question also included two potentially correct responses. The question asks: "What would you do if someone you did not know wanted to give you something?" Response categories were: (1) "Would you say no?" (2) "Would you take it?" (or 3) "Would you ask your mom if you could have it?" Again, responses 1 and 3 were considered correct as both reflect prevention-related behaviors.

Pre- and posttests were conducted in small groups with a trained staff administrator. The staff administrator read aloud each of the question and answer categories while pointing to each of the choices. Children could follow along on their own page or watch the administrator and mark the correct response on their answer sheet. Pilot testing showed that first graders appeared somewhat confused by the words on the page (at the beginning of the first-grade year, most children do not yet know how to read). Therefore, the questionnaire was read aloud to all children, although the written words were deleted from the pages for first-grade students.

## INTERVIEW

Children in the study also took part in an in-person interview with a trained interviewer. The instrument was based on the interview schedule designed for preschoolers in the earlier California study, although some important revisions were made to accommodate children's advanced developmental abilities.[7]

The first section of the interview included a picture book with images of four distinct interactions that often occur between adults and children. In the first picture, the adult and child were hugging; in the second picture, the adult was tickling the child. The third picture showed an adult tucking a child into bed, and the final picture depicted an adult spanking a child. Each picture book was either male- or female-specific, depending upon the gender of the child. To avoid cultural bias, each of the four pictures also featured one of four major cultural groups (white, black, Hispanic, and Asian). All books displayed androgynous adults; children could identify the gender of the adult as they chose.

The child and adult in each picture had an expressionless face. To the side of each picture were three faces, each with a different expression. One face was smiling (children were told that the picture represented a happy face). One face showed a mouth with a sideways S (they were told that this face represented a mixed-up feeling) and the third expression was that of a sad child. Third-grade children were asked to choose the face that best represented how the child might feel in each of the above situations. Because first-grade children demand greater interaction and because their abstract thinking is less developed, the faces in their picture books were represented on pieces of felt. Children were asked to choose the felt face that described the boy's (girl's) feelings and to place it on top of the face in the picture (a small piece of Velcro was attached to the picture so that the felt would remain in place).

The primary purpose of the four pictures was to determine the extent to which children understood the concept of the "touch continuum." They also tested the extent to which children's perceptions of regular human interactions changed after exposure to a prevention program.

This portion of the interview corresponded almost directly with the instrument used with preschool children. In that study, children were asked similar questions with regard to four interactions. The pictures used with preschoolers depicted rabbits rather than humans as preschool children were more likely to respond to pictures using animal stimuli.[8] Each picture in the preschool instrument corresponded to the elementary instrument except for two differences. Preschoolers were not asked about being "tucked in bed." Rather, they were asked about a picture of a big bunny bathing a little bunny. To this end, the elementary "tucking in bed" picture did not have a correlate in the preschool study. The elementary study also included a question regarding an adult spanking a child. The preschool study asked a related question regarding the little bunny's feelings about being "hit," but the two pictures could be only roughly compared.

The second portion of the interview continued with the use of the picture book, eliciting story completing from children. Children were shown three sequential pictures of children whose facial expressions were fixed. In the first picture, the child looked confused. The second picture depicted a sad child, and the third showed a happy child. Children were told: "Someone touched this boy (girl) and the boy feels sad (happy, mixed-up) about the touch. What happened?" These pictures corresponded directly to the preschool study and corroborated children's responses to the first set of pictures. They also elicited children's knowledge of support systems, an essential component of child abuse prevention programs; as they were asked, "What can he (she) do to get help? . . . What could make him (her) feel better?"

Following the picture book, children were presented with various wooden figurines resembling children and adults. Children were asked to choose the figure that might represent themselves. The interviewer then chose another figure to act as the adult. The vignettes that were acted out between the child's figurine and the interviewer's covered a number of areas central to the prevention programs. Children were asked how they might respond if they were touched inappropriately by a friend of the family, how they would respond to a bribe, how they would handle feelings of guilt or blame, and how they might manage if a stranger offered them a cookie. Using the vignettes, children's prevention-related responses were tested as closely as possible without provoking undue fear or anxiety.

Before conducting interviews, the researcher was introduced to students by the classroom teacher so that the children understood that the research was taking place with the teacher's approval. Written questionnaires lasted approximately 15 minutes. Interviews generally took place on the following day and also lasted approximately 15 minutes. Interviews with all children were audiorecorded; tapes were kept in a locked file cabinet at the research office. A different research assistant coded each of the oral interviews following a detailed code book that was developed early in the study. All responses that did not correspond to a clear code were reviewed by the project director for consistency in coding.

## NOTES

1. K. A. Kearney, R. H. Hopkins, A. L. Mauss, and R. A. Weisheit, "Sample Bias Resulting from a Requirement for Written Parental Consent," *Public Opinion Quarterly*, 47 (1983):

96–102; L. Lueptow, S. A. Mueller, R. R. Hammes, and L. S. Master, "The Impact of Informed Consent Regulations on Response Rate and Response Bias," *Sociological Methods and Research*, 6(2) (1977): 183–204.

2. Much of the instrument design was developed and tested by Dr. Nina Nyman.

3. M. Kovacs, *Children's Depression Inventory* (Pittsburgh, PA: University of Pittsburgh School of Medicine, Department of Psychiatry, 1987); E. Piers and D. Harris, *The Piers-Harris Children's Self-Concept Scale* (Nashville, TN: Counselor Recordings and Tests, 1969).

4. Avebury Research and Consulting Ltd., *Child Abuse Prevention Evaluation,* (Toronto: Author, 1986) (available from author, 20 Eglinton Ave. East, Suite 406, Toronto, Ontario, Canada.

5. A. Hazzard, C. Webb, and C. Kleemeier, *Child Sexual Assault Prevention Programs: Helpful or Harmful?* (Paper presented at the Southeastern Psychological Association, New Orleans, 1988).

6. Instrument consultation was provided by Francis Stott, Ann Hazzard, Deborah Daro, Dave Foster, and Danita Sorenson.

7. N. Gilbert, J. Duerr Berrick, N. LeProhn, and N. Nyman, *Protecting Young Children from Sexual Abuse: Does Preschool Training Work?* (Lexington, MA: Lexington Books, 1989).

8. L. Bellak, *The TAT, the CAT, and the SAT in Clinical Use* (New York: Grune & Stratten, 1975).

# Index